THE
WRITING CRAFT

Second Edition

Edward D. Yates

College of Journalism and Communications
University
of
Florida

CPC **CONTEMPORARY PUBLISHING COMPANY**
508 St. Mary's Street   Raleigh, North Carolina 27605

Publisher: Charles E. Grantham
Production Editor: Susan K. Taylor
Photographer: Tom Burton

Acknowledgement is made to Wide World of Photos/Associated Press for permission to use the following photographs:
The Playboy Advisor in Person, Page 7
Bee Beards, Page 77
One Hundred and One and Still Counting, Page 77
Lee Iacocca, Chrysler Corporation's Chairman with new product, Page 115
Brooke Shields with a travel bag, Page 115
Marine Leaving Lebanon with full pack, Page 175
Famous Sisters, Dear Abby and Ann Landers, Page 185
Ronald Reagan as a Sportscaster in the 1930's and today, Page 214

Other Photography in the text is taken of students at the University of Florida.

ISBN: 0-89892-042-6

Copyright © 1981, 1985, Contemporary Publishing Company of Raleigh.

Printed in the United States of America

DEDICATION:

For Shannon and Douglas.

PREFACE

Writing news and feature stories for print, writing news and feature stories for broadcast, and writing advertisements for print or broadcast require many of the same basic skills. If students understand and successfully practice the basic skills of one form, they can easily transfer the acquired skills to other forms.

This versatility in basic writing skills can be terribly important in the early years of professional education. Decisions about career goals are just being made by many freshmen and sophomores. An approach that emphasizes the similarity of basic skills can serve several purposes. It can:

—Help a student determine if he or she really wants to be a writer.
—Help a student determine which area of mass media writing he or she would like to follow.
—Help a student who is already committed to a specific area understand the basic similarity of all forms of writing for the media.
—Help students understand that decisions they have made on media jobs can be changed; that it is not all that hard, or all that unusual, to make career changes taking acquired skills with them to other areas.
—Help students carry added skills in the basics to their other courses.
Few books take a media-wide approach to writing. Most books are highly specialized. Specialization is appropriate in later courses. But in a first course, students should be taught the basic ways in which all writing for the mass media differs from other types of writing. Writers for all forms of mass media:
—Deal in facts.
—Must be interesting and serve the reader/listener/viewer.
—Must use sentences that are clear, short, logical, emphatic, and correct in style, grammar and punctuation.
—Must use paragraphs that are clear, and shorter than for other forms of writing; yet, are logical and effective.
—Must use appropriate words—words that are familiar, specific, standard and colorful.
—Must avoid inappropriate words—cliches, slang, vulgarity, jargon, provincialisms, euphemisms and unnecessary words.
—Must bring people into the writing as sources, case histories, examples, and in anecdotes.
—Must show professionalism in attaining accuracy, responsibility in the practice of ethics and standards, and objectivity in news selection and presentation.
—Must show skill in gathering information through research and interviewing.

Changes From the First Edition

This second edition of *The Writing Craft*, first published in 1981, has been extensively altered from the first edition to reflect two things:

—Suggestions made by instructors at several colleges and universities around the country which have adopted and used the book for the past three years. The suggestions were made in answer to a survey conducted by the publisher.

—Decisions by the author and the publisher that the first edition had shortcomings in organization and emphasis on certain materials included in the book.

The writing of *Leads* was moved up from *Chapter 3* to *Chapter 1* because many courses in which this book is used have writing labs or assignments beginning the first week of classes. Discussion of proper *Identification* of subjects and sources in stories was expanded and moved from *Specifics* to *Leads* because identification often is made in the lead.

The chapter on *gathering information* was moved back from Chapter 2 to Chapter 10 because beginning writers are rarely called upon to do extensive reporting or research in early assignments. Early assignments are usually done from fact sheets provided by instructors or from work books. Interviewing, which had been near the end of the chapter, was moved near the beginning of the chapter. New information was added on interviewing both live or by telephone.

The chapter on *Values and Interests*, Chapter 1 in the first edition, becomes Chapter 2.

Copy Preparation, which had been *Appendix A*, was moved up to Chapter 3, because it was felt that students must learn early the correct methods of preparing copy. New material on free-lance copy preparation and procedures was included for magazine writers.

Organization remains Chapter 4. The chapter was changed extensively and illustrated with new examples. There is more on outlining and more on feature writing, with new examples.

Writing Types, which illustrates all of the forms used in mass media writing brought to bear on one event, was moved from Chapter 10 to Chapter 5 to augment the organization chapter.

Word Usage, which had been Chapter 7, becomes Chapter 6, moving it ahead of *Sentences*, now Chapter 7 and *Paragraphs*, now Chapter 8. An expanded discussion of spelling has been given more emphasis in the *Words* chapter, and discussion of wordiness has been moved from the *Specifics* chapter to the chapter on words.

New information on the use of quotations and quotation marks has been included in the *Specifics* chapter, formerly Chapter 8 and now Chapter 9.

The chapter on *Discipline and Professionalism*, formerly Chapter 9 and now Chapter 11, has been extensively altered. Instruction on how to achieve discipline and professionalism has received new emphasis. The codes of ethics and standards, which had been at the front of the chapter, have been removed from the chapter and become Appendix B. This places the more important instruction on how to put the codes in action into better perspective.

In the first edition, the author was guilty of allowing some sexist wording to mar the book. Every attempt has been made to eliminate sexist identifications or cliches in this edition.

Intended uses of the book are as follows:

—A *text* for courses in writing for the mass media.

—An *auxiliary text* for survey of communications courses in which writing instruction and exercises are required.

—A *self-help text* for the free-lancer, the professional without journalism education, the nonjournalism student seeking to improve writing skills, the public relations volunteer.

The book is not intended for students who have had advanced specialized courses in mass media writing, nor professionals with substantial experience in the same areas.

Acknowledgements

My thanks go to many associates at the University of Florida's College of Journalism and Communications who have helped in the original edition of this book or the present one.

Many thanks to faculty members at schools throughout the country who suggested changes and improvements for the second edition. Special thanks go to Walter Jaehnig and his faculty at the University of Wyoming, Michael Shapiro at Cornell and Ted Stannard at Western Washington University. Their inputs were particularly helpful.

And thanks, especially, to the thousands of students who have helped by testing and refining the philosophy and principles to be expounded herein.

While many have contributed, directly and indirectly, the author alone is responsible for whatever shortcomings may be present in the book.

Edward D. Yates
Gainesville, Florida
May, 1984

TABLE OF CONTENTS

INTRODUCTION:
A WORD ABOUT PROFESSIONAL WRITING

Writing is not a new experience for you. You have been writing most of your life. You've moved from crayons to electronic typewriters. You have written school assignments and letters to family and friends. Some of you have written news and advertisements for high school and community college publications. A few of you have written fiction, both poetry and prose, some published, most unpublished. The more writing you have done as an amateur, the better prepared you should · be to write as a professional. But the transition from amateur to professional is a big one. It demands that you:

—**Learn the craft and art of writing.**
—**Learn to write for a different audience.**
—**Learn the guidelines to measure your writing.**

The Craft and Art of Writing

Writing is both an *art* and a *craft*. Art, of course, is rooted in talent. You come by talent and the ability to create art through an accident of birth. If you have talent, you cannot take any credit for it any more than you can take credit for the color of your eyes or the shape of your nose. If you do not have it, you can't acquire it in college. You have to do without it.

Craftsmanship, however, is an *acquired asset*. It is there for you to achieve if you are willing to work at it. As a craftsman you can take pride in skill acquired by your efforts. This book will concentrate on the craftsmanship in writing. That craftsmanship does not come easily. It takes constant work and constant dedication.

When you set out to become a professional writer, you begin a task you will never finish. *Dissatisfaction* is the *constant companion* of the writer. He never really finishes anything. He just reaches *deadlines* when he has to give an unfinished piece to an editor. Only mediocre writers are satisfied with their efforts. Good writers just do the best they can in the time they have. Someone told *Truman Capote*, author and journalist, about another writer who reportedly never changed a word of his writing, but insisted the first draft be printed as is. Capote retorted scornfully, "That is not writing. That is typing!"

While this book will *emphasize* writing as a craft which can be learned, you are urged to bring your talent and your art to your efforts. Many young people feel that courses and books in beginning writing pay so much attention to writing as a craft that art is stifled. That probably is a needless worry. Art can not be so easily stifled. It has an energy of its own and it will emerge.

While art cannot be denied, it requires a *framework*, a *showcase*, a *support system*. The craft supplies the framework. Most great artists are also great craftsmen. Kurt Vonnegut has given credit to editors on newspapers for improving his writing. Many other gifted writers have polished their talents on newspapers or in ad agencies while preparing to write more lasting novels and dramas. Some better-known journalists who turned authors are Theodore Dreiser, Ernest Hemingway, Winston Churchill, Lillian Hellman, Claire Boothe Luce, Dorothy Parker, Sinclair Lewis, John Steinbeck, Mark Twain, Walt Whitman and Stephen Crane. It could be argued that they were journalists because they were writers. This may be true, but their journalism certainly did not inhibit their talent. Don't be worried about losing your talent by learning the craft of writing. Learning the craft just might nurture the art.

With the point made that journalism is *both craft and art,* be forewarned that art is not always for the mass audience. It is not always simple, direct nor necessarily effective with everyone. It might take much study to comprehend and appreciate a fine poem or a great painting, but the art lover will devote the time necessary to get the emotional and intellectual message. He might, and probably will, return to the work of art again and again.

The mass media consumer *does not look for art* in reading/listening/viewing. He or she will not take the time to decipher the message if it is abstract, subtle or elusive. He or she is seeking the information quickly, information that is clear, concise, complete and effective.

So bring whatever talent you can muster to your writing. Be *original, creative, clever, "artistic,"* but not if it stands in the way of getting information to the reader/listener/viewer effectively.

As you are undoubtedly aware, there is little done for the mass media that is great art. There are certain conditions, you will learn, that inhibit the cultivation of art in the mass media. They are:

—**Time.** Art has a slow, tortuous incubation; mass media writing is usually done hurriedly, directly and under pressure.

—**Purpose.** Art appeals to the intellect and the emotions usually in a profound way; mass media writing provides information, and sometimes entertainment, in a more shallow way for a less profound purpose.

—**Reader/listener/viewer involvement.** Art calls on the reader/listener/viewer's complete concentration and involvement. Mass media reading/listening/viewing is most often casual with limited concentration and involvement.

Craftsmanship is a desirable attribute. Most of you will reach the conclusion with experience and maturity that creativity comes in many forms, some not related to your profession. And if you find that you are a good craftsman as a writer, but not really an artist, that discovery will be no great tragedy. It is much better to find you are a good craftsman without great talent than an unexpressed artist without craftsmanship. The latter discovery is tragic.

WRITING FOR A DIFFERENT AUDIENCE

Up to the point you decided to launch a professional writing career, you have been writing for a *limited* audience which has been *committed* to reading your writing and/or *forgiving* its shortcomings. You have been writing for school teachers who are *paid* to read your writing, regardless of its quality, and family and friends who will read whatever you write *because they love you.*

You are now ready to write for a different audience, one made up of *strangers* who are *not paid,* who have *no commitment* to you and who will be *unforgiving* of your writing shortcomings. You are preparing to write for a *mass media audience.* To satisfy the readers/listeners/viewers of that audience you must make your writing *interesting, clear, direct* and *effective.* Your writing now is probably not interesting, clear, direct or effective because it does not need those qualities to secure readership. But you must learn new rules. The public reader/listener/viewer deserves and demands interesting, clear, direct and effective writing.

Guidelines to Measure Your Writing

This book *will not* teach you to write. *No book, no course, no person* can teach you to write. But books, courses, and teachers can *help you learn* to write. This book will give you *guidelines* to help you criticize your own writing and improve it. You will be asked to:

—**Start to read critically,** asking yourself why you like certain examples of writing and analyzing how those qualities can be utilized in your own writing.

—**Determine to write only as a professional,** realizing that excellence is not something you can turn on or turn off on a whim, but a quality you work at constantly. (If you write a note for the milkman, make it the best note ever written to a milkman.)

—**Write factually** only, dedicating yourself to developing skills in gathering information from a great variety of sources.

—**Determine to write for the readers/listeners/viewers** to interest them, inform them, entertain them by emphasizing their needs and desires.

—**Learn new writing habits** that will lead you to write pieces that are accurate, complete, brief, objective, fair, in good taste and legal.

—**Learn to write effective beginnings** that will attract the readers/listeners/viewers and induce them to continue.

—**Learn to use logic in organizing** material for effective presentation in the various mass media forms.

—**Learn the anatomy of effective sentences** and **paragraphs** including desired lengths, structures, and varieties for the mass media forms.

—**Learn to love** and **use** effectively clear, concise, specific and appropriate words.

—**Learn the mechanics** of **copy preparation** and **style** for the various forms of mass media writing.

The book will present the principles of writing for the mass media and try to explain the reason for them and how they are applied. Attempting to present the application of the principles of writing is dangerous. While writing for mass media is primarily a craft, it is an art in the sense that every story and every advertisement is unique. Two different stories may seem identical, but always there will be different facts involved. Thus *examples* used to illustrate *writing principles* are not nearly as satisfactory as examples presented to illustrate other disciplines. But students want examples to put the principles in proper perspective. For this reason examples are used throughout the book. The reader must be cautioned that the *examples illustrate the principles* as applied to a *specific* set of facts. The *examples help* the student understand the principles if the student remembers that with a different set of facts, the principle might also be applied differently. The *examples can be harmful* if the student ignores the principle and applies the example to a different set of facts.

What is demanded of you in professional writing is not easy. Good writing requires a tremendous display of *self-discipline*. Sitting at a typewriter with a blank sheet of paper is a *lonely challenge*. The only way to meet the challenge is to have the motivation necessary to overcome the overpowering urge to just get up and walk away. *Procrastination* is the writer's private satan, one the writer has to conquer *every* time he or she sits at the typewriter.

But there are *compensations*. The writer performs a *vital* service. The reporter brings to the reader/listener/viewer the vital *information* that person needs to function in his or her community, state, nation or world. That is satisfying. The advertisement writer brings vital *consumer news* to the reader/listener/viewer and plays a key role in the functioning of the economic system. That is satisfying. The public information writer serves as a vital *link* between a client and the public. That is satisfying. All of the effort and headaches may pass with publication of your first professional piece. No reporter ever forgets that first byline. There it is. His or her name at the top of a story. It is an exhilarating experience that can provide motivation for a lifetime.

Chapter I

GOOD BEGINNINGS: NOT EASY BUT CRUCIAL

The dictionary defines the word "begin" in this way: To do the first act or the first part of an action; to take the first step; to start. There is a maxim which holds: A trip of a thousand miles begins with the first step.

It sounds pretty easy, doesn't it? Just start, begin, step out. But as a writer, you will find that the first step is a crucial one. The beginning of your article, ad or script has to perform several functions and can betray you in many ways.

First, the beginning, or lead, as it is usually called in journalistic writing, has to perform these functions:

—It must attract attention of the reader/listener/viewer.

—It must have action.

—It must set the tone of the piece.

—It must give the theme and angle of the piece.

GAINING ATTENTION

You should take the information with the strongest interest to the most people and display it in your lead. Don't save the best for last as you would with dessert at dinner or as you might do if you were writing a novel or short story. Put the best in the lead to attract the reader/listener/viewer. You have to convince him or her immediately that it is worthwhile to read or listen to what you have to say. Give him or her something: information, entertainment, titillation.

In a news story:

> Most of the residents of the city have been assigned to different polling sites for the upcoming election in a new voting district plan outlined today by the county supervisor of elections.

(If you were a voter, wouldn't you want to read on to see how this affected you?)

In an ad:

> Want 70 percent less cholesterol?

(Wonder how you can protect yourself against that demon, cholesterol? Better read on and find out.)

In a feature story:

Topless dancer Joy Bountiful was a radiant bride wearing only a smile and carrying a bouquet of daisies in an all-nude wedding yesterday at the Kit Kat Klub.

(Could you resist reading on?)

GETTING ACTION IN THE LEAD

You should always get some sort of action in your lead. You should also look for the unique thing about your story that sets it apart from other similar stories which may appear in the same issue of the newspaper or be heard on the same newscast.

For example, the media cover a wide range of meetings and speeches. You should look for the unique aspect of the meeting story (either advance story or followup story) you are working on. Let's assume you work on both an advance story and a followup story about a Chamber of Commerce meeting. This is the way *NOT* to do the leads:

The advance—

John Jones, a solar energy adviser for the state, will speak at the meeting of the Chamber of Commerce in the Main Street Hotel Monday at noon.

The followup—

John Jones, a solar energy adviser for the state, spoke at a meeting of the Chamber of Commerce in the Main Street Hotel Monday.

All that has changed in the leads is the tense—the advance is in the future tense and the followup is in the past tense. In a sense, you are saying nothing exciting happened or was said at the meeting. Otherwise, why wasn't it in the lead? Obviously something happened, or Jones said something, to make the followup a different story from the advance. If not, why write about it? Furthermore, why expect anyone to read it or listen to it?

The followup should have focused on something that happened at the meeting or something Jones said about solar energy. For example, a possible lead might have been about other items of business that took place at the meeting if, indeed, Jones said nothing:

—Were new officers elected?

—Were there any other distinguished visitors there?

—Did the group plan some activity of news value during the meeting?

Or if nothing happened, Jones must have said something of interest about solar energy:

—Did he say the future would see an increase in solar energy?

—Did he announce any specific plans the state may have to encourage use of solar energy?

—Did he make any comments about solar energy in response to questions from the audience?

THE PLAYBOY ADVISOR IN PERSON. Did this lead get your attention? It was designed to do so just as James Peterson, the 36-year-old bachelor better known as "The Playboy Advisor" does in his monthly offering. His "leads" certainly induce further reading. (Courtesy Wide World of Photos/AP.)

There just has to be something that happened, or you should tell your editor to forget the followup. There is no point in printing or broadcasting "no news" stories. There is not enough space or time for stories *with* news.

Even the advance story could be improved upon. It merely says that Jones will speak. Why not say what he will speak about? Wouldn't this be more likely to be read?

State solar energy consultant John Jones is expected to warn a hometown audience Monday that home utility costs will double or triple unless more use is made of solar energy in the next ten years.

...Then in a second paragraph you could identify the group and occasion for the talk. Your reader/listener/viewer is more apt (especially if he or she is a homeowner) to read on.

The followup lead could have read:

The state will launch a program to increase use of solar energy to offset an expected doubling or tripling of conventional utility costs over the next ten years, the state's solar energy consultant said Monday.

...Then in the second or third paragraph you can identify the speaker further and tell the reader/listener/viewer to whom he spoke and on what occasion. You have action and something new in the lead—something that is not likely to be duplicated in any other story that day.

INDUCE FURTHER READING

Always give the reader/listener/viewer something in the lead to make him or her want to read on. You can do this in several ways:

—You can lure someone to read on if in the lead you raise the question in his or her mind that he or she wants answered. The lead about solar energy would make the reader/listener/viewer want to read on to find out just what the state plans to do.

—You can use the values to make the reader/listener/viewer read on. If a prominent person is mentioned in the lead, that will hold attention. If something is happening nearby, it will induce further reading. If something of consequence is mentioned in the lead, the reader/listener/viewer will want to know more.

—You can involve the reader/listener/viewer by pointing out in the lead that something is going to affect him or her. He or she will stay with you.

—You can titillate the reader/listener/viewer into continuing by stimulating an emotional response in the lead—sexual interest, sympathy, anger, humor.

Some leads that do these things:

Using prominence—

Tom Selleck will stop briefly at UCLA today on his way back to Hawaii to begin a new T.V. season.

Wouldn't the students at UCLA want to know why Tom is returning, even briefly, to his alma mater? They would read on or listen to the rest.

Involving the reader/listener/viewer—
Our earlier example of changing polling sites for voters certainly would involve the voters. They would want to know if and how it affects them. Another example, from an advertisement:

While you've been growing up, your skin's been growing older.

That would inspire people concerned about their skin to look for more information.

Stimulating an emotional response—
The earlier example of a feature story about a nude wedding would be likely to stir a sexually inspired curiosity about the ceremony and its details if they are kept within the bounds of good taste and, as the Supreme Court says, meet contemporary community standards. Another example of stimulating an emotional response that would inspire further interest would be this:

An 80-year-old widow who said she could not afford both food and heat for her house was found huddled in blankets in her freezing home Tuesday by neighbors concerned about her welfare during the current cold spell.

That lead would certainly arouse sympathy in anyone without antifreeze in his or her veins.

SET THE TONE OF THE PIECE

The tone of anything you write ought to be appropriate for the type of story or ad you are preparing. You don't kid mother nature, or about tragedy. You don't treat frivolity with a sober tone or a serious approach. The tone should always be consistent with the material you are writing. If you are going to be funny, make the reader/listener/viewer laugh early. If you are trying to evoke tears, be sad at the beginning.

Some examples of leads appropriate in tone and some examples of leads inappropriate in tone:

In the end you might find investment in a piece of our real estate valuable.

This lead would be *appropriate* for a developer preparing an ad, brochure or story about new home sites. It would be most *inappropriate* for a cemetery trying to sell burial plots.

A cowboy who was right at home as long as he was on the range became a lost little dogie when his horse chased a steer into a pond during a roundup and dumped the cowhand into the water.

The above lead would be *appropriate* if the story then said the cowhand suffered nothing worse than embarrassment and a dousing.

9

The lead would be most *inappropriate* if the story went on to say that the cowboy, unable to swim, drowned and became a candidate for the cemetery plot mentioned above. (This sentence itself is an example of a sentence in poor taste.)

Burglars messed up a burglary Saturday at a beer distributor's warehouse in the city, but they left a neat scene of the crime.

This would be *appropriate* if the story went on to say that the burglars had piled cases of beer neatly on the loading dock but were chased off by police before they could load the beer into their truck.

However, the lead would be most *inappropriate* if in chasing off the burglars a policeman had a fatal heart attack.

Maintaining the proper tone in the lead involves exercising good taste, but it also involves letting the reader know whether the story to follow will be serious, sad, nostalgic, humorous, etc.

INDICATE YOUR THEME IN THE LEAD

As you should have learned in previous writing courses, each composition should have a theme. Journalistic writing, while more structured and more dictated by the facts, must still have that theme, that thread running through the story to give it unity. The main difference, of course, from writing an essay, or a fictional piece, is that the theme and the facts of a news story are thrust upon the writer. In writing an essay, you can choose your theme and then choose the facts to expand, explain and flesh out the theme. In writing a news story or an advertisement, you are given the facts and you have to determine the main thrust of the piece and fit the predetermined facts to that theme. In journalistic writing your starting point and your boundaries are dictated by the situation in general and the specifics.

Journalists sometimes refer to the *angle* of a story. The angle is about the same as the theme, with a slight difference. Both really refer to what material will be emphasized in the story by the amount of attention given it and the way it is treated. For example, you could emphasize some fact by placing it in a certain position in the story you write. The most emphasis you can give to material is to put it at the beginning—in the lead. You can emphasize material also by how much of it you use in the story. If you devote a great portion of your piece, no matter the size of the piece, to particular facts, then you have emphasized those facts and made them the theme of your piece.

If you want to differentiate between theme and angle, and it is a very fine distinction, you might say that what you emphasize is the theme and how you emphasize it is the angle.

Angle is not only how you use the material you wish to emphasize but the tone you use, the language you use and the reader/listener/viewer for whom you are writing. Let's assume you are doing a free-lance article on the tourist attractions in your city. If you are going to try to sell it to Family magazine, you would emphasize those things about your city that would be suitable for family visits—historic landmarks, natural wonders (falls, mountains, caves), recreational parks, lakes, oceans, family restaurants. However, if you were writing your piece for Playboy magazine, you would emphasize night clubs, adult entertainment, gourmet dining places and life in the fast lane in general. Different audience—different theme, angle and tone.

Before we leave the discussion of the theme, let's emphasize again that the theme should be introduced in the lead, and then become the string that holds the rest of the story together. For example, if you set out to do a profile feature story on an individual and you decide to concentrate on some aspect of that person's personality—his good humor, his absent-mindedness, his zest for life—you write a lead that played up that personality trait. Then you would return to that theme periodically throughout the piece.

VARY THE LENGTH OF THE LEAD

The length of the lead can vary considerably depending on the nature of the piece. A print ad may have a lead of only a few words. A lead for a profile, most often an anecdote about the person, could run several lines or paragraphs. A lead for a depth story, which might be the presentation of a single case history or a series of case histories, might run more than a page.

An advertising lead is almost always short. The advertising lead is the headline of the ad, and usually runs only a few words. Examples:

—Come alive, come and drive the first Nissan 300 ZX Turbo.
—Soda, rocks or neat, Bacardi makes it just right.
—Blue Diamond almonds . . . when hunger strikes at the office.
—Real gold. Tell her how much you love her without saying a word.

News story leads for newspapers or broadcast outlets are usually summary leads that are relatively short. A good rule to follow on a summary lead is to make it no longer than three typewritten lines, with occasional exceptions. Examples of summary leads taken from one issue of a newspaper:

Two hours after he was hired Wednesday, a salesman at an Orlando car dealership fled with his first customer's $5,000 down payment and the man's new car, police said.

***

KENNEDY SPACE CENTER—NASA's five-man repair team leaves today to capture and fix a solar observatory, hoping to prove that broken satellites no longer have to remain losses in space.

***

11

For the first time since the U.S. Supreme Court reinstated the death penalty in 1976, two death row inmates were executed on the same day Thursday.

***

WASHINGTON—The House Thursday rejected a Republican deficit-reduction package and moved to adopt a budget blueprint that accommodates a $182 billion Democratic plan for cutting federal red ink.

To summarize, leads for ads are extremely short; leads for news stories are usually of medium length; leads for feature stories and depth stories can be extremely long. However, leads for each of the forms of writing can vary widely.

THE HEADLINE IS NOT THE LEAD

We might point out here that when referring to news stories or feature stories, the headline is *NOT* the lead. In news and features the lead is usually the first paragraph of the story. The reporter who writes the story writes the lead. He cannot write the headline because he does not know what kind of headline the editor will want or what size. The headline is often written from the material in the lead of the story and summarizes the lead. Here would be a typical headline and lead:

Headline

Judge Refuses to let Sheriff Skip
Testifying in Court Suit

Lead

A judge Monday refused to let Hometown Police Chief John
Jones dodge a subpoena to testify in the Civic Association lawsuit
against his department.

As you can see, the headline written by the editor summarizes, in less space and fewer words, the lead written by the reporter. Because headlines fall into the province of editing, not writing, we will not go any further into headlines in this book, at least as they relate to print news or feature stories or broadcast news.

However, we have pointed out that in advertising, the headline and the lead are often one and the same. The ad is written usually by one person, and the headline often functions as the lead. The headline in an ad can move right into the copy that follows. For example:

Ad headline (Lead)

The cost of energy just tumbled.

Body of ad copy

If you are willing to use your appliances at off-peak hours, you
can now save power dollars under our new pricing policies.

In some print media ads, the headline will resemble a news story headline. Commericals for radio often have no headlines. The announcer begins with the first sentence of the body copy.

SUMMARY LEAD

The summary lead is the type of lead most often used in newspaper stories. Simply, it summarizes what the story is going to be about, either in a general or specific way. It usually is one paragraph, often just one sentence. A typical summary lead might read:

A fiery automobile crash killed one man and injured two others near here today.

That lead would summarize for the reader/listener/viewer what happened. In a general way it tells *WHAT* happened, to *WHOM*, *WHERE* it happened and *WHEN*. It might have told *HOW* and *WHY*, in which case it would have illustrated the "five W's" lead, which you may have heard about in past readings. At one time, many reporters considered it necessary to include in every news story lead the *WHO, WHAT, WHEN, WHERE, WHY* and *HOW*. That requirement no longer exists among editors.

The modern newspaper summary lead makes use only of those "W" elements that seem appropriate for the story being written. It may use them all in the lead of a very short story, or item. More often, the lead will include only some of the elements. Usually the *WHAT* and the *WHO* are included, at least in a general way if not in a specific way. The *WHEN* and *WHERE* are almost always included, again in a general way if not specifically. The *HOW* and the *WHY* are included when they are important elements of the story. In the following examples, look for the emphasis on different "W" elements and varied use of specific elements and general elements.

To repeat the earlier lead:

A fiery automobile crash killed one man and injured two others near here today.

Note that the *WHAT, WHO, WHERE* and *WHEN* are general. The lead does not give specific details of *WHAT* happened because accidents are usually complicated and hard to explain in a lead. The lead does not give the names and identification of the dead and injured, probably because they were not well-known persons, and their names, addresses and ages would clutter up the lead. The word "here" is a specific *WHERE*, in that it means the city in which the newspaper story will appear. The street and block in which the accident happened would add to the clutter of the lead and can be given later in explaining the accident. "Today" may be as specific a *WHEN* as you need if the hour of the accident was not important in the total story. Or you could give the hour in a later paragraph.

Now let's assume the person killed was prominent. You might want to emphasize the *WHO* by placing it first in the story and giving the specific *WHO*, thusly:

13

Mayor Thomas Dwyer was killed in a fiery automobile crash here today.

Or it is possible the *WHEN* might be an important element in the story:

Just 30 minutes after he accepted delivery of his new automobile, a man was killed in a fiery crash here today.

The *WHERE* could be the most important element of the story and deserve emphasis:

At the blind corner of Main and First streets, where five people have died in automobile accidents in the past five months, a man was killed in a fiery crash today.

We haven't forgotten about the *WHY* and the *HOW*. Circumstances might dictate they get the emphasis as in the following:

Why Lead

Because he wanted to spend Christmas with his family, a local serviceman drove all night from his base in Virginia to his home here. He didn't make it. He apparently went to sleep at the wheel, and his car crashed early today, killing him instantly.

How Lead

Skidding on a freshly oiled road, a local man's car went out of control and smashed into a tree here today, killing him instantly.

In using the summary lead, you must analyze your material and use the general or specific elements that seem called for by the circumstances. It should be short, probably no more than 25 words. It should summarize what is to follow. It should give proper emphasis to the elements that are important.

IDENTIFICATION IN THE LEAD

There are two problems of identification in constructing the news summary lead. You have to decide how to identify the subject of the story, or the subjects if there are more than one. You also have the problem of identifying the source of your story, and attributing the source to the story. This book will offer more on attribution later, but here we will discuss attribution as it applies to the lead.

Specific identification in the lead of the subject, or subjects, the story is about is preferred by most newswriters, but only if that identification is not too long and cumbersome. Some examples follow:

Effective specific identification in the lead—

Hometown Police Sgt. Mike Strong was honored Tuesday for his efforts in capturing two armed men charged with burglary of the Ninth National Bank.

The policeman is a vital part of the story, and a specific identification is not that much longer than a general one, "A Hometown police sergeant." On the other hand, there would be no attempt to identify the robbery suspects. It would take too much space and clutter up the lead, which is about as long as a summary lead should be.

14

Ineffective specific identification in the lead—

Andrew Peter Judressiack, 30, an assistant maintenance supervisor at the Westside Utility Plant, and Frederick Holmes Cunningham, an employee of the city utility department....

... well, you get the idea. The lead is already longer than it should be, and there has been no mention of the WHAT, WHERE, or WHEN.

It would be much better to make the lead say, "Two city utility workmen...," then you would have room for the rest of the lead. You can give the specific names and job titles later in the story.

It is always better to give the source of your information in a summary lead, at least in a general way, if you can. Where it would result in an overlong, cluttered lead, you can postpone the identification of your source to the second paragraph, but you need to tie the attribution into the lead so the reader/listener/viewer will know who the source is for the material in the lead paragraph. It would work this way:

Identification of the source in the lead—

An increase of two mills in the real estate tax may be needed to balance the city's budget, Mayor Thomas Dwyer said Wednesday.

Identification of the source postponed until the second paragraph—

An increase of two mills in the real estate tax may be needed to bring in the $6 million which city budget director Alfred Baker estimates will be needed to balance the budget for fiscal year 1980-81.

In announcing the possible tax increase, Mayor Thomas Dwyer said it would provide needed services at a cost of only $70 more a year in taxes for the average homeowner.

Although the attribution is postponed until the second paragraph, to keep the lead from being too cumbersome, it will be clear to the reader/listener/viewer that the need for the tax was expressed by the mayor and not the budget director.

In determining whether you should put the specific WHO, WHAT, WHEN or WHERE in the lead, be guided by the following rule:

If you can be specific in as short a space as you can be general, you might as well be specific.

As to the WHY and the HOW: If you feel they are important enough to be in the lead, you should be specific.

People Have Many Identifications

You should also remember that everyone has more than one identification, and the identification you use should fit the story you are working on at the time. For example, all people have certain general identifications such as:

—A name. (This is an individual identification, but can be duplicated. There are many Mary Smiths.)

—An address. (Almost everyone has a home, be it ever so humble, or a palace.)

—An occupation. (Everyone is working at a specific job, is retired, is unemployed, is a student, or has a profession.)

The more of these general identifications you use about a person in the news, the better. There could be two Mary Smiths living at an apartment complex, so a name and an address might not be enough. If you add the occupation, then readers know it is Mary Smith, the teacher, and not Mary Smith, the lawyer. Another element you can add is the age. If Mary Smith, the teacher, is 58 and Mary Smith, who also happens to be a teacher and lives at the same apartment complex, is 36, the age makes the identification accurate.

In addition to the general identifications all people have in common, most have specific identifications that might be more appropriate to use in certain stories about them. For example, people often are active in civic affairs. So Banker James Brown, who is a banker in most stories, may become chairman of the United Fund during the drive for funds for that organization.

Other people will have other specific identifications in different situations in which they might be in the news. A university student, who is also a member of the debate club, will become a debater when he wins the debate contest. The machinist in a factory, who is president of his plant's union, becomes a union representative during contract negotiations. The lawyer who heads the city's Boy Scout Council, becomes a scouting official when the Boy Scouts are in the news. When you are writing about or quoting a person with a specific identity other than the general name, age, address and occupation, use the appropriate identification that fits the particular story. When the age, address, or occupation will do, use the general identification.

OTHER TYPES OF LEADS

While the summary lead is the one most often used to begin news stories, there are many other types of leads that can be used for news stories but are more commonly used for feature stories and/or advertisements. Hugh W. Cunningham, a professor of journalism at the University of Florida, categorized these types of leads in his book "Writing for the Reader, Listener, Viewer" several years ago. He listed the most common:

—The modified summary lead.
—The quotation lead.
—The question lead.
—The narrative lead.
—The punch or jolt lead.
—The analogy lead.
—The suspended interest lead.
—The cumulative lead.

—The flashback lead.
—The contrast lead.
—The direct address lead.
—The dialogue lead.
—The freak lead.

These categories are simply guidelines. Leads may seem to fit into more than one category and often do. A quotation may be part of a narrative lead. A question may be a direct address lead. A punch lead may read like a summary lead. But the classifications are good for study purposes and for analyzing writing—something every aspiring writer must do if he or she wishes to improve his or her own writing and style.

Modified Summary Lead

The modified summary lead is used when you want to dramatize and strongly emphasize one element, or possibly two, of the story. It is usually reserved for rather momentous events:

World War III started today.

President Kennedy is dead, the victim of an assassin's bullet.

The nation's railroads are running once more.

Quotation Lead

Use the quotation lead sparingly. Most quotes are not worthy of being played up in the lead. But occasionally a good quote can make an effective lead. There are two types of quotation leads that are effective:

—When the quotation sums up the story as well as you could paraphrase it.

—When the quote is short and startling and is in harmony with the general theme of the piece.

A good example of the first type is the following lead that might have been written over a century ago:

"If nominated, I will not run. If elected, I will not serve."

Thus, Gen. William T. Sherman took himself out of the presidential race yesterday.

An example of the second type of quotation lead might be this advertisement:

"Yeah, I use Listerine, but I hate it."

Don't hesitate to use the quotation lead, but use it with care. You can probably summarize shorter and better than the quote, but not always.

Question Lead

The question lead is one that beginning writers tend to overuse. Again, it should be used sparingly, and only if it fits into one of two categories:

—The question is one that has no answer—a moot question.

—The question is one that can be and is answered immediately after it is posed.

An example of the moot question:

Will a guaranteed annual income solve the myriad problems in the American welfare system?

That is the question Congress will debate in the coming weeks.

Or the question for which there is an immediate answer:

Do the dangers of not taking birth control pills outweigh the dangers of taking them?

"Yes," agreed a panel of doctors at a conference here yesterday.

Narrative Lead

A narrative lead, usually in the form of an anecdote, is an excellent lead for a feature story. It develops interests, provides the tone and angle of the piece, and can set the theme. Magazine writers probably use the anecdote lead more than any other kind, especially in personality or profile stories. But it can be used effectively in news stories, as the following narrative lead illustrates:

As a student editor of his college newspaper, John Jones covered the execution of a prisoner.

"It left me physically ill and mentally shaken," he recalled. "I swore I would do everything I could to end such a barbaric practice."

Monday, Gov. John Jones fulfilled that oath. He signed legislation outlawing capital punishment in the state.

Punch or Jolt Lead

Inasmuch as one of the functions of the lead is to get the attention of the reader/listener/viewer and induce him or her to read on, there is no better way to do so than to give a piece of astonishing information. This will certainly grab attention. Some examples:

The low temperature this morning in Fairbanks, Alaska was 28 degrees; the low temperature in Atlanta, Ga. was 22 degrees!

***

In a poll taken in a political science class, only one college student in five could name his or her Congressional representative.

***

Americans spend more money annually to keep their cars running than they do to keep themselves healthy.

The punch line is effective, but it must be used with care. The lead should represent the theme of the story, and not be a sensational side issue used in the lead only to attract attention.

18

Analogy Lead

In an analogy lead, the writer draws a comparison between the situation he is writing about and a similar situation, usually one that would be known to the reader/listener/viewer. The analogy usually involves something from literature (Shakespeare is a favorite), the Bible, a song title, an advertising slogan in vogue, a nursery rhyme—anything from the reader/listener/viewer's background. The advantage of this is the reference to something with which the reader is familiar, makes him or her comfortable reading your piece, and he'll read on.

An ad might read:

Humpty-Dumpty should have had Blue Cross. When all the king's men failed him, his Blue Cross would have paid for the best hospital and doctors to get him back into shape.

Obviously, the analogy lead is most often used with light-hearted stories or ads. You must take care not be be frivolous with a serious story.

Suspended Interest Lead

The suspended interest lead is a lead in which you gain the interest of the reader/listener/viewer without revealing immediately what the story is about. But you usually do not keep him waiting too long. By the second or third paragraph, clear up the suspense.

The County Safety Council was discussing stricter safety observance through increased educational efforts last night.

Chairman Tom Smith leaned back in his chair as he listened to a colleague. His chair flipped over backward.

Today he is resting comfortably at home with a broken right arm and a keener appreciation for safety.

Cumulative Lead

The cumulative lead, as its name implies, is a lead in which you use several items to make your theme or point:

A grade school teacher lives in Hometown and must drive 40 miles each day to her school in Yourtown. An independent bread man drives 60 miles daily to cover his route. A construction superintendent often drives up to 30 miles a day to oversee jobs he has under way.

All of them are wondering if the high price of gasoline will keep them from making a living.

Flashback Lead

A flashback lead is a lead in which the writer refers to an earlier time when a situation existed similar to the one being written about. It might read like this:

In the prosperous 50's and 60's, people thought the prospects for economic improvement for all Americans were unlimited. Today, many wonder whether that American dream is slipping away for large segments of the population.

Contrast Lead

The opposite of the analogy lead, which shows similarities between the subject being written about and something the reader/listener/viewer would be familiar with, is the contrast lead, which shows how things differ.

Cows used to graze peacefully on the rolling hills south of Hometown. Now those hills are covered with suburban homes as the population continues to expand.

Direct Address Lead

The direct address lead, wherein you, the writer, speak directly to the reader/listener/viewer, is an especially effective lead for advertisements and, to a lesser degree, for broadcasters. Direct address establishes or confirms a close relationship between the writer and the reader/listener/viewer and between the product or service being advertised and the reader/listener/viewer. The relationship is helpful in selling. Some examples of the direct address lead as used in advertisements:

Ever wonder why the phone works when the lights go out?

Spend a milder moment with Raleigh.

If after 30 days your kids aren't still playing with our toy more than others, we'll send you your money back.

Are you passing your courses, but flunking life?

A most effective lead in advertisements, the direct address has other uses. It is good for how-to-do-it articles (like the book you are reading. Notice how many times the word YOU has been used.) The direct address can also be used in a news story, as in this:

As a Hometown taxpayer, you can expect to pay about $30 more per year in real estate taxes because of a record city budget adopted Monday by the city commission.

The Dialogue Lead

The dialogue lead is perhaps used most often in media writing by the writers of commercials for radio or television. You are probably all too familiar with television commercials which feature conversations between the housewife and any number of strange characters who seem to pop into her kitchen, often to be heard but not seen. The same sort of thing is heard often on radio, sometimes the same dialogue without video. You have heard it:

STRANGE VOICE: Madam, why are you cleaning your oven with that Brand X cleaner?

HOUSEWIFE: Oh, hello, whadya say? (She expresses no alarm that this disembodied voice is loose in her kitchen.)

STRANGE VOICE: Why don't you use our brand and save yourself work, money and blisters on those soft hands?

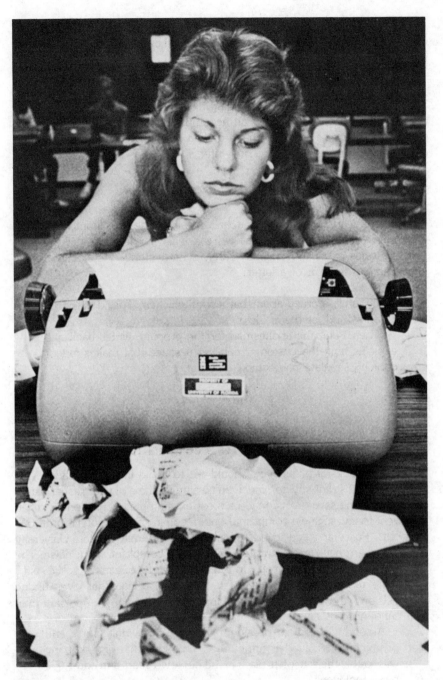

THE LEAD IS NOT ALWAYS AN EASY TASK. Remember that using information with the strongest interest to the most people is a good general rule. Follow it and you will be on target more often than not. (Courtesy Wide World of Photos)

The housewife then says something that reveals she didn't know about this wonderful product and that she will ditch her old brand immediately. (Housewives in commercials are not very loyal.)

But seriously, the dialogue approach to advertising is effective.

It is, however, a more difficult form of writing than straight exposition, so beginners ought to steer clear of using dialogue writing. Aside from advertising, dialogue can be used by an accomplished writer to begin a feature story. Care must be taken to make certain the conversation rings true, no easy achievement. Ask any fiction writer.

Freak Lead

The freak lead category is a catchall. If a lead does not fit into any other category it could be classified as a freak lead. These are usually used in feature stories, or advertisements—rarely in news stories. An example would be an ad in the form of a letter:

Dear Pete:

My family's crazy about barbecued chicken. They'd barbecue indoors if I'd let them. Help!

...Then Pete, the spokesman for the product, writes back and explains how the customer can get a sauce that makes indoor cooking simulate barbecuing.

SOME THINGS TO AVOID IN LEADS

There are several pitfalls you should try to avoid in writing leads.

—*Avoid leads that say nothing.* Don't waste the time of your reader/listener/viewer. Don't say, "Police made a most exciting discovery Monday when they went to investigate a complaint of noise coming from a motel room." Say right out: "Police arrested several members of a fraternity at State University Monday when they raided a motel room after a complaint about noise. The students were having a pot party to celebrate the end of exams, police said."

—*Avoid what might be called the P.R. lead,* a lead that gives undue emphasis on the source, when what happened is much more important than who announced it. An example might be:

Amos L. Bossman, president of the Ajax Widgit Corp. and prominent civic leader, announced Thursday that his company will double the size of its plant in the next two years and add 1,000 new employees.

The public is much more interested in the news that there will be 1,000 new jobs in town than who made the announcement.

Write it:

The Ajax Widgit Corporation will double its manufacturing capacity in the next two years and create 1,000 new jobs in Hometown.

You can say who made the announcement in the next paragraph.

—*Avoid anecdote leads that are too long.* If an anecdote lead takes a page and a half to complete and the entire story is to be only two pages, you have the tail shaking the wombat. A long anecdote would be fine for a long magazine story. But always keep things in proportion.

—*Avoid disassociated and hypothetical leads.* Only a beginning writer would start a piece: "Can you imagine what it would be like to be . .?" Avoid it.

—*Avoid exaggerating unimportant incidents in the lead.* Even if an incident is funny, tragic or poignant, do not give it undue emphasis unless it is related to the theme of the story. An example—somewhat exaggerated ala Saturday Night Live—would be:

President Awkward, returning from a Summit Meeting called to try to avert an impending war in the Mideast, slipped on the exit stairs from Air Force One and almost fell.

Embarrassed, he drew himself to his full height and walked toward the microphone to address the nation, but he slipped on the ice and fell on his fanny. He was helped to his feet and then proceeded to the microphone and made this announcement:

"We have been unsuccessful in our efforts to mediate this dispute. In all likelihood, war will break out within a day or two. I am declaring a national alert. We must be prepared for anything. We could be at a full state of war within a week."

As said, this is an exaggeration. Few of the rawest amateur writers would be apt to so distort the news. But there have been lead stories about presidents hitting their heads on helicopter doors, presidential candidates having holes in their shoes, and other similar trivia. So make certain that when you write a lead you play up what is important, not what is incidental.

—*Avoid using pointless anecdotes.* There is always a temptation to use a particularly good anecdote if you are doing a feature story or personality profile, whether or not the anecdote applies to the theme of your piece. Resist that temptation. It is hard to do, but often you have to discard a good anecdote because it doesn't fit into the theme. For example, if you are writing a story about a professor who is devoted to his job, playing up his good relationships with students and the excellence of his teaching and research, there just may not be any place in the story for the tale about the time he captured 25 German soldiers during World War II.

—*Avoid putting too many details in your lead.* As we have already illustrated, too many specific details in a lead can clutter it so badly the reader will have trouble making it out. Summarize in the lead and leave the details until later. Don't do this:

Mary P. Schroeckengost, 23, of 2634 NW 41st St., Hometown, an assistant teller at the West 29th Street branch of the Ninth National Bank, a subsidiary of the Hometown National Bank and Trust Company, suffered a broken rib, a bruised left arm, contusions and abrasions to the face and body, and shock at 10 a.m. Thursday when her 1979 subcompact automobile, proceeding north on the Boulevard of the Americas, blew the right front tire, careened across the median strip and collided with a 1978 sedan driven by...

This, of course, is also an exaggeration. But it may serve to make the point that you cannot crowd too many details into a lead without making it gibberish. The lead could have read:

A Hometown bank employee was injured, not seriously, in a two car collision on the Boulevard of the Americas Thursday, a police representative said.

Avoid letting your lead stand alone. A lead must be smoothly joined to the story that follows. Here are examples of how to tie a lead in with what follows and what not to do:

Two men were arrested Wednesday and charged with armed robbery in the holdup of three liquor stores in a two-hour period, a police representative said.

Police identified the two men as etc....

* * *

Two men were arrested Wednesday and charged with armed robbery in the holdup of three liquor stores in a two-hour period, a police spokesman said.

John Smith, manager of the Fifth Avenue Liquor store, arrived at work at 8 a.m. and was preparing to open for the day when he noticed a car pull up outside the store.

In the first example, the lead is tied to the rest of the story through the reference in the second paragraph of the two men discussed in the first. However, in the second example there is nothing to tie the second paragraph to the first. It is almost as though you are starting another story. Remember: link your lead clearly to the rest of the story.

SUGGESTED EXERCISES

1. Look through the newspaper and pick out several leads you think could be improved. Look for those that violate some of the rules we have discussed, such as being too long and cluttered, using poor quotations or inappropriate questions. Rewrite them using either the same type of lead but improving on it, or choosing another type of lead that might be more appropriate.

2. Working with another student or an instructor, have the other person choose several leads that are, in his or her estimation, good ones. Have him or her break the lead up into its various WHO, WHAT, WHERE, WHEN, WHY and HOW elements and retype these. Then write leads from the facts given and compare what you did to what the leads were originally.

3. From the following information, write several different leads playing up different angles of the story. Write one summary lead featuring the WHO and WHAT. Write another summary lead featuring the WHY. Write another lead featuring the HOW. Finally, write a quotation lead. Pay attention to keeping the leads short and tying the leads into a second paragraph. Analyze the leads to determine which is the best and why and under what slightly different circumstances the others would be preferable.

WHO: Hometown University student, Mary P. Brown, 22, senior in the College of Nursing. Hometown Miami. Local residence - 1428 NW 6th Avenue

WHAT: Was killed in automobile accident.

WHEN: This morning at 7:15 a.m.

WHERE: Corner of University Avenue and 17th Street.

HOW: Her Volkswagen was struck broadside by a Hometown bus.

WHY: She failed to stop for red light as she entered University Avenue from 17th Street.

SOURCE: Patrolman Fred P. Wright

ADDITIONAL INFORMATION:

—She apparently died instantly

—Was pinned in car for an hour before body could be released.

—"It was the grimmest thing I have seen in my two years on the force," Wright said. "She didn't have a chance. The car was crumpled as though it had been smashed by a giant hammer."

—A friend, Gladys Schmidt, said she did not understand why Miss Brown even was out driving at 7:15 a.m. because she had no class today until 10:10 a.m.

4. From the following notes about certain stories, write summary leads that seem most suitable for the material:

WHO: The state.

WHAT: Must increase its water reserves and cut down on waste.

WHY: To insure enough fresh water for growing population.

SOURCE: Professor Dewey Aquifer, meterology department, Hometown U.

* * *

WHO:	Hometown Police chief John Jones.
WHAT:	Retained his position as Chief despite move by mayor to fire him.
WHEN:	Last night (Monday) at city commission meeting.
HOW:	Commissioners voted 4 to 1 against the mayor's motion.
SOURCE:	Reporter at the meeting.

* * *

WHO:	Seven men
WHAT:	Were arrested on I-75, just outside Hometown with truck loaded with 300 bales of marijuana.
HOW:	State Police stopped the truck for routine check
WHEN:	Friday night at 10 p.m.

* * *

WHO:	Prison inmate Floyd Fowler
WHAT:	Given death penalty for fatally stabbing another inmate
WHEN:	Tuesday at 3 p.m.
WHERE:	Hometown County Courthouse

* * *

WHO:	Members of Hometown Recreation Authority
WHAT:	Told construction of Jones Park will be completed March 1
WHEN:	Thursday
WHERE:	Luncheon meeting in the General Hotel
SOURCE:	City engineer P.J. Pelland

5. The following are examples of poor leads for the reason given. Rewrite the leads to improve them following the principles discussed in this chapter:

(P.R. Lead)

Police Chief John Jones yesterday announced the promotion to captain of Lt. Caldwell K. Jennings, head of the police detective squad, for his work in capturing a murder suspect last week.

(Cluttered Lead)

Robert Q. Charles, 33, William J. Quimby, 25, and Carole Viola Crenshaw, 22, all of High Springs, have been charged with grand theft, breaking and entering, resisting arrest, and unlawful use of firearms for the robbery on Thursday, March 26, last year of $46,000 in currency and $20,000 in checks from the office of Fred Albertson, president of Hometown County Community College.

(Say-nothing Lead)

Dr. Francis Roberts, of Hometown University, talked last night to the annual banquet of the Hometown Founder's Club in the Hotel Bostwick.

"Young men who smoke marijuana over a period of years, even though they smoke it infrequently, run a risk of permanent impotence in middle years," said Roberts, a research professor in the Ourstate University Medical School.

(Hypothetical Lead)

If you could change places with rock singer Danny Digitalis your life would be one of incessant travel, constant hiding out in hotels from overzealous fans and making more money than you have any chance to spend.

(Pointless Anecdote Lead)

When Jane Mapleoak was just ten, her mother caught her taking 50 cents from her brother's piggy bank to buy candy from the grocer.

She promised her mother that she would never again steal a penny from anyone.

She broke her promise. Tuesday, Jane, now 23, was arrested by police along with two others for the armed robbery of the North Hometown Building and Loan Association office of $10,000.

(Letting Your Lead Stand Alone)

A Pennsylvania study on how people use pesticides has prompted a national study of the practice.

Dr. David Pilson, Pennsylvania State University biochemist, last night addressed a record crowd of scientists attending the yearly science fair and seminar in Pittsburgh.

Chapter II

VALUES AND INTERESTS: CAPTURING YOUR AUDIENCE

Think for a moment about how you read a newspaper or magazine and how you listen to television news. Do you bring the same intensity and attention to those reading and listening moments as you would bring to reading a recipe you are using to prepare a dinner for guests, or reading a love letter, or listening to a recording of your favorite vocalist? Not likely.

You probably read, listen and watch with something less than full commitment. You probably are a scanner. You shop through the paper looking for those things that will register high on your attention scale. You listen or watch broadcasts only partly tuned in—until something grabs you. Most people do that.

Why do you scan printed material and half listen to broadcast material? Think about the circumstances under which you read mass media messages—the newspaper story, magazine article, brochure or advertising circular. You scan because you are busy. You have many things to do that are as important to you, or more important, than the broadcast, but you want to be informed. So you challenge the printed word or the picture and sound from the broadcasters. You say: "Interest me, or I will play golf, or work in the yard, or read a novel, or listen to music, or take a nap."

So you scan; you pick and choose. The writer of news stories and advertisements for print or broadcast consumers must realize that potential customers will be doing the same thing. The writer must capture the interest of the reader/listener/viewer so the latter will pay attention to the news, feature article or advertisement.

THE BASIC INTERESTS: AN OVERVIEW

Fortunately, there are many basic interests that all people share. The writer can make use of these to capture the attention of the reader/listener/viewer, and hold that attention to the end. These universal *interests* include:

—Self.
—Other people.
—Conflict.
—Competition.
—Progress.
—Suspense.

—Drama.

—Sex.

—Fear.

—Sympathy.

—Oddity.

There are probably other universal and basic interests, but these are the ones used most by writers to touch and attract the reader/listener/viewer.

Let's talk about them individually and see how you can utilize them in your writing.

Self Interest

When your high school yearbook was delivered, what did you do first? Did you look quickly at your own picture? Certainly you did. When the new phone book was delivered, you turned to your listing and read your name. You looked after your own interests first. It is a natural thing to do. Your reader will do the same. He or she will look for anything in your story that applies to his or her self interest.

In your writing make use of that self interest in any way you can:

—The city is going to raise taxes by $2 million. In your newspaper or broadcast story tell the reader/listener/viewer that; but, more important, tell him or her that a typical taxpayer will pay $34.50 more a year in real estate taxes. That figure is of more concern to him or her than the $2 million because the $34.50 is near and dear to his or her heart.

In your advertisement, tell the reader/listener/viewer how your product or service will make him or her healthier, happier, wealthier, more attractive, or more efficient.

—Tell the student how much the tuition increase will cost while you are telling how much money will accrue to the university.

—Tell the investor where to get the best return for his or her dollar while you are telling about the general conditions of the economy.

—Tell the homeowner what steps to take to protect himself or herself from dishonest repair operators while you are telling what has been done to other homeowners.

The list is endless. In every story, broadcast, or ad you write, you should think of the audience. If you write to satisfy the interests of the audience, it will respond.

Other People

The reader/listener/viewer is interested in other people. This is what is called human interest. So bring other people into your writing. Tell your story in relationship to people. Bring people into your ad. Use them:

—Quote them. The reader/listener/viewer wants to know what other people think about a situation, product, or set of facts. It helps reinforce his or her thoughts or feelings. It helps him or her identify with the situation, product, or information.

—Describe their experiences. What happened to others in a given situation? It, or something similar, may have happened to the reader/listener/viewer or someone close to him or her. Or it may happen in the future. Or if it couldn't happen to him or her, he or she will still be intrigued because it happened to someone else.

—Show people in action. Have someone eating the hamburger you are advertising. Have someone enjoying the vacation facilities you are promoting. Have someone take the new driver's examination you are telling about in a news story.

Sometimes the only reason for writing a story is that it is about a person, and that is enough of a reason. If two sisters who were separated in childhood get together again after 50 years, it is of no great importance in the world's scheme of things. It really doesn't have any great significance to the reader/listener/viewer. But he or she will be interested because it is happening to other people.

Conflict and Competition

Don't you like a good fight? Oh, maybe not with blood and black eyes, but how about conflict and competition? Do you enjoy detective stories on television? Westerns at the movies? Football games? Quiz shows? Do you read about the ups and downs in the stormy marriage of some celebrity? Is it intriguing to you that Avis is second, and "trying harder?"

Of course you are interested in many or all of these things. You are human, and humans relish conflict. Your reader will like it, too. Bring it into your writing when it is there and you will interest and hold your audience.

What is the most interesting crime story to most people? The story of the ultimate conflict: a murder, a kidnapping, a shootout between police and bandits, a chase? Which would you read first and most thoroughly—a story about a mild-mannered bookkeeper who managed to steal $1,000 over a period of time from his employer and submitted meekly when caught, or a story about a gunman who beat and robbed a shopkeeper of $8.19, fled from police in a stolen car, and was captured after a wild chase and gun battle?

It may be an indictment of the human animal that most would be attracted to the violent crime rather than the peaceful one, but it is a fact of life. The writer does not create human nature. He or she may uplift it at times, but usually he or she caters to it.

A word of caution. A reputable writer does not exploit conflict. But if conflict is present, the writer must recognize the universal interest in it and utilize it in a story.

Conflict appears in many forms:

—The conflict between politicians and parties in political races.

—The conflict between products in competition with each other.

—The conflict between people and the bureaucracy of their government agencies.

—The conflict people have within themselves in controlling their emotions, desires and compulsions.

—The conflict between ideals and practicality.
Conflict can be wholesome and progressive:
—The conflict of science with disease and ignorance.
—The conflict inherent in most sports—that part of the conflict which expresses disciplined training, the character qualities of persistence, dedication, team play and self sacrifice, good sportsmanship.
—The inherent adversary relationship between the press and government which makes the press the watchdog for the people over public servants.
—The demonstrations and petitions of people to obtain or protect their human freedoms and rights.

Living is a conflict from birth to death. Readers/listeners/viewers understand that fact and are interested in conflict, competition, the struggle that is living. The writer who doesn't understand the nature of conflict, and the strong interest it has for all people, had better learn to bring it to his or her writing where it is called for.

Progress

After reading about people's inherent interest in conflict and turmoil, you may have drawn the conclusion that people are just no damned good. Not true. That is just the Mr. Hyde side. The Dr. Jekyll in people also makes them interested in human progress in its many forms.

People are interested in the way humans manage to better themselves in small and big ways, and, critics to the contrary notwithstanding, newspapers, magazines, radio and television devote much time and space to this progress. You, as an aspiring professional writer, should be aware of this interest in progress and appeal to it in your writing.

There are so many examples of it:

The biggest stories in sports are about great human effort in achieving championship performances. Everyone likes to see records broken. When Kareem Abdul-Jabbar of the Los Angeles Lakers basketball team broke the career scoring record of Wilt Chamberlain on April 5, 1984, every basketball fan was thrilled, and most of them were in Salt Lake City to witness the feat. Abdul-Jabbar's parents were on hand to see Abdul Jabbar surpass the 31,419 career points scored by Chamberlain 11 years earlier. National Basketball Association Commissioner David Stern was on hand. And the house was sold out.

The same thrill swept the country during the 1984 Winter Olympics at Sarajevo when American Skiers Debbie Armstrong, Bill Johnson and Phil Mahre won gold medals. And it happened on numerous occasions earlier when:

—Henry Aaron broke Babe Ruth's career home run record.
—Mark Spitz won a host of gold medals in swimming in a summer Olympics in 1976.

—Eric Heiden took a fistful of ice skating medals and when a tenacious group of young hockey players defeated the Russians and went on to win a gold medal in the 1980 Winter Olympics.

People love to honor achievements in any area. Great human achievement raises the spirit of all humanity.

—The reader/listener/viewer applauds the intellectual achievements of a Thomas Edison, an Albert Einstein, or any of many Nobel Prize winning scientists, humanitarians and writers.

—The reader/listener/viewer rejoices in the courage of the handicapped person who overcomes his affliction to gain personal success.

—And while skepticism may dampen his enthusiasm somewhat, the reader/listener/viewer is still interested that the child has fewer cavities because he uses a certain toothpaste.

Progress comes in all areas of human activity. Look for it in whatever you are writing about. It can come in the human condition—health, happiness, personal achievement. It can come in a social context with the environment, general welfare, education, government. It can come through discovery, invention, insight. It can affect your reader/listener/viewer, or it can affect others. But your reader/listener/viewer will be interested. Tell him about it.

Suspense and Drama

If you are reading a murder mystery, do you read the last chapter first? Probably not. It would spoil the story for you. Do you make an attempt to get to the movie as it begins rather than as it is ending? Of course, because you want to enjoy any suspense in the plot. Drama often depends on the element of suspense which is the spice of the entertainment. Suspense holds the reader's or viewer's interest through to the end.

This fact is often true in writing for the various forms of mass media. The police story in which the identity of the slayer or bank robber is not known has an added element of interest to the audience. The teaser advertising campaign wherein the audience is alerted that some big announcement is coming is a productive form of the use of suspense.

Suspense and drama are not as basic to writing for the mass media as they are for writing literature. For the most part, mass media news and advertising attempt to give the audience all of the facts immediately and clearly. But there are situations in which the use of suspense is necessary because the answer is not known; and there are cases in which suspense is useful in building interest. Some examples:

—Future events. You should search for any suspense you can find in trying to make stories about future events more interesting to the reader. Will the injured star quarterback be able to play in the upcoming game? Will the coy politician eventually announce he will run and when? Will the astronauts return safely from their orbit around the moon? Will the union go out on strike on the deadline it has set?

—Continuing mysteries. Where do flying saucers come from? Is marijuana dangerous to your health? Why can't Johnny spell?

—Unsolved past mysteries. Did Lee Harvey Oswald act alone in slaying President Kennedy, or were others involved? Did Hitler commit suicide in a bunker in Berlin at the end of World War II or live out his life in Argentina? Was Muhammad Ali a better fighter than Jack Dempsey or Joe Louis?

The list is endless, but these should illustrate the interest people have in drama and how much they are intrigued by suspense. Use the interests with care, however. Your main function is to give your reader/listener/viewer the facts, but he also enjoys speculation if it is not sensational and if it is handled with care.

Sex

If you are normal and healthy you think about sex a lot. Sex is a basic emotion in all humans and of intense interest to them.

The advertising writer utilizes the human preoccupation with sex to gain interest in his product or service and to motivate the reader to buy. Sex is just one of the motivations used, but it is used widely and effectively.

The news writer, too, makes use of sex to create interest in his story. If the murder was the result of a love triangle, you have a more interesting story than if it was the result of most other motives.

While sex can be used with caution when it is an integral part of a story or a natural part of an ad, it has often been exploited. Obviously, there is nothing wrong in using an attractive woman to model swimsuits for an ad or in using baseball pitcher Jim Palmer to model Jockey shorts. But you should probably avoid exploiting sex to sell unrelated items. Cigarettes and liquor advertisements are the worst offenders today in using sex exploitatively in advertising. It seems that scantily clad voluptuous women and bare-chested, macho men are the only purchasers of cigarettes or liquor. Most products today avoid forcing sex into advertisements in an artificial way.

Editors, too, are more sensitive to feminist complaints that women have often been exploited in the press. If the story does not hinge on an obvious sexual theme, editors will probably cut out any attempt on the part of the writer to give sex undue emphasis.

Sex is universal. There is a great interest in sex. If it is present in a story, or necessary to an ad, go ahead and use it with good taste and proper emphasis.

Fear

Fear is utilized in the mass media, sometimes in a constructive way and sometimes in a destructive way.

Constructively, fear is used to establish respect in adults for those things that may be dangerous to themselves or to their children:

—Carelessness in driving or walking in areas adjacent to heavy traffic.

—The perils of smoking cigarettes, driving while drunk, using drugs to excess, eating foods that may be hazardous to health.

—The dangers small children may face from medicines left within their reach, cleaning materials with caustic chemicals, unsafe toys, pajamas that may catch fire and burn quickly.

Unfortunately, fear can also be used in a less helpful way. Unscrupulous advertisers may sometimes use fear to influence people to buy things they may not need, or which may actually be harmful to them:

—There is the case of the insurance ads that sold an elderly woman various kinds of insurance—health, accident, damage—which cost her more than $5,000 in annual premiums and was unlikely to pay much, if anything, in benefits.

—Some medical firms advertise that people should use their products not only when they have symptoms, but also as a preventive when they do not have symptoms.

—Some not very reputable publications publish undocumented stories that spread false fears of everything from killer bees to creatures from alien planets.

Fear is a powerful and often uncontrollable emotion, and ethical writers will shrink from exploiting fear in news stories or advertisements. Readers should be made aware of real peril, but the writer who cries "fire" in a crowded theater when no fire exists is misusing writing talents and violating responsibility as a journalist.

Sympathy

Sympathy for others is always present among most people. It is easy for a skilled writer to touch the sympathy button with stories of people in some sort of deep trouble—poor health, dire economic straits, untimely loss of a family member.

Sympathy is not a bad tune to play. It is one of the bright notes in the human behavior pattern that brings people closer together. Appeals to sympathy can do many things including:

—Calling attention to the plight of the elderly poor who have to choose between keeping their houses warm in an era of high energy costs, and having enough food to eat.

—Bringing offers of financial aid when a youngster needs medical attention his parents cannot afford.

—Bringing volunteers to the local blood bank when supplies run low.

Oddity

There is a definition of news that holds: If a dog bites a man, it is not news; but if a man bites a dog, it is news. The definition has acquired the status of cliché, but it does illustrate that oddity is a universal interest. Everyone is interested in the unusual, the exotic, the bizarre. The circus sideshow still does good business even in this sophisticated age. The unusual job, the unusual attire (costume parties are popular on Halloween), the unusual philosophy, the unusual anything arouses the interest of the reader/listener/viewer.

Evidence? How about this:

—One of the television shows popular while this was being written was "That's Incredible!"

—Among guests on Johnny Carson's TV show was one man who set fire to his "lemon" car on the lawn of the district office of the manufacturer, and another man who "shot to death" a vending machine that failed to give him his purchase.

—Many theater and television dramas involve encounters with creatures from other planets, children whose bodies have been taken over by satanic figures, and heroes and heroines who are put together with a screw driver and wrench. Everyone loved E.T.

More mundane oddities that might appear in the paper or on the evening news are:

—A story of the 99-year-old man who is celebrating his birthday in his prison cell.

—A story about an Italian groom-to-be who forced his fiancee to undergo a physical examination, and when told by the doctor she might not be as pure as the Alpine snow, shot and wounded her and himself.

—The story about the volunteer firemen who answered the alarm but were unable to fight the fire because all of their equipment was in the firehouse, which was being destroyed by flames.

Unusual things happen all the time. And while oddity is only one facet of news, it is a universal interest you can use to capture attention of the reader/listener/viewer.

To sum up, in all forms of writing for the mass media consumer, you can call on various universal interests to make your stories and your publication or broadcast more appealing. To repeat, these interests are:

—Self Interest.
—Other people.
—Conflict.
—Competition.
—Progress.
—Suspense.
—Drama.
—Sex.
—Fear.
—Sympathy.
—Oddity.

Just knowing and appealing to these universal interests in an objective way is all that is necessary for the writer of news or feature stories for print or broadcast delivery. Writers of advertisements or editorials, both of which want not only to inform the reader/listener/viewer, but also to influence him, have a more complex problem.

Advertisements, public relations promotions, and editorials must not only interest the person they are aimed at, but must try to:
— Convince him or her to adopt a position.
— Convince him or her to change his or her mind.
— Convince him or her that he or she wants or needs what you are selling.
— Move him or her to action—to purchase something, write a letter to a congressman, vote for your candidate, send a check to your charity.

To so move a person requires more than merely interesting that person in reading your effort, it takes a precise knowledge of and use of subtle psychological needs and motivations.

You have to appeal to the reader's specific desires for the necessities of life—food, shelter, health care, money, security, and recognition as an individual. You must also appeal to desires for approval of and contact with the opposite sex, entertainment of various kinds, philosophical fulfillment, and a sense of being useful in contact with others and civic and humanitarian sense of duty.

The accomplishment of such aims requires much more training than is covered by the scope of this book. But you should be aware that you must use appeals to these needs in your writing and should be aware of your response to these appeals as a consumer of media output. How such attempts to motivate the reader are put into practice will be discussed in later chapters.

MEASURING THE INTERESTS

In writing you must not only ascertain what the basic interests are in a given set of facts, but you must also measure the intensity of the interest to a given reader/listener/viewer so you can make best use of the information. There are certain values you can use to measure the strength of the interest. Reporters call them news values, but they are more basic than that; they apply to much more than news. These values are:
— Timeliness.
— Proximity (nearness).
— Prominence.
— Consequence.

Timeliness

Think how important timeliness is to you. Have you ever stood in line to see a new movie even though you knew that if you were willing to wait a few weeks you could walk right into the theater? Why do they call it a NEWSpaper? Why does everyone want to read the latest, wear the newest, drive this year's model? Why is an entire age group referred to by many advertisers as the NOW GENERATION?

The answer is obvious. People are interested in the PRESENT more than the past or future. And after the present they are interested in that which is closest to the present—the NEAR FUTURE and then the NEAR PAST. People are less interested in the DISTANT FUTURE and least interested in the DISTANT PAST. In trying to measure the intensity of an interest, remember that, all else being equal, the reader/listener/viewer interest varies according to that time order.

News media and advertising people are well aware of the importance of timeliness. In advertising, for example, the word NEW is regarded as a key motivational word. Did you ever hear of an OLD soap product? It is always the NEW BRAND X, or the ALL NEW BRAND Y, or the NEWER THAN NEW BRAND Z.

In news writing and editing, print and broadcast journalists strive to get the latest news in the paper or on the air. The strength of radio news is that it is usually first with whatever news occurs. Because radio is more flexible in its programming, it can and does go on the air immediately when an important story breaks. Television is more reluctant to interrupt programming unless the station has really vital news to present. Newspapers take longer to get the news to their customers because of production and delivery demands, but they still strive to be as timely as possible.

Media outlets will also strive to make news that is not the latest sound fresh by writing it in such a way that the time element is not emphasized.

An example of the way in which a newspaper will attempt to play down the lack of timeliness in news is the way afternoon newspapers write about sports events. Deadlines for newspapers that will be delivered in the late afternoon to be read in the evening are too early to permit those papers to carry results of sports events held in the afternoon or evening. Consequently, the morning newspaper always has the first story giving the results of the games played the previous day, so the afternoon newspapers will not lead off with the results and details of yesterday's games. They concentrate on what is going to happen in today's game, or next week's game. They give the details of yesterday's game, but down a bit in the story.

In those depth stories or feature stories which do not have time as an important element, other values will be played up.

Proximity

In determining the extent of your reader/listener/viewer's interest in the people, conflict, oddity, progress, suspense, etc., you can turn to a second measurement of evaluation—nearness of the event. Everything else being equal, interest will be the most intense in that which is close, and less intense for that which is distant.

For example, your reader/listener/viewer will be intensely interested if the person living next door to him is killed in an automobile crash, less interested if the person is from the other end of town, a different town, the next state, or another country.

Again, nearness enhances all of your interests; and distance, in most instances, diminishes interest. For example:

—What sports team do most people root for? The closest.

—What newspaper are you more likely to read? The one from your city.

—Which advertisements are of the most interest to you? The ones of merchants near enough that you can patronize their stores and take advantage of their bargains.

Modern newspapers understand this interest in your own world, your own environment. In seeking to increase circulation beyond their immediate publication area, newspapers will insert special sections with news and advertisements of interest to persons in those outlying areas.

Magazines circulated nationally recognize the value of localized advertising. While much of their advertising may be national in scope, many of them run different regional ads for the different regions of the country.

Prominence

Why do newspapers, magazines and broadcasters publicize everything, even insignificant things, that happen to celebrities? Simply because the people are prominent, and while the reader/listener/viewer is interested in all people, his interest is heightened when the people are well known. The importance of prominence applies not only to people but also to cities, states and nations, institutions, and even ideas. There are many examples:

—Almost anything that happens to members of the President's family is of interest worldwide.

—Advertisers have found that endorsements by celebrities of their products increase sales dramatically. Everyone from movie stars and sports figures to retired politicians with American Express credit cards is pushing products and services.

—On the local level, the mayor of your city finds there is much demand of his or her time in presenting keys to the city, cutting ribbons at openings of businesses, and eating a lot of rubbery chicken at local organizations, only because he or she is the mayor.

It is all prominence at work. People like to read, listen to, and hear about prominent people. As a writer of news and advertisements, you need to be aware of this phenomenon and take advantage of it.

Consequence

The final measurement you should be aware of and utilize is the consequence of the event of situation; consequence often has an inherent interest. The consequence is measured in two ways.

1. The number of people affected.
2. The extent of the consequence, or the seriousness of it.

A few examples will illustrate the play of consequence in determining the value of an interest in an event of situation:

—An automobile crashes, but no one is hurt. Consequence is low. The car crashes, and someone is hurt. Consequence is higher. The car crashes, and someone is killed. The consequence is high. The car crashes, and several are killed. The consequence is extremely high.

—A river overflows its banks in a remote area, and the water covers unused land. The consequence is low. The river overflows as it goes through a city, and several families are made homeless. The consequence is high. A dam breaks, and several people are killed in a flash flood. The consequence is highest.

—A child has his tonsils removed in routine surgery. The consequence is low. A child undergoes experimental surgery, and his life is saved. The consequence is higher. Dr. Jonas Salk discovers a vaccine for polio, and thousands of children are saved from death or crippling. The consequence is maximum.

Journalists occasionally are asked to speculate on what would be the biggest stories they could imagine. The lists almost always contain stories of great consequence:

> World War III
> A cure for cancer
> The assassination of a president
> The approach of the end of the world

USING THE VALUES IN YOUR WRITING

Utilize the four values in analyzing the data from which you will write your news story, feature, advertisement, or promotion. The values bear on one another and each set of circumstances can differ just by a change in the values by which they are measured.

The best story or ad will have strong ratings in all four of the values. For example, the ultimate news story would be for something of great CONSEQUENCE to happen to several PROMINENT people CLOSE to your reader TODAY. If an airplane carrying several of the city's political, cultural and social leaders crashes today at the local airport, that would be the story of the year for that city.

Be aware that a low reading in one or more of the value measurements can be overcome by high readings in one or more of the other measurements. Something of great CONSEQUENCE doesn't have to be NEAR nor involve PROMINENT people. The eruption of Mount St. Helen's in Washington did not involve PROMINENT people, but was news all over the world.

If the people involved in a news story are PROMINENT, the locale of the story does not have to be CLOSE and the story does not have to be terribly CONSEQUENTIAL. In the great scheme of things, does it really matter to the world that some entertainer is going to take unto himself an eighth wife? If something happens NEARBY, it can be weak in CONSEQUENCE, PROMINENCE, and even TIMELINESS.

News writers can use the four values in several ways:

—If mentioning several people in a story and everything else is of equal value, a writer could put the people in his story in order of PROMINENCE. Or he or she might, if they were not all local, put them in the story in order of NEARNESS to the reader.

—If a reporter is writing a story of accidents that took place over a weekend, he or she could discuss them in order of CONSEQUENCE—the most serious first, less serious second, and least serious last. Or, again using proximity as a guideline, he or she could put the accident closest to the reader/listener/viewer (in his city) first, the one in the suburbs second, and the one in the country last. Or he or she could use PROMINENCE to dictate the story order.

—The writer of an advertisement might try to get a PROMINENT person to appear in an ad to attract the reader/listener/viewer to a message. Or he or she might choose to emphasize NEARNESS to the prospective buyer by concentrating on the local status of an organization. Or the advertiser might choose CONSEQUENCE to emphasize. If the customer does not take immediate advantage of the tremendous sale prices, he or she will have to pay full price for a widgit after the sale ends.

If you are confused, perhaps you will also realize that writing is an intellectual exercise. You cannot use stereotypes as models and write your stories to a handy formula. Each function you perform takes a full analysis of the data available to determine what will interest the reader/listener/viewer the most and just how strong each interest is when measured by the values of CONSEQUENCE, PROXIMITY, PROMINENCE, and TIMELINESS. Once you place yourself in the shoes of the readers, listeners, and viewers, you will find it much easier to give them the information in which they are interested in the order and quantity to match the intensity of the interest. It is not easy. But no one promised you a rose garden, especially one without thorns.

SUGGESTED EXERCISES

1. Analysis of a news story:
   Clip a news story from the paper and analyze it for interest and value use. Try to determine:
   —How many of the interests were utilized by the writer of the story?
   —How did the writer use interests in organizing material and in giving priority to the data?
   —What values were apparent in the story?
   —How did the various values come into play in the organization of the story?

2. Analysis of an advertisement from the print media or a commercial from radio or television:
   —Do the same analysis of interests and values as suggested above for the news story.
   —In addition, analyze the advertisement for use of the subtler appeals to motivation and needs which are used to persuade and not just inform.

3. In reading the paper or watching television or listening to the radio, think about why certain stories were selected. What interests did they display, and how did the value of the interests determine the scope of coverage? Ask yourself:
   —What values overcome the fact that the story was from a distance place?
   —Why was the story used when it was of small consequence?
   —Why was the story used when it had low consequence and proximity?
   —Why was the story with low consequence and low prominence used?

4. Cut some stories from the paper. Then change the intensity of one of the values—TIMELINESS, NEARNESS, PROMINENCE, or CONSEQUENCE—and determine how the stories would have been handled differently under the changed values.

Chapter III

COPY PREPARATION: IDEAS INTO TYPE

The once popular jazz song offers these words of philosophy. "It ain't what you do. It's the way that you do it." There is much reason to doubt that the writer, in the throes of inspiration, was thinking of preparing copy for the reader/listener/viewer of the mass media. But there is an analogy. Various mass media writers will disagree widely as to what data they want to present, but the mechanical forms in which they present that data will be strikingly similar. Practicality dictates that an agreed upon set of forms, symbols, styles, usages be employed by publishers and broadcasters. The uniformity of mechanical matters facilitates understanding among professionals and movement of copy and people. Professionals generally agree on such matters as:

—*Copy preparations of news and feature stories for print.*
—*Copy preparations of news and feature stories for broadcasting.*
—*Copy preparation of public relations news releases.*
—*Copy and layout preparation of print advertisements.*
—*Copy preparation of radio commercials.*
—*Style and word usage for print stories.*
—*Style and usage for broadcast stories or commercials.*
—*Style for print advertisements.*
—*Copyediting marks and usage.*
—*Copy to be typeset by an electronic scanner.*
—*Use of video display terminals to write and edit copy electronically.*

COPY PREPARATION OF PRINT STORIES

In preparing news and feature stories for print, all work is *typewritten* on 8½ x 11 inch white paper. All *double spaced*, or preferably, *triple spaced*. Wide-spaced lines make editing easier. There is more room to add to or change copy between the lines. *Type on one side of the paper only.*

Typewriter *margin stops* should be placed at *10 and 75*, allowing *65 units* between the stops. This setting is used universally. It allows the editor to figure quickly the approximate length of a piece. This setting will leave about an *inch margin* on each side of the copy for the editor to make any editing or typesetting marks necessary. A *margin* of about an *inch* should be left at the *top of all pages* except the *first*. The *margin* at the *top* of the *first page* of a piece should be three or four inches. This wide margin at the top of page 1 leaves room for the editor to give *printing direction,* write a *byline,* give direction for a *headline, write* the *headline* or type in an *editor's note.*

Newspaper and magazine news stories or feature stories carry in the upper left hand part of the page: *the name* of the story, called the *"slugline"* or *"slug"* for short, and the *name of the writer* immediately under the *name of the story.* The *slug* is usually one word which indicates roughly what the story is about. For example, a story written about a fire could be slugged *"Fire."* However, if the newspaper had *two* stories *about fires* on a specific day and the *first* was slugged *"fire",* the *second* would have to have a *different name,* perhaps *"blaze,"* or if the fire took place at the "Quality Produce Store," the slug could be *"Quality."* The *slug* is used to keep track of each story. There cannot be duplicate slugs, or parts of two different stories may end up together. Computerized editing and printing systems will not accept duplicate slugs. The *name of the writer* is written on each story so the editor always knows who wrote a piece he is working on.

The *slug line* is repeated on *each page* of the piece *with* the *number* of the page. However, page 2 is *not* marked as *page 2.* Page 2 of the newspaper piece slugged *"fire"* would be marked *"fire, add 1,"* or *"fire, first add."* The *next page* would become *"fire, add 2,"* . . . etc.

There are some circumstances when you might have to furnish more information than the *slug* and your *name.* If you are a *freelance writer* who submits an article for publication you would write an accompanying letter giving your *address, phone number* and other information the editor would want. You would tell him if he has the article *exclusively* or if you have submitted it to others, either in the same area or in other parts of the state or country. If you are a student writing a class assignment your instructor would want you to write, perhaps in the upper right corner, such things as the class, section number, date, and perhaps the instructor's name. The format of a story for newspapers would look like this:

Slug:
Name:

The story would begin roughly three inches from the top maintaining *one inch margins* on the *sides* and the *bottom.* You would *double* or *triple space* all copy.

You could make corrections in your copy using *copy correction symbols* and marks. *Make* such corrections *between the lines of type only.* Do *NOT* add information vertically in the margins. If additions do not fit between the lines, rewrite that part of the story.

As you near the bottom of the page, remember to end the page on a paragraph. In some circumstances, different printers

PRINT ADVERTISING REQUIRES ADDITIONAL SKILLS. Unlike news writers, advertising writers must also write the headlines of their ads. They also must either layout the ad or work closely with the person who does the layout. (Courtesy Wide World of Photos)

may handle different pages of the story. A printer cannot begin a block of type in the middle of the paragraph. At the end of the page, write a (30) if the story is finished. If the store will continue, type (more) at the end of each page until the last.

The Freelance Article

The process for preparing copy for magazines is similar to that for preparing copy for newspapers, but there are differences. Stories to be sent to magazines are manuscripts that represent a much higher investment in time than news stories for newspapers. They should be given more formal treatment. They would be neatly typed without penciled corrections as might be found on a newspaper story. This is especially true of the freelance writer who is submitting work to an editor for the first time. The editor might forgive a talented and experienced writer some sloppiness of preparation, but a new writer needs to make a good impression in every area.

The Query Letter

Before submitting a finished article to a magazine editor, the freelance writer should send the editor what is called a query letter. This should be done before a writer does any extensive work on an article. It doesn't make much sense to devote a lot of work researching and writing an article until you have determined there is a market for that article. The query letter would explain just what you, the writer, are proposing to submit to the editor for publication. The letter would define the basic idea, tell the editor how you propose to pursue the information for the article, what angle the article will take, how long it will run, what photographs might accompany it, and an accounting of the expenses the editor would be expected to pay whether he accepts the article or not. Add anything else that might convince him to buy the article. The query letter has a sales purpose also.

If the editor is apt to be unfamiliar with you or your work, the query letter should include information on your experience such as a list of articles you have already published and the magazines in which they appeared. It should list editors who have run your articles in the past, and any evidence of expertise you can present that would qualify you to write the article you are proposing. You should not mention payment for your work in the query letter. Pay can be determined in later negotiations. Organization of the query depends on what you want to emphasize. If it is your first contact, you will want to stress your qualifications. If the editor already knows your work, you can concentrate on explaining the idea and why you think it would make a good article. If the query letter is sincere, informative and well written, it should be effective. But only if the editor really likes the idea.

PREPARATION OF BROADCAST NEWS AND FEATURE COPY

Most of the rules cited for print copy preparations apply to broadcast copy preparation. There are some differences, however. You should always *triple space* broadcast copy. And because broadcast copy is usually shorter than print copy *don't* be tempted to type *more than one story* on the *same sheet* of paper. Use *separate* sheets for *each story*. If a broadcast story takes more than a page, some writers rather than use the word "more" will draw a *heavy line* along the bottom of the first page with an *arrow* at the end as:

Never split words in writing for broadcasting. If you can't finish a word on one line, *do not hyphenate* and continue it on the next line. Write the *entire word* on the next line. To aid the news director in timing a newscast, the writer *should write* in pencil at the *top right* of each page the number of lines on the page. In determining *how long* a story will run or how much time it will take, count 16 *lines for each minute of airtime*. The broadcast writer should also *type the date* of the story at the top left. On newspapers, the story date is usually added by an editor rather than the writer.

The top of the page of a broadcast story would look like this:

Slug:

Name: _____ lines

Date:

The story would then be written as would a story for print, but in some instances IT WOULD BE TYPED IN ALL CAPITAL LETTERS. THE POLICY OF INDIVIDUAL STATIONS WOULD DETERMINE WHETHER ALL CAPITAL, or capital and lower case letters are used.

PREPARING PUBLIC RELATIONS RELEASES

Copy preparation of public relations releases would *follow* the rules for *print* publication if the release is to be sent to a newspaper or magazine. It would follow the *rules* of *broadcast* copy if it is to be sent to a *radio* or *television* station. The public relations handout differs from a news story in that it will sometimes be accompanied by a cover letter, or the release will have additional information typed at the top. Understanding that editors will not take time to read unnecessary letters, public relations writers send most releases *without* cover letters. In releases *not issued* with cover letters, you should *type* at the top of the release your *name, phone number*, the *earliest date* the item is to be published, and whether the release *is exclusive* for that publication or broadcaster. The top of the release might look like this:

Slug — Date

Name — Phone Number

Release: *Date,* or *Immediate,* or *At Will.*

If the release is sent from a firm or organization, you should use *letterhead stationery so the editor can see at once the source of the information. If you do not use letterhead stationery you might want to type the source as from "The United Fund" or from "Company Name."*

PREPARING COPY AND LAYOUT
FOR PRINT ADVERTISEMENTS

Unlike news writers, who only write the stories, *advertising writers* must also *write the headlines* of their ads. And the advertising writer must either *layout the ad* himself or *work closely* with the person who does the layout. Sometimes the *headline* and *copy* are typed on the *layout sheet.* More often, the copy of the ad is *typed* on a *separate sheet* of paper, and *lines* are *drawn* on the *layout sheet* to show where the copy goes. Thus most ads would consist of two sheets—the *copy sheet* and the *layout sheet.*

At the top of *both* the *copy sheet* and the *layout sheet* you would type the *advertiser's name, name of the publication* in which the ad will be run, the *date* it will be run, your *name* and *phone number* and such additional information as necessary. Additional information might include the *section* or even the *page* on which you want the ad to appear. Rates are higher when specific pages or sections are requested. The cheapest rate, or the "run of paper" rate means the ad will be run on the page most convenient for the newspaper or magazine. A copy sheet for a newspaper ad might look like this:

Copy Sheet — Advertiser

Publication Name

Date ad will run—section—and/or page

Writer's name and phone number

Copy A:
   Then you, as a writer would type the first block of copy for the ad. It could be just a few lines or several lines if all of the copy will be in one block.
Copy B:
   If you have a block of copy that goes elsewhere in the ad than Copy A, you would call it Copy B as done here. You would type more blocks of copy (Copy C and Copy D, etc.) if your ad had type dispersed elsewhere in the layout.

The *layout sheet*, which should be the size of the finished ad, would have about the same information at the top as the copy sheet. You would *draw in* the *headline* in the size and style of type you wished. You would *dummy* in the illustration. You could *paste down* an illustration, *draw one,* or indicate the area where the illustration will go. The placement of blocks of copy is often illustrated by drawn lines and the slugs: Copy A, Copy B, etc. The logotype— *nameplate* of the advertising business and run at the bottom of the page with the business name would also give the *address* and *telephone number.* The layout sheet for a simple, basic ad would look something like this:

Layout Sheet—Advertiser

Publication

Date ad will run, section, page

Writer's name and phone number

THE HEADLINE WOULD BE ACROSS TOP

The illustration would be here.

Copy A

NAME OF THE ADVERTISER
Address
Phone Number

All sorts of variations are possible. There could be more than one picture, the illustration could be to one side with the head on the other, etc. But the basics would remain the same.

COPY PREPARATION OF RADIO COMMERCIALS

Preparation of *commercials* for radio follows many of the rules of preparation of news stories. Copy should be *double-spaced* or *triple-spaced.* There should be only one commercial to each page. *Do not split words* from one line to the next with a hyphen. The top of the page should include: the name of the advertiser; *date* the commercial starts; *length* of the commercial, usually 30 seconds or 60 seconds; and because commercials are repeated many times on radio, the *date* the commercial *ends.* (The commercial will be placed in the schedule to appear at a given time each date of the sales contract.) Other items that might appear at the top of the page would be *directions* on whether the commercial is to run on *AM* or *FM* or *both, any warnings* that might *avert a mistake,* and *information* about possible *musical preludes, backgrounds,* or postludes. A commercial would look like this:

ADVERTISER'S NAME   NOTE: BROWN'S SHOES
(60 seconds)   *NOT*
                   BROWN'S *HARDWARE*

Start: date

Stop: date

Cartridge: *No* music. Both AM and FM

THE COMMERCIAL WOULD BEGIN HERE. NOTICE THAT THE WRITER TELLS THE ANNOUNCER THAT THIS IS A COMMERCIAL FOR BROWN'S SHOES, WHICH HAS NOT ADVERTISED BEFORE, AND NOT BROWN'S HARDWARE, A LONGTIME ADVERTISER. THIS WARNING MAY PRE-VENT A MISTAKE. AT THE END OF THE AD YOU WOULD PLACE A (30) OR ITS EQUIVALENT, (##).

STYLE AND WORD USAGE FOR PRINT STORIES

All publications attempt to maintain *consistent style* in such matters as *abbreviations, capitalization, grammar, punctuation, spelling of numerals* and word usage. The *Associated Press* and the *United Press International,* the two chief wire services providing comprehensive state, national and international news to newspapers around the country and the world, have jointly compiled a stylebook that encompasses most style matters. Newspapers have, for the most part, adopted the same style. It is easier for newspaper editors to have local writers adopt AP/UPI style than to change all of the wire stories to agree with a different style. Most newspapers will depart from the stylebook on certain rules. But such departures are minimal and can easily be learned by new staff members.

A summary of the stylebook, including most of the commonly used rules, can be found as Appendix A. Students or writers in journalism or public relations are urged to purchase the AP or the UPI stylebook and become accustomed to using it. Students and writers of broadcasting or advertising will find the stylebook rules for news stories and features do not apply in most broadcast or advertising writing situations. However, broadcasting and advertising writers, sometimes called upon to write for print, might want to have a stylebook in their libraries as a reference book. Cost of the book is minimal.

STYLE AND USAGE FOR BROADCAST STORIES, COMMERCIALS

Broadcast copy is written to be heard, as is emphasized throughout this book. Therefore, broadcast style differs in many ways from print style. Broadcast style differs from print style in *abbreviations, word usage, use of numerals, spelling* and *use of capitals.*

—*Broadcast abbreviations*—Avoid abbreviations in most instances because an abbreviation can make an announcer stumble. You should use only well-known abbreviations, such as *C.I.O., Y.M.C.A., G.O.P., F.C.C.* And when you write them, make certain the announcer will not try to pronounce them as words. Write such abbreviations with hyphens separating each letter: *C-I-O, Y-M-C-A,* or *G-O-P.* When the initials form an *acronym* (a pronounceable word), as in NATO or NASA, *omit* the hyphens.

—*Word Usage*—You can be *informal* in broadcasting, using *contractions* in situations where you would not use contractions for print. *Doesn't, won't, can't, it's* are all natural in speech and should be used. You can omit *middle initials* or *names entirely* in broadcast style. You would be more likely to give *titles* instead of, or *ahead of,* names. You would *avoid* overuse of *pronouns.* In writing broadcast copy *use a pronoun only* if it is *very close* to the *noun* it replaces and *clearly refers only to that noun.* Remember that while a *reader* can *look back* to see what a pronoun refers to, the *listener cannot.* In general, choose *familiar words* that will be easily *recognized* by the listener.

—*Use of numerals*—Use *numerals* where they will not cause the announcer any difficulty, but *spell out* numerals if that will aid pronunciation. *Spell out fractions*—*three-fourths, not 3/4; one-half, not 1/2. Spell out* numbers where each number in the series is not be be pronounced separately: i.e., *addresses* as in *twenty sixty-one* Main Street; or *years* as in *nineteen eighty.* If *each number in a series* is to be pronounced as in *license numbers* or *phone numbers,* use *numerals separated by hyphens;* i.e.,—his license was Florida *P-W-C-7-5-2.* His phone number was *3-7-6-5-4-2-2.* Avoid using *statistics,* except in the simplest form. The listener just cannot absorb a *statistical listing.* A single reference, properly explained, is acceptable. *Results* of sports events are given, but not box scores. *Round out* large figures. It is somewhat meaningless to the listener to say the city budget will be *$9,748,640.* Say it will be *nine and three-quarter million dollars.* In writing the time of events, do not use newspaper style, *7:30 p.m.* Instead write *seven-thirty last night.*

—Spelling—Words in broadcast stories or commercials should be *spelled correctly* even though they will not be viewed by the public. *Misspelled words can cause mispronunciations.* There is one important *exception to correct spelling.* When you use words that are not familiar (usually names of persons or places), you should *spell the words phonetically* for the announcer. The proper way to do this is to spell the word correctly, and then *spell it phonetically in parentheses above the correct spelling:* i.e.—He is from

(Core-eee-OPP-pole-iss)

Coraopolis, Pennsylvania.

*—Capitals—*Use of capital letters or capital and lower case letters seems to be *optional* in broadcasting. At some stations everything is written *all caps.* At other stations, *capitals and small letters* are used, with capitals used occasionally for *emphasis.* Writers must adjust to practices followed by individual stations.

*—Miscellaneous style points—*All *directions* not intended to be *read aloud* should be *placed in brackets or circled. Direct quotes* other than those on tape should be *used sparingly. Sentences* should be *short* and of *uncomplicated structure.* Words used should be the words the *listener will readily understand.*

STYLE FOR PRINT ADVERTISEMENTS

In all ways, advertising is more creative and free-wheeling than are other forms of writing for the mass media. Style in advertising should be consistent with a single advertisement, or perhaps in all advertisements in a single campaign, but there are not too many general rules. Each advertisement is an individual composition. One style may be used by a writer in one advertisement and a different style in another.

Even rules of grammar do not always apply to advertisements. Sentence fragments abound in advertising writing. And it is not difficult to find improper comparisons, incorrect punctuation and improper word usage. English teachers and language purists may deplore the improper use of "like" in the advertising slogan "Winstons taste good like a cigarette should," but few readers/listeners/viewers have problems with the usage. Advertising writers not only use popular idiomatic expressions, but they often create the expressions. Specific style rules for abbreviations, capitalization, punctuation, grammar, use of numerals, and word usage just do not apply to the writing of advertisements.

In taking creative license with the language, writers of advertisements should, at least, show restraint. Proper language should be used unless there is a compelling reason to ignore the conventional rules. Modern advertising, especially that on television and radio, has a tremendous impact on young people. Advertising style should be informal. It should be colorful. It should be effective. But it can be all of these without being irresponsible and destructive.

There are some rules that do apply to writing advertisements. Words should be spelled correctly at all times. Sentences should be short. Paragraphs should be short. Headlines should read into the body copy. The imperative mood should be widely used with the direct address word "you" appearing frequently. Words should be specific and, in most instances, familiar to the reader/listener/viewer.

USE OF COPYEDITING MARKS

Copy written for print publication should be as clean as is possible, but it does not have to be flawless. The reporter can use copy editor's symbols to make minor corrections to his story or feature before handing it in to his editor. A reporter should be familiar with the universally understood copy editing symbols and use them for corrections. Copy symbols and their uses are:

Indicate transposition of letters, words.

The car new was

Insert words, letters, phrases.

The meeting was today

Deletion

John started school.

Delete words, letters, phrases.

School school started.

Building bridges across gaps.

The officer who was a colonel resigned.

Delete a paragraph.

He attended school in Pittsburgh before becoming an accountant. He then moved to Nebraska.

Abbreviate or spell out.

Senator John Smith serves

Colo.

6 earned diplomas.

One was over forty.

☰	Capitalize.	He lives in michigan.
/	Make lower case letters.	She Loves Ice Cream.
/	Insert space between words.	The letter arrived late.
⌃	Insert comma.	John a Virgo married early.
⌄	Insert apostrophe.	Its Mables coat.
⊙ ⊗	Insert period.	This is the end⊗
⌄	Insert quotation marks.	He said, Not me.
⁾ ⌐	Indicate beginning and end. quotation marks.	She said, I will.
⌄	Insert a hyphen.	He bought a two ton truck.
⌄	Insert a dash.	He did not ask much of life just the moon.
? ! ⌄	Other punctuation.	Where It can't be Mary, a nurse Jane, a cook and Cecille, firefighter.
∟	Indicate a paragraph.	⌐The game was sensational from start to end.⌐It began with, etc.

) Indicate no paragraph, to run copy together.

and Jones struck out in the 7th inning.)

(The next batter up . . .

⌢ Close up space between words.

I'll have⌢the chicken.

⊂ Close up space within word.

I'll have the meatⅠoaf.

The preceding copy editing marks can be used to make minor corrections or minor improvements in news or feature stores for newspapers or magazines. If the changes are major or numerous, rewrite your copy.

COPY MARKS ARE NOT FOR BROADCAST OR ADVERTISING COPY

News stories or commercials for broadcasting should not be edited with print copy editing marks. To be read, copy must be clean and uncluttered. The announcer cannot pause to interpret the copy marks. About the only editing suited for broadcast copy would be the deletion of an entire word or an occasional insertion of no more than one or two words. For example, broadcast copy should look like this if there is not time to retype it:

THE PRESIDENT ANNOUNCED THURSDAY THAT HE WILL APPOINT A NEW SECRETARY ▪▪▪ OF ENERGY WITHIN THE NEXT TEN DAYS. IT IS EXPECTED THAT THE (FORMER REPUBLICAN/ JOB HAS BEEN OFFERED TO SENATOR JARVIS STENTTOR OF NEW MEXICO . . .

There should be *no copy editing* on *print advertisements* or *on public relations handouts.* All mistakes and editing changes should be made on preliminary drafts. The final draft should be free of errors or corrections.

PREPARING COPY FOR AN OPTICAL SCANNER TYPESETTER

Many newspapers set type by means of an *optical character scanner.* The scanner is an electronic device that can read typed characters and some simple editing marks turning a piece of copy into a punched tape. The tape can then be fed into a typesetting machine to create printed columns of type ready to be pasted onto a page layout dummy. Copy has to be relatively cleanly typed because the scanner can only *delete* characters and words or *insert* characters and words. Material to be deleted must be marked out with a special pencil. Characters inserted must be typed in below the line into which they are to be inserted. Specific editing marks such as slash (/) marks are typed in preceding and following the inserted material. The scanner has two electronic eyes that read across the copy. The top eye reads the characters and deletion marks. The bottom, traveling between the lines, reads the editing commands and the copy to be inserted. A combination of typesetting coded signals and traditional words would head the copy. The codes would vary with the paper and make use of the delta (Δ) mark and other characters. The copy could look like this copy prepared for the Gainesville (Florida) Sun.

Δ+1 Δ+n

+ΔBF   Union School Board Wed. 1-9 Area ΔLF

ΔPD   In response to a question from board member Donald

Dukes, Cason said budget proposals should be ready for board

consideration by September. The budget must be submitted to the

state by Oct. 1 .

On another subject, Cason reported that the new plan will

hopes~~jepm~~ draw more than $20,000 in interest money for the
/fully/
county schools nex⊄ year. Cason praised bank president Paul
/t/
Rinert for his cooperation in setting ~~up~~ up the daily interest savings

accounts. Cason said the ~~gu~~unty would also save money by paying
/co/
employees twice per~~mo~~ month.

Considerable time was spent in a discussion on the use of driver

eaacation cars. Dukes reported complaints about the use of
/du/
school cars for other than offical/business.
                    /school/
After much discussion about rumored abuses . . . etc.

The reporter who wrote the story above would probably not ready the story for the scanner. An editor or a production typist would prepare the copy. But the reporter's copy should be quite clean or the story would have to be retyped.

USE OF VIDEO DISPLAY TERMINALS

The computer has revolutionized the production of newspapers specifically and printing in general. Reporters now type stories directly into a computer rather than onto a sheet of paper. For those of you who have not yet been introduced to the computer data storage and retrieval systems, newsroom systems are designed to receive, store and transmit stories and headlines in electronic form.

Such systems feature *video display terminals* (VDT's) which resemble television sets with a keyboard attached. The keyboard is basically a typewriter with added keys to perform editing and typesetting functions. When a reporter types a story on a VDT, the characters appear on the screen. No carriage moves as in most standard and some electric typewriters. Nor does a typing ball move across the page as in an IBM Selectric typewriter. Instead, a *"cursor"* a blinking light, moves across the screen recording the characters as the reporter types them.

No copy editing marks are needed. The keyboard includes keys that delete characters, words, sentences or paragraphs. Another key allows the operator to insert material into the copy. The copy already on the screen moves over to make room for the inserted copy. Other keys allow the reporter to move words, sentences, paragraphs, or entire blocks of type from one place in a story to another. When the reporter finishes typing his story and correcting it, there will be no editing marks on the screen. The story will be clean, just as the reporter wants it to go to the editor. The reporter then punches another key that could be called "enter," "store" or "file", which will store the copy in the computer's memory systems. The editor can then call up the story on his VDT whenever he is ready to edit it.

As in other instances, the story is accompanied by additional information in the heading. This information would include the slug, the reporter's name, the edition the story is meant for, or the section of the paper, and the date. When the reporter gains access to the computer, usually by typing an identifying name or code, often known only to the reporter and the computer programmer, he will get an electronic "page" screen with a heading that might look like this one from the system used by the *Sentinel Star* in Orlando, Fla.:

CMD _____

ECHO _____

CR _____ SIDE _____ TO _____

CMD is the command field. That is where the reporter tells the system what he wants it to do.

ECHO is the area in which the machine *"talks back"* to the reporter. The ECHO is the "voice" of the computer. It may ask the operator a question, tell him he made a mistake, or give him instruction on what to do next.

CR stands for *cursor* and is a number telling the operator on which line the cursor is at any given moment. The number changes automatically as the cursor is moved around the screen.

SIDE tells the operator on *what side* of a *split screen* the cursor is at a given time. Most VDTs can be split into two screens, with separate stories, stories and corrections, or a directory of stories and an individual story on the screen at the same time. The split screen is used primarily by editors. Many reporter terminals do not have the split screen capacity.

TO is a place the reporter can tell the computer to send a story. Usually the story would be sent to the editor of the page or section for which the story was written.

Computer systems vary from newspaper to newspaper, but not in any basic way. Some systems have more capacity than others and are able to perform more functions. The *ATEX* system at the Orlando *Sentinel Star*, also used by the *Minneapolis Star and Tribune, Newsday, Newsweek, Chicago Sun Time,* and *Pittsburgh Press,* is a versatile system capable of many complicated operations. For example, after a reporter stores his copy in the system, a much more complete heading will appear on the story the next time it is called up. It would look like this:

CMD _____ EC _____

SL _____ MSG _____ PR ___ DA ___ ED ___ PG ___ VE# ___

BY _____ POPR _____ FROM _____

CUR ___ MAR ___ MO ___ FMT ___ HJ ___ DE ___ QU ___ TO ___

These headings, many of which are filled automatically, give the editor information he needs to perform his functions. The abbreviations stand for:

CMD is the *command field.*
EC is the *ECHO,* the *voice* of the computer.
SL is the *slug.*
MSG is for *messages* the editor might want to write.
PR is *priority* of the story.

DA gives the *publication date.*

ED is the *edition* or *section*.

PG is the *page number.*

VE# is the *version* of the story. Each time a story is changed a new version is stored in the computer memory. Each version, from the reporter's to the final edited version to be printed, is stored and can be recalled at any time.

BY is the *author* of the story and the *time* and *date* written.

POPR is the name of the *previous operator* who last worked on the story.

FROM is the *desk* or *person* who sent the story.

CUR indicates *line* cursor is on.

MA stands for *margin* or *width* story is being displayed.

MO stands for *video mode.* Tells whether type is being displayed in *regular light* type, *bold face* or *italic.*

FMT indicates the *type face and size* in which a story will be set.

HJ indicates whether the story has been *hyphenated* and *justified* (set to have even margins on both sides).

DE gives the exact *depth* of the story as it will appear in print ready to be pasted onto a layout sheet.

QU indicates the *queue* in which the operator is working. Queue would be equivalent to a *desk* of or *section* of the paper, such as city desk, sports, family, state, national, international, etc.

TO indicates the *person* or *desk* to whom the operator wants the story sent.

All of this may seem like a mystery to you, but it is an efficient way of handling copy. You should at least be aware that such technology exists and that you might be using it in your field.

Reporters can learn to write and file stories on VDTs with just a couple of hours of instruction and practice. Editing on VDTs is a bit more complicated, but an editor can master the system in a relatively short time.

Chapter IV

ORGANIZATION:
A STUDY IN LOGIC

"Good order is the foundation of all good things," Edmund Burke said in *Reflections on the Revolution in France*. He spoke of things political, but his observation applies as well to things written. After you have captured the attention of your reader/listener/viewer with a good beginning, you will want to give him the information or entertainment he desires in an orderly way and leave him with a sense of satisfaction. To achieve that end there are two functions you must perform:

—Select the best material to use.

—Organize the material logically.

SELECTION OF MATERIAL

If you have done a thorough job of research and reporting, you should have much more material than you will be able to use in your piece. This should not bother you. It means you will be able to use the small percentage of material that is top grade and eliminate that which is mediocre. It is like the basketball coach who has 50 players turn out for the first practice. From the 50, he is almost certain to come up with five who are tall enough, fast enough and adept enough to become good players. The coach who has only ten players turn out for practice will probably have to settle for some short, slow, untalented players.

In the selection process, the choosing of material you will use in your story, feature, advertisement or broadcast commercial, there are several things you must take into consideration:

—The *scope* of your piece.

—The *quantity* of material needed to fulfill your purpose.

—The *quality* of the material you have to work with.

—The *nature of your audience*.

—The *kinds of information* to suit the purpose of your piece.

All of these things have to be considered in the selection of material for your piece. The selection of certain material and elimination of other material is the first step in the process of organizing your writing effort. Each of these considerations helps in determining that selection in different ways.

The Scope of the Piece

The scope of the piece is determined by your informed judgment of the extent of the interest, desire, and need on the part of your reader/listener/viewer for the information or entertainment you will provide with your piece, whether it be story, feature, or advertisement. Scope can be determined by the old factors of interests and the value of those interests, plus the amount of space or time available for this particular message. While you can determine limits of the scope by analyzing the material realistically from your knowledge of the audience and your knowledge of the facts, the space available is usually out of your hands.

Space and time available are usually controlled by someone other than the writer. The editor of a paper has to determine how much space can be devoted to each category of editorial matter and each item within each category. The broadcast news director does the same things for news on radio or television. He or she has to divide the time available by the time needed for the categories of news and the individual items. In advertising, the budget usually determines the amount of space or time you will have for your ad or commercial.

Space and time available are extremely flexible things. They are different at different publications and broadcast stations, and different at different times. A few examples:

A small daily newspaper has less space than a large daily, but news emphasis may mean that the smaller daily has more room for local news than the large paper, which may devote more of its space to national and international news. A local broadcast station with a small budget and staff may not really have anyone to work on news extensively and may devote little time to local news, preferring to "rip and read"—tearing news stories from the wire service serving the station and reading it in the small amount of time devoted to news. A larger city television station may devote considerable time to local news. Some large television stations have news shows in the morning varying from 15 minutes to 30 minutes, a half hour news show in the middle of the day, an hour show in the early evening, and a half hour show at 11 p.m.

Advertising is more likely to vary by time of week or month or year. Food advertising is likely to be heavy on Wednesday and Thursday as most homemakers shop for groceries at the end of the week. Entertainment advertising will be heavier on Friday when people are planning their weekends. Travel advertising is heaviest in the summer when most people take their vacations. Gift products are advertised most heavily before holidays, Christmas, Easter, mother's and father's day, graduation, etc.

The factor of space and time is decided for you, the writer. You have to fit material into the strictures of this reality.

The practical effects on the scope of your piece can be that it will vary from: (in a news story) a few paragraphs to several pages; (in a print ad) a small display spot on a page with other ads to a half or full page ad all by itself; (in a commercial) from a 15-second spot of about 40 words to a one-minute commercial of 160 words. You have to be able to tailor your writing to the space and time demands. The smaller the space and time, the more selective you must be. A choice must be carefully made from a mass of material for limited space. You may have to be a bit more general in your approach, having to bypass more specific material, but you can't be too general. Every good story or ad needs specific information, no matter how limited the time and space. Later in this book we will talk more in detail about the need for specifics.

The Quantity of Material

The amount of material to be used in your piece is largely determined by the size of the article or ad. But, especially in the case of an ad, the amount the writer will devote to the space available is affected by several things. These include:

—*The amount of white space* used in the print ad, and space taken up by the headline, any pictures accompanying the ad and the logotype (nameplate of store or business).

—*The amount of dialogue* used in a commercial, plus the time needed for any musical precede or prologue or other sound effects that may accompany the dialogue.

—*The amount of space devoted to headlines, pictures or white space* in a newspaper or magazine.

Unless you are your own editor, as a writer for print outlets you will not be all that concerned about headlines, pictures, or other matters limiting the length of the story. Those decisions are made by the editor. You usually are informed of the amount of space you have. In writing advertisements or commercials that is not true. The writer of the copy usually also writes the headline, edits the pictures, and plans the white space. The writer has more control over the ultimate amount of copy to be devoted to the piece in relationship to the other elements.

The Quality of Material

Obviously you want always to use top quality material in anything you do, but sometimes your best material, for one reason or another, is not suited for the piece you are writing because it is in conflict with the emphasis of the piece, the theme, the tone or the purpose. You occasionally will have the painful task of eliminating something that is very good for something that is not as good in quality but is more suited to your purpose. This can happen in several ways:

—In an ad, a piece of information may seem good, but it may not suit the audience the ad is trying to reach.

—In a news story, a bit of material might seem terribly interesting, but it may be unsuitable on grounds of bad taste or possible libel. Or it may not apply too clearly to the theme of the story.

—In a broadcast news story, you may have a tape of a witness, spokesman or participant in an event, but the speaker might have such a broad accent or manner of speaking that what he or she has said when played and sent out over the air, may be completely unintelligible to the listener. It's better not to play the tape, but let the announcer sum up what was said. Don't leave the listener frustrated.

—In a photo for newspaper use or a video tape for television use, you may have excellent shots that, unfortunately, do not fit into the theme you are using in your story. Don't use them.

The emphasis must not be on how good a quality is the tape, photograph, film, feature ancedote, ad benefit, story quote, but how apropos it is to the piece being written. It is better to use a less humorous quote that fits the theme of the feature or a summary of what a source said rather than a tape no one can understand, a photo that tells a story rather than one that misses the story even though it is esthetically and professionally excellent. Use the best material you have that serves your ultimate purpose.

In selecting material, remember that only you as the writer are in a position to evaluate the material to do what you want to do with your piece. You will have a lot of volunteer help. Every news source is confident that he knows what should go into your story better than you do. He will be more than glad to tell you what to use, and how to use it. Resist the temptation you may feel to follow such suggestions. Each source is eager to get his version of the story printed or broadcast. You must take all information as raw data to be evaluated for accuracy, objectivity, taste, usefulness to the reader, and such technical things as grammar, punctuation, spelling, word usage. The only thing you owe the source of the material is the responsibility to reproduce what is said accurately (not word for word unless it is in quotation marks), fairly, efficiently and only in the amount you deem necessary to make your story a good one and one that will serve the reader/listener/viewer.

Selection of your own material should be strongly emphasized to beginning writers. Too many writers without experience lack confidence in their own abilities. They hesitate to change the wording of information they will use in their stories as well as the organization of the information. It may or may not come to them in the order it would be used in a story—probably not. For example, minutes of a meeting, which might be the reporter's source, are written chronologically. Seldom would a story written from such minutes be written in that order. A lawyer's brief builds his case under rules of argument, which may or may not be organized in the way a news writer would want to use them. And benefits of a product to be advertised could come to a writer in any haphazard way. They usually must be reorganized. Young writers are urged then to be their own judges of the quality of information they will be working with. Treat every bit of information, every source as raw data. You must supply the order in which the data will be used, the quantity, the wording, the sentence structure, the grammar, punctuation and spelling. Check it all for accuracy. You are responsible for what you write—not the person who gave you the information.

THE NATURE OF THE AUDIENCE

The professional writer must always be aware of the reader/listener/viewer for whom he or she is writing. You have to give the reader what he wants. And the better you know him, the better job you can do. Readers/listeners/viewers fall into two main categories:

—The mass reader/listener/viewer.

—The specialized reader/listener/viewer.

In selecting material for a piece, you must be guided by the nature of your audience—whether it is a mass or general audience where all members have pretty much the same interests, or whether it is a specialized audience which has interest or knowledge of the subject more intense than the general audience.

The Mass Audience

The mass audience, while made up of diverse people, becomes alike in a universal interest in certain news, features and products to be advertised. For example, all people are interested to some degree in news stories that provide information they must have to function in their daily lives—the weather, changes in laws, the deadlines for paying taxes, which offices will be closed on holidays, elections of local, state and national officials, changes in the public transportation routes, prices of groceries, sales of clothing, etc.

In selecting facts to include in news stories, features, ads or promotions for the mass reader/listener/viewer, you, as the writer, must choose those facts that apply to each of the diverse individuals who make up the mass. You must seek the *common denominator*. For this audience you shun the exotic, the less well known, the data that takes special knowledge to understand, the data that is less useful to the majority of readers/listeners/viewers. Anything done for a mass audience is done in the center of the spectrum. An analogy might be made to a product for sale to the masses—soup. Manufacturers of tomato soup want everyone who likes tomato soup to buy their brand. Consequently, there will be nothing in the soup that will turn a sizable number of the population off. There will be a blandness about the soup. It will be as good as the company can make it so as not to offend the individual tastes of too many soup lovers. But it can never be as good or as unusual as soup in an excellent restaurant, because it must satisfy unsophisticated palates as well as somewhat more sophisticated palates. It won't have a great deal of originality about it. It will be nourishing and not offend you. But it doesn't have that special tang that would delight you but might offend many with a different idea of good.

News and advertisements for a mass audience are like soup. They will feature material that everyone needs in a general way and that a majority of readers/listeners/viewers need in a specific way, but will probably not include items of interest to minorities in the general audience.

In a typical news story for a mass audience you *would include* the facts that a burglar broke into a certain home, and stole cash, a stamp collection, a painting and some silverware. You *would include* the fact that a suspect was arrested by police from fingerprint evidence and a description furnished by a neighbor.

In the story you *would not* be likely to include a detailed description of the stamps in the collection even though the stamp collectors in the audience might be interested. You *would not* include identity of the painter unless he was well-known, even though art students might want to know. You *would be unlikely* to identify the detective who checked the fingerprints even though his friends might want to know, and you *would give* the value of the silverware, but *be unlikely to give* the brand name or names of the people who gave the silverware to the young married couple whose home was burglarized. (Nosy neighbors might be interested in that.)

If you are writing a feature story about an individual's unusual occupation as a member of the police department's bomb disposal squad, you *would probably mention* that he relaxes from his tense and dangerous job by knitting as a hobby. You *might mention* that he is a member of the Kiwanis Club. However, you *would not* be likely to go into detail about knitting, even though knitters among your readers might want to know what techniques he uses and what kind of things he prefers to knit. You *would not* be likely to go into detail about the history and purpose of the Kiwanis club, even though that would be of much interest to the Kiwanians among your readers/listeners/viewers.

In an advertisement or commercial about a dishwasher you *would tell* the mass audience about the efficiency of your brand, its dependability, its flexibility if it is mobile, and its price if it is a good buy. You *would probably not* tell the reader/listener/viewer the machine was built in a certain city, although that would be of some interest to residents or former residents of that city. You *would probably not* tell a mass audience the type of steel used in the construction although that would be of interest to metallurgists. You *would probably not* tell a mass audience that some of the components were imported from Japan, although that would be of vital interest to members of the "Buy American" lobby.

In short, for a piece to be read by a diverse, but mass audience, you would select facts of interest for a majority of the readers/listeners/viewers making up that mass audience. Different people will be more interested in parts of that information than other people, and most people will not be interested in all parts of the piece, but all people will share some common interests in most of the facts that go into the story or advertisement aimed at a mass audience.

The Specialized Audience

As a writer for newspapers and broadcasting outlets, and perhaps even more so for magazines, you will have to write for audiences with specialized interests. Selection of material for specialized audiences will differ from selection of materials for mass audiences. For example, while much of the editorial material and the advertising in a daily newspaper is of interest to the mass of readers as we have already seen, the newspaper tries to provide many things for the specialized reader.

The Newspaper Audience

Think how a newspaper is divided up. The typical newspaper has four sections:

—*The front section.* This usually contains news of national and international interest, with a few outstanding state and local items included.

—*The second section.* This usually contains state and local news and perhaps the financial section with business news.

—*The third section.* This section usually includes the sports news and the classified advertisements.

—*The fourth section.* This section usually includes the entertainment aspects of the paper—feature stories, comics, television and movie news.

All of these sections have specialized readers, but the divisions are broad enough that the readers of each section constitute a mass audience of a sort. Spread throughout the paper are highly specialized types of items each with a relatively limited audience. Among such things are: crossword puzzles, horoscopes, news for people over 65, health columns, advice-to-the-troubled columns, bridge columns, essays on religion, psychology, and sociology.

The Radio Newscast

Radio news is designed to appeal almost exclusively to a mass audience. Rarely does radio have the time or inclination in its news presentation to present specialized news. The entertainment aspect of radio is highly specialized, of course. Some stations devote a major portion of the broadcast day to music for a selected audience. But radio is not designed nor is it inclined to devote much time to highly specialized information shows. There are exceptions. There are special shows heard occasionally on such varied topics as bird watching, gerontology, health, etc. But they are rare. Some radio audience participation call-in shows (an audience involvement is uniquely suited to radio using the telephone and the instant relay) are often devoted to information items involving government actions, social problems, financial matters, etc. But in almost all cases the questions are broad enough to apply to a mass audience, and no writing is involved.

Television

Television has both a mass audience, as we have seen, and many specialized audiences. The specialized audiences for news and information on television include:

—News for the homemaker—cooking news, home decorating, sewing, health, education, cultural—is often presented at or about noon along with the general news broadcast.

—News for the sports fan—presented along with the regular mass news-casts, but also presented in more detail on Saturdays, on special cable services and at times of special sports events such as the Olympics, the World Series, etc.

Most news on television is meant for the mass audience. The regular newscasts are meant for a general audience, as are documentaries, the Sunday interview shows such as Face the Nation and Meet the Press.

Advertising in Broadcasting

A brief study of *what* is advertised on television and *when illustrates that* advertisers buy time when they can reach the potential buyers for their products. Some clear examples:

—Soaps, food, household aids, health aids for the family are usually advertised during the day when the homemaker is likely to be the only television viewer at home.

—Automobiles and auto accessories, shaving aids, lawn mowers and other yard appliances are likely to be advertised during a sports event on the weekend when the male of the household is more likely to be watching the screen.

—Breakfast cereals accompanied by premiums, candy, toys are most likely to be advertised on Saturday morning when children will be in control of the channel selector.

The Magazine Audience

Magazines are much more likely to have an appeal to selected and specialized audiences than are newspapers, radio and television. In writing for magazines, you must adapt your theme and selection of materials to a special audience in almost all instances. Magazine writing demands a much broader study of the market and the audience than this book can devote to it. Those interested in writing for magazines are urged to make a thorough investigation into the market, either on their own or through a magazine writing course which devotes a considerable time to the marketplace as well as to the writing skills required.

There are a few general circulation magazines on the market today, but not nearly as many as in the years prior to television. The debut of television in the late 1940's and the 1950's led to a rapid decline in the general circulation magazines Saturday Evening Post, Collier's, Liberty, Life, Look, and others. All of these leading magazines closed down, although the Saturday Evening Post and Life have been revived with less expensive operations, less extensive circulation, and revised goals. The Reader's Digest kept its broad readership market. The news magazines, Time, Newsweek, and U.S. News and World Report stayed in business. But the news magazines and others that were not fatally affected by T.V. were specialized magazines, seeking a selected audience. Surviving long-lived magazines aimed at limited markets include Atlantic, Saturday Review of Literature, New Yorker. They adapted to newer generations.

And a host of new magazines aimed at specific audiences appeared in the 50's, 60's and 70's: *MS* for feminists, *Rolling Stone* for rock music fans, *T.V. Guide* for television fans, William Buckley's *National Review* for conservatives, the *Smithsonian* for culture-oriented readers and *Woman's Day* for homemakers. The vast majority of today's magazines strive to reach a limited audience. Some examples:

—Male audience—Playboy, Esquire, Gentlemen's Quarterly

—Female audience—Cosmopolitan, Woman's Day, Family Circle, McCalls, Glamour, Good Housekeeping

—Sports fans—Sports Illustrated

The list is almost endless. There are magazines for gourmets and dieters; for hedonists and esthetes; for children and the elderly; for the urban dweller and the farmer; for laborers and managers; for the deeply religious and the agnostic; for the scientist and the mystic; for the adventurer and the homebody; for the hobbyist and the workaholic; for the photographer and the writer. For everyone.

Selecting material for a specialized audience entails additional audience research. You must know the reader of the magazine before you can hope to write an article for the magazine, or write an ad for the magazine.

SELECTION OF MATERIAL FOR NEWS STORIES

Most news stories are made up of two general types of facts:

—*New material.* This includes the facts of the event that becomes the news story. The facts about the accident, the fire, the city commission meeting yesterday, the city commission meeting scheduled for tomorrow, a speech. It is the WHO, WHAT, WHEN, WHERE, HOW, AND WHY of the immediate event.

—*Background material.* This includes facts from past events, future events, or sources that will make the new facts more easily understood by the reader/listener/viewer.

Most news stories need a combination of both new facts and background facts to be clear to the reader. However, there is an occasional story that can be made up only of new facts. The following story is an example:

A Hometown youth was killed early Monday when his car crashed into a bride abutment on I-75 near the University Avenue interchange.

The State Highway Patrol identified the youth as Peter Hammond, 18, of High Street Extension Apartments.

A spokesman for General Hospital said death resulted from a fractured skull. Hammond was pronounced dead about 30 minutes after admittance, the hospital official said.

The above story is made up only of the details of the event. WHAT happened is included, to WHOM it happened, and, in a general way,

WHEN, WHERE, and *HOW.* Other circumstances could have been involved that would have called for inclusion of background facts. For example the story might have included such things as:
—The victim was driving without a valid driver's license.
—The driver had been arrested for speeding three times in the past year.
—The driver's older brother was killed in nearly the same spot just a year ago.
—Several fatal accidents have occurred in the same place because the roadway there is curved and poorly banked.

In other words, almost all stories can be made clearer, placed in better perspective and become more informative with some background facts. Most stories require background material to be effective. For example, here is a story about an increase in city taxes that must have extensive background information to make it a complete story for the reader/listener/viewer. The new facts will be *CAPITALIZED* and the background set in *small letters.*

THE CITY COMMISSION VOTED, 3 TO 2, MONDAY NIGHT TO INCREASE TAXES TWO MILLS TO RAISE FUNDS the state has mandated the city must pay back in misused highway construction funds.

THE TAX INCREASE WILL BRING IN $2 MILLION OVER THE NEXT TWO YEARS. THAT WILL COST THE AVERAGE HOMEOWNER IN THE CITY ABOUT $30 A YEAR IN INCREASED PROPERTY TAXES, TAX ASSESSOR JAMES ABBOTT SAID.

Commissioners had a choice of cutting back on city services for the next two years—the time the state has given the city to pay back the misused funds—or increasing the tax rate. THEY CHOSE THE LATTER ALTHOUGH SEVERAL CITIZENS ARGUED AGAINST A TAX INCREASE.

COMMISSIONERS JAMES BROOKS, HARRY KRANTZ AND ROBERT STEIN ARGUED THAT A $2 MILLION CUT IN CITY SERVICES OVER THE NEXT TWO YEARS WAS IMPOSSIBLE WITH THE RISING INFLATION RATE.

The problem arose two weeks ago when the state refused to postpone payment of the debt another year. Discovery that the city had diverted funds earmarked for repairing state highways in the city to building a parking garage downtown was made three years ago by state auditors.

Last year the state Supreme Court upheld a lower court order that the funds be paid back to the state.

COMMISSIONER KRANTZ MOVED AT THE MEETING MONDAY THAT THE TAX INCREASE BE LEVIED. HE SAID THE STATE HAS AGREED TO ALLOW THE CITY TO PAY BACK THE FUNDS OVER THE NEXT TWO YEARS.

In furnishing background material, the writer must estimate how much the reader/listener/viewer read or heard about the stories that took place earlier and are related to the current story in which the writer is working. There is a tendency for beginning writers to assume the audience knows more about the event than in fact the consumer of the news may know. In light of that tendency, it is better to over-explain than under-explain. If you give the reader/listener/viewer information he or she already has, no great harm is done. If you fail to give the background needed to help him or her understand the story, he or she will find it confusing. The longer the story has been running, the less background is needed, for the reader/listener/viewer can be expected to be fairly familiar with the background. In doing a continuing story during the first few days it is in the news, however, or picking up an old story in which there have been new developments, the writer must give sufficient background so the average reader/listener/viewer can place that new information in the correct perspective with what has gone before.

KINDS OF MATERIAL TO SELECT FOR ADVERTISEMENTS

The advertisement has a different function than does the news story. The ad must persuade the reader/listener/viewer to use a service or buy a product. Its main function is to motivate, not provide information objectively. Ads do, of course, provide information, but only to help the sales pitch. Advertisements in print or the electronic media are substitutes for salespeople. The merchant cannot afford to send a sales person to call on all potential users of his product or service. So he sends an ad. The ad is a poor substitute for a salesman, but a practical one.

In selecting material for ads you must select material which will perform the sales function, attract ATTENTION, arouse INTEREST, create DESIRE and move the potential customer to ACTION. This A-I-D-A formula is universally used in selecting material for ads and in organizing the ads. The first two functions of the AIDA formula are true in all forms of communicating. You must always attract ATTENTION and arouse INTEREST, in ads, news stories, feature stories, etc. But the final two functions, creating DESIRE and moving the consumer to ACTION, not present in news stories, are the key functions of an advertisement. The kinds of material you select must perform these persuasive functions to be effective.

Ads Must Have A Theme

Just as in a news story, the advertisement must have a theme, a unity provided by using only material that will reflect the theme. You arrive at a theme in an ad usually by choosing a specific benefit that the particular product will provide for the reader/listener/viewer. Once you have selected a theme, the material you select to use in the ad must advance and enhance that theme. You should put nothing in the ad that would detract from the theme or divert the attention of the consumer from the theme.

The theme can be anything that is likely to persuade the reader/listener/viewer to purchase the product being advertised or to use the service being advertised. The benefit can be anything that appeals to the reader/listener/viewer's need or desire for amusement, good health, recognition, food or drink, security, comfort, approval of the opposite sex and friends of the same sex, a chance to make or save money, a chance to save time, a chance to gain relief from labor, etc. In other words, anything that will improve life or the perception of life.

The theme of an advertisement, unlike the theme of a news story, is more likely to be an appeal to an emotional response than it is an intellectual response. Thus, the need to create a *desire* for the item or service advertised and the need to move the reader/listener/viewer to *action* often will take precedence in determining the theme than the need to attract attention and gain interest.

In achieving the appeal to emotions needed in an advertisement, the writer should select words with a connotative value rather than denotative value. That means the words and material in an ad do not have to mean something definite that will be the same for each reader, as it should in a news story. Instead, the material and words used might not be quite clear to most persons, and each could be expected to make his own emotional (rather than intellectual) interpretation of the words. Semanticist S. I Hayakawa once likened writing for advertising to poetry. He pointed out that in addition to using connotative words rather than denotative words, both forms also make use of rhyme and rhythm as evident in singing commercials. Hayakawa cited such examples as the stomach aid that contains "Simethicone." Hayakawa says no one really knows what Simethicone is. Each person can determine just what to make of that word, and many might determine that the word adds some mysterious or magical quality to the preparation. He also said that advertising, like poetry, thrives on ambiguity. Smirnoff's vodka leaves you *breathless*, a Datsun *sets you free*, Schlitz beer helps you lead a life with *gusto*. Everyone can give his own definition to those words. With these differences in the purpose of the materials selected for ads, let's touch on some decisions that might be made, and how, in achieving each of the A-I-D-A purposes in writing an ad.

Ads Must Attract Attention

As discussed earlier, an advertisement has to be considered as a whole in its preparation. The illustration, if any, and the headline play a more important part in the function of the ad than they do in the writing of a story. It could be said that headlines and illustrations are an *adjunct* to print and broadcast news story, but illustrations and headlines are a *vital* part of a print advertisement or a commercial. Thus the headline and/or illustration can and often do carry out some of the chief purposes of the advertisement.

One of those functions, of course, is *attracting the attention* of the reader/listener/viewer. The illustration and the headline of an advertisement are almost always used to attract the attention of the consumer. If you think about it, you can see that this is true in many ways.

—A picture of a baby, pretty woman, handsome man, or a cute animal will almost always draw the attention of the reader/listener/viewer, whether the picture has much to do with the product or service being advertised or not.

—A headline that entertains, intrigues, startles, amuses the reader/listener/viewer, or that offers him some reward for his deep emotional cravings will certainly attract the potential consumer of the product or service.

The absence of something the reader/listener/viewer is expecting will also draw his attention. Therefore *white space* in a print ad or *dead space* in a broadcast ad will attract the reader/listener/viewer. A short message with a small illustration framed in a sea of white space is often appealing to the reader and effective in drawing his attention. You might compare a newspaper page of advertisements from a department store featuring high fashion to a large ad for a grocery store. The former is likely to have large areas of white space to frame its attractive illustrations and brief copy. The latter will be loaded with as many items as possible featuring prices, the main motivating force for the grocery shopper.

The body copy of the ad is not used to attract attention because it is usually too inconspicuous. So in making up an advertisement you should select illustrations, write headlines, and create layouts which will *attract attention.*

They Must Arouse Interest

In addition to *attracting attention,* the headline and illustrations in advertisements can *arouse the interest* of the potential consumer. They should induce him or her to read the body type of the advertisement, for it is there that the ad should *arouse his or her desire* to have the product or service and *move him or her* to purchase it.

The best way to raise interest is to select data for your headline (and to a lesser degree, illustrations), that will give the reader/listener/viewer a *promise,* give *information,* provoke his or her *curiosity.*

The best way to do that is to focus your headline especially on the *theme* of your ad, the chief benefit your ad offers to the consumer. Some ways to arouse interest:

—*Intriguing headline.* "The computer radio. At 6:00 a.m. it's smarter than you are."

—*Headline appeal to basic desire.* Free! (We all want this.)

—*Subtle blending of illustration and headline.* "Have you ever seen a grown man cry?" (Headline accompanied by illustration of whiskey bottle broken on floor with contents spreading in puddles.)

—*Headline appeal to snobbery.* "For those who ask how good a whiskey is. Not how much it costs."

—A picture of a noted author seated on a beach in Hawaii. The headline urges you to "Fly the Friendly Skies of United."

—A photograph of a rugged male standing out in the snow with a long haired sheep beside him. The headline advertises a shirt that is "rugged but blissfully soft."

—A photo of a man peacefully asleep in the luxurious first class seat of an airliner. And Thai Airline suggests you "Fly through the air with the greatest of zzzzz's."

—A gorgeous landscape scene with grass in the foreground and snow-capped mountains in the background. It is an invitation to visit New Zealand.

—A picture of Jimmy Stewart in a Boy Scout uniform. The caption says, "When you help a Scout troop, there's no guarantee one of the Scouts will grow up to be in the movies. But you never know."

—A picture of two hands, one male and one female, holding liquor glasses. The picture and caption take up only about a fifth of the page. The rest of the page is all black framing the subtle photo. The framing effect of the "picture on black" forces your eyes to the hands and the liquor.

There are countless other examples of pictures and heads fulfilling their functions: The healthy baby eating his special food. The mouth-watering desserts pictured in the food company ads; the beautiful girl in the perfume ads; the photo of the sleek automobile; the headline that promises the "price of power just went down"; and the headline that promises you your "money back" if a product turns out less than thrilling.

Arousing Desire Is Important

An advertisement is a uniquely integrated message. Often the same headline or picture that *attracts attention* and *arouses interest* also creates *desire* in the reader/listener/viewer. But if that has not happened in the headline or the picture (or even if it has to a limited extent) the writer can arouse or enhance desire in the body copy of the advertisement. Some instances of this might be:

—The copy of the snob headline above about the whiskey tries to raise desire to have some by telling the consumer if you "serve your friends . . . , you've told them that you know they appreciate the very best." (You all want the best for your friends.)

—The copy accompanying the picture of the author on the beach in Hawaii enhances the reader's desire to accept United Airlines' invitation by telling of the charms of the islands other than Oahu—Kauai, Molokai, Maui, and Hawaii.

—The shirt ad enhances desire by telling the reader that the Hathaway shirt "is so soft, your skin will think you've invested in cashmere. The imported fabric is of incredibly smooth texture. The purest combed cotton and just the tops—the softest part—of wool are spun together in every strand." Doesn't that feel "comfy" just reading about it?

—And, finally, the Galliano ad of the touching hands holding glasses of sparkling liquor carries this copy: "Close friends. Close talk. Close feelings. Just say the word, and the evening doesn't have to end." Does that increase desire for something? You bet your Saturday night.

Ads Should Promote Action

Advertisers have many ways to move the reader/listener/viewer to action. For example:

—United Airlines tells the consumer to call a travel agent.

—Hathaway shirts reminds the consumer there is a supply shortage and suggests "you make haste, while your haberdasher still has your favorite color."

—The Boy Scouts of America suggests the reader of the ad call them to find out how to sponsor a Boy Scout troop.

There are commonly used methods advertisers use to move the consumer to action. They include:

—Giving the consumer a coupon to fill out.

—Giving the consumer a telephone number to call, usually in big type in a print ad, repeated several times on a radio commercial, and shown in a graphic on a television commercial.

—Giving the consumer a choice of models, pay plans, or service contracts, implying that he or she has already decided to participate.

—Giving the consumer *BOTH* a coupon to fill out and a toll free number to call.

—Giving the consumer a delayed-action subliminal urge to act at a future time.

The delayed motivation to act is used when the purpose of the ad is to give the consumers a good feeling about the product so when they have a future need for such a product they will remember the brand in the ad. An example of such an approach is the toothpaste ad which makes a comparison of the qualities the advertised brand has with the less qualified competing brands. The reader/listener/viewer will not run out and buy a tube of toothpaste immediately especially if he or she has a full tube in the bathroom. But when he or she is in the market for a tube, he or she may switch to the brand advertised.

Another example of the delayed action ad is the ad which has a specific food ingredient used in cooking named by trade name in a recipe the advertiser offers to the homemaker. The advertiser hopes the reader/listener/viewer will be convinced to buy the specific brand of sugar, baking soda, flour, margarine, when he or she tries out the recipe.

The ultimate success in an advertisement is whether or not it invokes action, or sells the product. While all four phases of the *A-I-D-A* formula help to sell the product or service being advertised, the ad usually contains an implied or stated urge to action.

The Print Ad

The print ad usually *attracts attention* with a headline and/or an illustration. It *gains interest* either with the illustration and headline or the early part of the body type. It usually *arouses desire* and *moves to action* within the body copy. There are some exceptions. Sometimes all of the functions are performed with illustrations and headline with little body copy. In other instances, where desire and interest are already present, as with grocery shoppers, illustrations and heads may be absent, and only body type designed to move the consumer to action will be present.

A typical organization for a print ad would be the organization in the following ad:

(Illustration shows a bar of soap in its package, name visible on a plain background.)

(The Headline.) THE WORD IS GENTLY

(Body copy)

Modern advice of skin specialists is that you should wash your face with soap.

Soap that is mild. Soap that is gentle.

Dewdrop Soap is more than mild and gentle. It is skinproof.

Dewdrop can not harm your skin. It caresses it as it cleanses. Dewdrop softens your skin. It lifts out the dirt so gently, it leaves behind a glow, a tingle, a natural fragrance.

It acts so gently.

Dewdrop is as close as your nearest toiletries counter. Where gentleness is sold. Be kind to your skin. Treat it to Dewdrop.

The Broadcast Commercial

The broadcast advertisement is organized with the same purpose in mind as the print ad—to *attract attention, gain interest, arouse desire* and *move to action*. But the form for the commercial, especially for television showing can vary greatly. It is not nearly as restricted as is the print advertisement. The radio commercial is often quite similar to the print ad without the picture. It quite often has a headline and then copy expanding the message, and an ending suggesting action. You could take the print ad illustrated above and rewrite it rather easily for voice delivery in a commercial.

Radio does, of course, have the use of sound to attract attention and rouse interest, much as the illustration does in a print ad. A voice can be excited, sober, enthusiastic, sexy, commanding, condescending, bored, etc. In addition, other sounds can be utilized to gain attention. You can use music to set almost any mood. You can use any number of sound effects—water running, boiling, steaming, the sound of automobiles, airplanes, trains, sirens, horses' hoofs, barking dogs, howling wolves, popping corks, breaking bottles, packages being unwrapped. The list is endless. Sound effects can replace illustrations and headlines and they can enhance body copy in the ad.

IN A FEATURE STORY, THE IMMEDIACY OF THE EVENT IS SECONDARY. Instead, human interest, mood, atmosphere, irony, humor or emotion are used to give the reader pleasure and entertainment. ABOVE, *Bee Beards* in Orono, Maine make an interesting subject for a feature. BELOW, Lucy Brown Coleman and her twin sister Lizzy Brown English celebrate their 101st birthdays together in McRae, Georgia, another good feature topic. (Courtesy Wide World of Photos/AP.)

The television commercial is much too complicated for the aims of this book. The television commercial achieves the same purposes as print and radio advertisements, but it has many more possibilities for variety of organization and use of sight, sound, movement, dialogue, and dramatic presentation. Often commercials are little dramas in themselves, produced by sophisticated means and highly talented professionals. The principles are the same but the package is much different.

Selection of Materials for Features Stories

A news story almost always begins with an évent or is tied to an event in some way. A feature, however, usually begins with an idea. Rene Cappon in his book, *The Word, An Associated Press Guide to Good News Writing*, says that in features related to news events "the immediacy of the event is secondary. The plain ladder of descending news values is replaced by human interest, mood, atmosphere, emotion, irony, humor. Features aim to give the readers pleasure and entertainment along with (and, on the fluffier side, sometimes in lieu of) information." You must select materials for features with that in mind.

In one sense the feature defies description. It can take almost any form and be on almost any subject of interest. But while specific features can escape classification, there are two general categories into which features fall. They are:

—*News Features.*
—*Straight Features.*

As you can guess from these broad categories, *news features* are feature stories that are in some way related to the news. Like news stories, news features are only good at a certain time and perhaps for a certain audience. News features are stories that either precede, accompany, or follow some news event. If they accompany a news story, they are often called *sidebar* stories. An example of news features are the many stories that accompany the main story when a famous person dies. Such stories, containing almost every conceivable bit of information and/or photograph, and/or film clip, accompanied the deaths of Elvis Presley and John Lennon. The fans of these famous singers were so legion that editors and news directors chased down every scrap of history, commentary, and remembrance to publish along with and immediately following the deaths of the two rock musicians. So, in gathering information in such cases—*anything goes.* Another example of profuse use of feature stories to precede, accompany and follow an event is, in the words of Howard Cosell, the "veritable plethora" of stories that are written about a World Series or a Super Bowl in sports. The reader wants every preparation recorded, every star or coach interviewed, every record broken or threatened cited, and a broad cross section of the fans attending given a chance to express their views on air or in print. *Anything goes.*

Another type of news feature is the localized story accompanying a story that is centered elsewhere. For example, hometown newspapers, radio stations and television stations carried everything they could about individual Marines when they were being killed, injured and kept under siege in Lebanon. Hometown neighbors were eager to read all they could about their friends' ordeals in the crisis. Just as all Americans were interested in the overall story, neighbors were interested in the individual Marine and his fate. The fact that nothing had happened to an individual Marine from a specific city became news in that city.

Straight features are stories that are not necessarily related to a news story. They may be timely or seasonal as feature stories about holidays, hunting, planting flowers, planning vacations, saving energy, or filing your income tax returns are, but not directly related to a specific news event. Often they are not timely at all, but can run at any time of the year. One of the most successful enterprises built on feature stories is the Reader's Digest. A perusal of the table of contents of a typical issue is a seminar on feature story types. The April, 1984 edition contains:

—A child/animal story, a touching tale of how a three-year-old befriended an injured wolf.

—A sad story about a mother's fight to accept the death of her baby.

—Personal Glimpses, short anecdotes about a variety of people including the late David Niven, retired anchorman Walter Cronkite and pop star Bette Midler.

—A scientific story about the eclipse of the sun.

—A health story, a short compilation of short items about advances in medicine.

—A psychological "confession" of a woman's inner growth from child to woman.

—A political piece by Carl Rowan decrying President Reagan's Directive 84 aimed at preventing his aides from writing about their administration in the future without approval from a government review board.

—An inspirational story, *Mother's Bible,* telling how a dying mother ended a long-standing feud between two of her children by leaving her Bible marked at passages that ended the ill feeling.

—A story of heroic rescue telling how teenagers risked their lives to save a friend following a swimming accident.

—A humorous piece defining fishing terms in an unconventional manner.

—A sports profile about the late great baseball legend, Satchel Paige.

—An international story asking whether Scandinavia is the newest Russian target.

—Other stories of a similar nature, plus many small departments of humor, self help, and items, items and more items about people at home, at work, and at leisure.

In all of these stories the information selected was that information which would make the piece an effective one. It was information that was pertinent to the purpose of the piece. Specifically, it might have been:

—Good *anecdotes* and *quotes* for a *profile.*
—*Case histories* and *examples* for *life style* or *inspirational* stories.
—Sage *advice* for experts in a *how-to-do-it* article or a *self-improvement* piece.
—*Jokes* or *humorous situations in a humor* article.
—*Unusual facts* in an *oddity* piece.
—*Dramatic events* in an *adventure* article.

The list could go on, but these are examples of specific kinds of information you would select for feature stories of various kinds. The information chosen should *interest* the reader/listener/viewer. The information should *carry out the theme* of the feature article, and the information should *entertain* as well as *inform.*

ORGANIZING THE MATERIAL YOU HAVE SELECTED

Once you have selected the best material for your news or feature story, your advertisement or promotion piece, you must organize the material into an effective order and form to achieve your purpose. You can do that most efficiently if you follow these steps:

—*Make an outline to bring order to the material.*
—*Arrange the material in the outline in a logical sequence.*

OUTLINING

Outlining your material before you write is essential. The form the outline takes is a matter of individual choice. In a short story, the outlining might well be done mentally. In a longer piece it pays to use some sort of outline to aid in the organization. There are various methods:

—*Formal.* You are all familiar with the formal outline in which you use Roman numerals, I, II, III for major divisions; capital letters, A, B, C for major sections under divisions; and numerals 1, 2, 3 and small letters a, b, c, for a more detailed breakdown. Try it for long pieces. It would look like this:

I. Major division.
   A. Major sections under divisions.
      1. Important details.
         a. Less important details.
II. Second major division, etc . . . .

In the informal outline, you might make a list of only the major points to be covered, filling in the details by reference to your notes and from memory. For instance, it might look like this in a news story about a city commission meeting action:

1. Zoning plea voted down.
2. Vote count.
3. Mayor's comment.
4. Arguments for zoning change.
   Developers
   Councilmen Brown and Jones
5. Arguments against.
   Residents of area.
6. Audience reaction.

As an experienced reporter you would not bother jotting down the outline above. You would keep it in your head, and organize as you write. With beginners, however, suddenly confronted with a lot of facts, the idea of trying to keep an outline in your head might not work. A few minutes analyzing the facts and organizing a brief outline could be helpful in writing a more effective story. The story from the outline could read:

City commissioners voted down last night a petition by a Hometown developer for a zoning variance which would have allowed him to build a roller skating rink in a residential area near Eastside High School.

Commissioners voted 3 to 2 to deny the petition of developer Harry Hodges to allow the rink to be built at N.W. 3rd Street and College Avenue in the Suburban Heights section of the city.

Mayor Thomas Dwyer, who had indicated he was opposed to building the rink at the proposed site, praised the commission vote. "As public officials, we have a duty to protect the residential neighborhoods of the city from the encroachment of commercial enterprises which could destroy the residential atmosphere," he said.

Developer Hodges expressed his disappointment but said he would not appeal the decision in court. "It is my city, too," he said. "If opposition to my plan is this strong, I will look elsewhere to build the rink."

Commissioner James Brown said he voted for the rink because "The kids need it. We have to provide youngsters with wholesome recreational facilities. I hope the decision tonight does not delay too long construction of this and other such facilities for young people."

Commissioner Hubert J. Jones said he voted for the zoning variance because "We have no right to deny a property owner the chance to earn a fair return on the money he has invested in property. Government needs to encourage business enterprise, not deny it."

Several property owners near the site for the proposed rink told commissioners the rink would reduce the value of their houses.

Bruce McKay, who lives across the street from the site, said bluntly, "It will ruin the neighborhood. Who wants a bunch of teenagers racing their cars up and down the street all evening? They can skate in their driveways. At night, they should be home studying anyway."

Five or six young people loudly booed McKay and chanted, "We want our rink. We're citizens, too. We want our rink." Leader of the delegates of teenagers was Gail Goodman, president of the Student Council of Eastside High. She quieted her group and said to the commissioners, "We will accept your decision tonight, but we do need more places where we can go to have fun. We hope you will remember that in the future."

Index Cards

Some writers make individual notes on index cards or small sheets of paper, then they organize the cards in the order they wish to use the data in the piece they are writing.

The important thing is to use whatever outlining tools work best for you. The best organizer is your brain. If you think about your material and think how best it can serve the reader, you can't go far wrong. Use whatever organizing method works for you. You get credit or criticism for what you write. Noboby cares whether you use an outline or what form that outline takes.

USING INFORMATION LOGICALLY

In deciding how you will use information in a piece of writing, use logical organization. Some examples of being logical in use of information:

News Stories for Print or Broadcast Outlets

—If you were writing a news story about an accident in which one person was slightly injured, one was seriously injured, and one was killed, in which order would you write about the victims in the story? Logically, you would discuss the dead person first, the seriously injured second, and the slightly injured last.

—But suppose the story had elements that dictated a different organization, could you still be logical? Let's see. Suppose the man killed in the above story was not well-known, but the seriously injured man was the mayor. Wouldn't it still be logical to discuss the most prominent first, then the less prominent?

—Suppose you were writing a roundup story of football action in the Big Ten Conference to be published all over the Midwest for the Associated Press. You would write about the leading teams first, runners-up second, and alsorans third. It is logical.

—But suppose you were writing the roundup for a newspaper in Wisconsin. Regardless of their standing, you would discuss first the University of Wisconsin Badgers, the state's team. It is also logical. You might then follow up with the rest of the league in the order of team standings in the conference. Or you might give the second priority to those teams in the conference which will be future opponents of the Badgers. Either order would be logical.

—You are doing a series of interviews of candidates for local offices. You would probably turn the spotlight on the candidates for mayor first; then turn to the candidates for lesser offices later. It is logical. But if the mayor has only token opposition and is a shoo-in, and there is a hot contest for one of the city commission seats—sorry, Mr. Mayor, you'll have to take second place. It is logical.

Advertisements

—You are called upon to write an ad for a clothing store which is having a sale featuring slacks reduced 10 percent, shirts reduced 50 percent, suits reduced 20 percent. The logical way to organize the ad would be by size of the reduction. Men buy all three items regularly, so play up the 50 percent reduction on the shirts, then the 20 percent reduction on suits, and finally the 10 percent reduction on slacks. It is logical.

—But you are writing an ad for a drug store which is reducing Evening in Paris perfume $5 a bottle and cigarettes $1 a carton. Would you organize the ad by size of reduction to be logical? Maybe not. You might remind yourself that relatively few of your readers are interested in Evening in Paris perfume even at reduced price, while a high percentage of your readers are interested in a bargain in cigarettes. You might want to put the cigarettes first, but for a good logical reason.

—You are writing a commercial for a shoe store which wants to feature a new type of shoe copied from a pair worn by Tom Selleck in his latest movie. They cost $75 a pair. Obviously, no one is going to buy them to save money, so logically your ad would play up the hero worship angle that they had graced the Selleck feet. If price is mentioned at all, it should be played down.

Feature Stories

—You are doing a profile on a local citizen who has just won some high honor—a Nobel Prize, a Pulitzer Prize, football's Heisman Trophy or the local Citizen of the Year award. You lead off with an anecdote that illustrates the quality of the person which won the award. You might follow that with a quote from the awardee about his or her feelings on being honored. Farther down in the story would come material about the other aspects of the person's life, comments from others, and lesser material about the award. Then you might end with a quote about the award or an anecdote bearing on the award. That sort of arrangement of materials would be logical.

—In a feature about compulsions that make people do odd things, such as always leaving a building by the same door they entered, or folding clothes neatly before throwing them in the dirty clothes hamper, you could start with a question that will bring the reader into the story immediately. Ask the reader if he has any such compulsive actions he must take, reasonable or not. Then go on and list various compulsions others have in order of strangeness. It finishes with a reassurance to the reader that if he has an odd compulsion, he has lots of company. It is logical even if the compulsions are not.

—A feature story on fire safety tips catches the reader's interest by asking the reader the question, "When was the great Chicago fire?" It then gives the date and uses that as a springboard to give other facts about the widespread damage and danger from fire. It lists the chief causes of fires, and then gives a series of tips on how the reader can prevent fire. This is a logical way to present the information.

LOGIC AT WORK

Let's look at some examples of writing that have been organized in a logical order. First example is a news story about an art show.

Graph 1:
Overall summary, the general who, what, when, where

Creators of arts and crafts walked off with 37 awards worth $2,000 at Hometown's first City Art Festival, sponsored by merchants on Tuesday in Jones Park.

Graph 2:
Important specific data, top awards, local winners

The Best of Show award, $250, went to Jane Shaw of Hometown, for an oil painting. The Chamber of Commerce award, $200, went to Tom Orwell, also of Hometown for his sculpture. He also won the York Restaurant award of $50.

Graph 3:
Secondary award, but local winners

Homer Ferrara of Yourtown took the Ninth National Bank award of $50 for work in any medium. Dave McDonald, also of Hometown, won the Auto Dealer's Association award of $50 for his water colors.

Graph 4, 5:
Out of town winners, and winners of less Important Categories

Two out-of-towners also won prizes. Dan Small of Theirtown, won the $150 Art Society award for an oil painting, and the $100 Women's Club award went to Linda Bond of Neartown.

Best graphics award went to Mike Brown of Theirtown. Blue ribbon for photography went to Gerald Coover of Hometown.

Graph 6:
Also-rans: less important awards and winners

In addition, those who earned second or third place or honorable mention received 18 awards— merchant gift certificates or U.S. Savings Bonds.

Logic was used in the story above in organizing a lot of facts into a natural way. The reader is interested in the most prestigious awards, or most valuable, and in the winners close to home. These were all emphasized in organization of the material.

An example of how the logical organization in an advertisement is best used as follows:

Headline:
(Attention "A" interest "I" of advertising's AIDA aroused.)

For larger sizes:
smart evening wear
by Carol Chic
of Pere of Paris

Body Copy A:
(Desire to buy aroused, the "D" of AIDA.)

Great news for you stately women. Drab is out; delightful is in. Carol Chic brings lovely, only semi-muted colors to your wardrobe. Breathless blue, radiant rose, vibrant violet. Sizes 18 and up. Chiffons and Crepes.

Body Copy B:
(Urge to action aroused, the final "A" of AIDA.)

Shop today at the Grand Boutique in Hometown Department Store, Elm Tree Mall. Just say charge it.

A 60 second radio commercial that is organized logically to fulfill its purpose follows:

The Beginning:
(Gaining attention, arousing interest, the "A", "I" of AIDA.)

Don't put up with the *cold!* Don't sweat out the summer *heat!* Solar Energy Limited can *switch off* high electric rates . . . *now!* Stop by our display room at twenty three forty five North Elm Street and *learn how you* can install solar energy units in your home

The Middle:
(Arousing desire, the "D" of AIDA.)

or business. Solar energy is *plentiful, silent, non-polluting* . . . and *free!* Products from Solar Energy Limited can provide you heating and cooling *better* and at *less cost.* Be *ready* with *solar energy!* Call

The end:
(Moving listener to action, the "A" of AIDA.)

46-S.O.L.A.R. *today* for more information. Or *visit* Solar Energy Limited at twenty-three forty five North Elm Street in Hometown. That phone number again is 46-S.O.L.A.R. *Call now!*

As you can see from these examples, logical organization can take any form, so long as it is orderly. It can be chronological—from now to then. It can be reverse chronology—from then to now. It can be in order of consequence, prominence, nearness. One set of facts can be organized in various ways for various purposes, and various readers, and each of the organizations can be logical for its purpose.

A thing that should come across to you strongly, is that as a writer you must analyze your material, think about your audience, its desires and needs, consider your purpose in writing the piece, and choose the logical arrangement that works best.

THE NEWS STORY FORMS

While each piece of writing you do has unique organizational aspects, and that is more true today than in the past, there are some basic forms you should be aware of. Straight informational news stories are often written in what has been called the *INVERTED PYRAMID* form. In this organization, the information most important to the reader/listener/viewer is at the *top;* the least important at the *bottom* of the story. The material is organized in a descending order of importance from *most important* first to *least important* last. While this *formula* organization is not as universal as it once was, it is widely used.

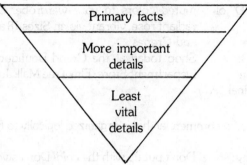

Primary facts

More important details

Least vital details

The Inverted Pyramid Story

A typical three paragraph inverted pyramid story, with most important facts in the first paragraph, more important details in second paragraph, and least important details in third paragraph, might read like this:

New officers will be elected at a meeting of the Westside Civic Club in the Lincoln High School Tuesday at 8 p.m.

The nominating committee has named its candidates: Joseph Jones for president; Patrick Smith, vice-president; Alice Johnson, secretary-treasurer. Other nominations can be made from the floor.

Retiring officers are: George Swanson, president; Martha Stein, vice-president; James McCarthy, secretary-treasurer.

The inverted pyramid form of the news story is effective for several reasons:

—It is the natural way to tell a news story. When you relate a newsworthy event you have witnessed to your friend, you blurt out the exciting, most important details first, then come the secondary details. The minor details you might skip altogether, or give at the end of your recitation, or upon being questioned. If you tell about seeing a bank robber running out of a bank with his loot and dashing down the street, you wouldn't describe how he was dressed before you told your friend about the shootout that followed with the patrolman on the corner. Of course not.

—It is helpful to the reader/listener/viewer. To paraphrase an expression— some will read all of your story; all will read some of your story; but not all will read all of your story. And what is wrong with that? If you write your story in an inverted pyramid form, all of the readers are happy: those who want only the primary details can move on to other stories after the first paragraph or two; those who want full details can read on through the story.

—It aids in production. An inverted pyramid story is easier for the editor or news director to cut to fit the space or time available, if space or time is in short supply. The editor merely has to chop the less important details from the end of the story. And that can ease the pressure when decision time is close to action time.

The inverted pyramid story is a favorite of the wire service organizations which furnish national and international news to newspapers and broadcast stations. When several stories are ready to go on the wire at the same time, if they are written in inverted pyramid style, they can be sent in short takes. The editors and news directors thus can have parts of several stories rather than all of one. The rest of the stories can follow. Also, with hundreds of outlets receiving the same news stories, the editors and news directors can cut easily to fit their needs. Some may want to use only a couple of paragraphs, some half the story, and others the entire story.

The inverted pyramid form got its start during the American Civil War when the telegraph wire was just coming into its own. Because the wire was not always dependable, war correspondents learned to write their dispatches with the most important news up front, so that in the probable event of a wire failure, the important facts were more likely to get through. The inverted pyramid is an effective way to write news. Learn its construction and use it.

While the inverted pyramid story is used so often in news writing it could be called a "formula" story, there are many forms a news story can take. Editors and news directors are becoming more receptive to more creative approaches to news. And there are situations in which the inverted pyramid can be improved upon. Some alternatives are:
—*The modified inverted pyramid.*
—*The straight chronological form.*
—*The featurized approach.*

The Modified Inverted Pyramid

There are stories which can best be told in a chronological order except for emphasizing a few highlights in the beginning. Many sports stories lend themselves to this type of organization. In reporting a football game, you would want to tell the reader early who won, by how much, and the big plays and star performers who contributed the winning points. Then you might want to revert to a straight chronological order to tell about the rest of the action. The same treatment might be appropriate in covering a parade, some convention activities, or some meetings. An obituary is often told in a modified inverted pyramid form. The beginning would identify the person who died, tell about the circumstances of the death and summarize the highlights of the victim's life, whether personal, career or public service. The story might then revert to a chronological telling of the person's life. The following example shows how that is done:

(FIRST PART OF STORY ORGANIZED IN INVERTED PYRAMID)

Robert J. Croswell, superintendent of schools here for 12 years, died Friday of injuries he received two weeks ago in a boating accident.

Crosswell received a fractured skull when his head struck a dock at Lake Butler as he slipped trying to leap from his small boat to the dock. In a coma since the accident, he died at 5:30 p.m., a Hometown General Hospital representative said.

Appointed to succeed the late Elmer James as superintendent in 1972, Croswell headed the school district during its period of greatest growth. He twice was named the leading educator in the state, in 1980 and in 1983. He served as secretary to the National Association of School Superintendents from 1977 to his death.

(LAST PART OF STORY BECOMES PREDOMINANTLY CHRONOLOGICAL)

Croswell, who was born in Chicago, got his early education in the public schools of Boston where his family moved when he was 4. He attended Harvard College, majoring in the classics. He earned master's and doctoral degrees in education from the University of Pennsylvania in 1948 and 1956.

Croswell served in Korea as an intelligence officer, earning the Distinguished Service Medal.

After the war, Croswell taught at Northwestern University College of Education for ten years. From 1963 to 1972 he was superintendent of schools in Neartown.

Croswell was a member of the Hometown Kiwanis Club, chairman of the Hometown Library executive committee, a member of the Boy Scouts Council, and past president of the Mental Health Society.

He is survived by his wife, Hazel. Services will be held at 2 p.m. Monday at the Smock Funeral Home.

Straight Chronological Report

The straight chronological arrangement is not used often in a news story, but on occasion it can be a dramatic device to tell certain types of stories. It is a handy method of "updating" a story the reader may already be aware of from earlier accounts. For example, an afternoon newspaper may have carried an inverted pyramid account of a story, and the reporter on the morning newspaper may want to present the information the next day in a new way. He might adopt this treatment:

Tommy Burns awoke before dawn yesterday. He was more eager to go to school than on any day of the three years he had attended Lincoln Elementary. The teacher had given him permission to bring Elmo, his pet rabbit, for science class.

Tommy, 9, wanted to skip breakfast, but his mother, Mrs. Fred Burns, of 2642 W. 3rd. St., insisted her only son eat his cereal and drink his orange juice. Even so, he left at 7:45 a.m., half an hour before his usual departure time, with Elmo safely tucked away in a covered wicker basket.

At 8 a.m., just a block from school, Tommy met his friend Bobby. He couldn't resist showing his pet. As he lifted the lid of the basket, the rabbit leaped out and bolted for busy Main Street. Tommy ran after his pet.

Mrs. Elsie Hartman, driving home after her night's work as a waitress at the All-Nite Diner, told police she never saw the boy darting from between parked cars. Tommy was knocked to the street unconscious.

After several hours, Tommy regained consciousness at General Hospital. Doctors said he suffered a severe concussion and a broken left arm, but will be fine in a couple of weeks.

There was no sign of Elmo. If the rabbit is not found by the time Tommy is due home, Burns said Tommy will get a new pet "of his choice."

Featurized Story

Some stories can be best told in a featurized way. They are humorous or poignant, but still involve news events. They can be improved by a bit of writing skill into a featurized news story that will be more interesting to the reader than a bare recitation of the facts. Some examples:

—Forced cancellation of a scheduled plane flight when several lizards escaped from the storage area and were skittering about the plane.

—Sentencing of a man charged with uttering "dirty words" to wash his mouth out with soap as an alternative to ten days in jail.

—The miraculous recovery of a youth badly injured in an automobile accident and given one chance in a hundred to survive.

An example of this type of story:

When volunteer firemen from Hometown responded to an emergency call Friday, they had a hard time fighting the blaze they found. It was in the firehouse.

Firemen rounded up garden hoses from nearby homes to battle the blaze after flames kept them from their own equipment.

Damage to the firehouse was estimated at $25,000. An adjoining office building suffered $5,000 in damages.

The Depth Story

The academic or term paper form of organization is not often used in mass media writing, but in writing a depth story such a form might be suitable. In general, this organization would:

—State the problem.

—Introduce evidence to show the scope of the problem.

—Suggest solutions for the problem.

—Arrive at the conclusion pointing out the obvious solution, giving the reader optional solutions, or pointing out why no pat solution is possible.

This is the procedure you would use for doing a term paper, and with only slight variations it is the method reporters use when exploring an economic, political or social problem. But be cautioned. If you take this approach, make certain your story, including the lead, is interesting, tightly written, and relatively informal. For example, documentation would be included in the text of the piece, not in footnotes. The reader would accept such an organization in a depth story because he would realize from the subject matter, headline and display treatment of the story, and probably the length, that it was a depth treatment. He would expect to read the entire piece.

A syndicated story about the continued emotional suffering of some of the veterans of Vietnam's "police action" was written by Carole Agus for Newsday and published in the St. Petersburg Times. (March 30, 1984, Page 1). With headlines and illustrations, the story runs 40 column inches on page 1A and 66 column inches on page 16A. It is a long story for a newspaper, but it covers a complex subject in a comprehensive manner. The beginning of the piece presents the problem in a dramatic way:

OLYMPIA PENINSULA, Wash.—There is fire in the quiet: hellfire and holocaust, rocket and mortar fire of the mind.

Bombs explode in the hush of the forest, but all is silent. Tracer bullets stream through the black skies, and the smoke is colored by the tracers. There is no smoke, but they can see it. It chokes them, it sears their eyes, it burns their flesh.

In the still green forest, in the evergreen forest, in forests without even the sound of crickets, they hear grenades exploding. Firefights rage in the minds of these veterans—lonely, angry tortured men. Sitting in the chill of the northern wilderness, they burn with the fever of Vietnam. Platoons of them, brigades of them, yet each alone in a separate army.

They are living in exile in America.

* * *

The story then goes on to tell of the private hell and personal anguish suffered by these self-termed Bush Vets, who have been "hiding out" since they left Vietnam 12 years ago. The author spells out the problems more specifically by telling of the particular nightmares and hallucinations that bedevil individual veterans and of the Vietnam experience they relive.

The author describes the therapy being conducted by the Veteran's Administration on the victims of what is termed Post-traumatic Stress Syndrome, the nervous disorder that is an outgrowth of the Vietnam experience. The story tells how the illness, characterized by 24-hour fear, has made it impossible for the victims to function in society and explains why they can only cope in the wilderness of the Northwest Rockies. The story relates the problems and attempts at a cure through interviews with therapists and victims. The story is grim, offering not a great deal of hope.

Other stories that might begin like this one by pointing out a problem in society might end differently. The other stories might offer solutions. All depth stories define and flesh out problems; not all can offer solutions.

The Feature Story

Organization of the feature story can take almost any form. It is usually adapted to the material and purpose of the piece. It can take a structured form such as:

—A question and answer format in an interview in either print or broadcast media.

—A narrative format using anecdotes, description, or dialogue to achieve its end.

—A loose news story form in which the facts are presented in inverted pyramid style, but garnished with anecdotes, quotes, observations, and colorful language.

Or, a feature story may have no formal structure that represents anything used in other types of writing for the news media. For example, a feature story might:

—Be a letter to a person or the public in general.

—Be a dramatic or comic dialogue between two people, real or imaginary.

—A listing of strange facts, funny facts, sad facts, eerie facts, or even mundane facts if presented in an interesting way.

A feature story can take any form. You can let your creativity show in a feature story. Most features are based on interesting facts, but you have the freedom to take a few minor facts and with creativity turn out an entertaining feature. A reporter visited the zoo in his city on a quiet Sunday looking for anything that would make a story for Monday morning's paper. He noticed two cats in adjoining cages snarling at each other and asked the zookeeper why they were not separated as they seemed anything but friends. The zookeeper said that the male cat had been borrowed from a nearby zoo to be mated with the female, hopefully to produce some cubs for the zoo. However, the cats did not take to each other immediately, and the adjacent cages, it was hoped, would make the cats amenable to romance. With those few facts, the reporter, using the letter technique mentioned above, came up with this story:

DEAR MISS LOVELORN:

I have just spent $750 for a boy cat for my girl cat, but they don't seem to get along very well. Do you have any suggestions as to how I can encourage them to swallow their hatred for a few days and establish a relationship.

Sincerely,
Zookeeper Sam Jones

DEAR MR. JONES:

I can't imagine anyone paying $750 for a male cat, but I guess that is your right. Why not just keep the cats in the kitchen so if they fight they won't hurt the furniture. Maybe eventually they will get to like each other. If not, I'm afraid you will just have to sell one. But I doubt you will get back your $750. There aren't many suckers like you around these days. Good luck, and why not stick to canaries?

Ann Lovelorn

DEAR MISS LOVELORN:

You misunderstand. I am director of the city zoo. The male cat I rented is a 130-pound Fels Pardus (that's Latin for black leopard) and he's really a bargain. Stud service for a black leopard can run more than $1,000, so please wipe that smirk off your face.

This 18-month-old Fels Pardus (we never name our cats) arrived here on November 3. We placed him in a cage next to our female Fels Pardus, who is a widow. Her first mate died earlier this year. She is 10-years-old and eager to make a good rematch. She is still in her prime and a good breeder as they say.

Now the problem is, so far they snarl at each other. Not so much as a smile, let alone a leer. How do I kindle the flame of love in their hearts? I have to justify that $750.

Prayerfully,
Sam Jones

DEAR MR. JONES:

We hear from a lot of weirdos in this business, but you take the croissant. If you had told me this in the first letter, I wouldn't have answered. But I will try to help you even if you came close to violating current community standards for sleaze in describing this disgusting affair.

As you introduced Latin into this whole thing I will quote a Latin proverb: Tempus Fugit, E Pluribus Unum, Semper Fidelis and Caveat Emptor. Loosely translated, that means, "Be patient. They will get it together." If you have any more problems, do not consult me.

Ann Lovelorn

The story, accompanied by a photograph of the reluctant lovers, made everyone happy. The city editor had a story to brighten the paper on a dull news day. The reader had a chuckle to lighten a heavy Monday. The reporter got a byline and reasserted his value to the paper. Having the ability and initiative to make an interesting feature story out of a few facts increases the value of a reporter to the newspaper that hires him or her.

CONSISTENCY IN ORGANIZATION

To make certain the organization you use for your writing performs its chief purpose to make the piece easier for the reader/listener/viewer to understand, always be consistent in organization.

Keep your piece in the same tense, voice, mood, person and number unless there is a clear call for a change, such as in quoted material or other inserted material.

Be consistent in the order in which you present material if you treat the same material in more than one place in a piece. If you summarize items in the beginning of a story or ad, treat them in the same order later when you return to give specifics. For example, note the following story beginning:

Three new faculty members have joined the staff of the Hometown Community College, it was announced today by college president Dr. Fred James. They are:

—Dr. Michael Smith, assistant professor of math.

—Dr. Hershel Wright, assistant professor of English.

—Dr. John Engbert, assistant professor of history.

In the item shown, the names have been listed randomly, for all are of the same rank, all have doctorates, and the listing is not alphabetical. It may become clear later why that listing was chosen, but for whatever reason, when you return to the names later in the story to give additional information about the three men, begin with Dr. Smith and end with Dr. Engbert to be consistent. Or rearrange the order in which they are first mentioned if you change your mind about the organization and wish to discuss Dr. Wright first because his credentials are best, or he is a Hometown man, or for whatever reason.

Always be consistent.

ADEQUATE TRANSITIONS

In writing, you must remember that you have to carry the reader wherever your writing carries you. You have to build bridges from one idea to another, from one time to another, one place to another, one person to another. That can be a real problem in mass media writing because of some of the organizational forms. The inverted pyramid style, for example, does not have the simple transitional qualities of a chronological order. You must carry the reader along from paragraph to paragraph by using transitional devices carefully.

—You can do it with words such as "but," "still," "yet," "however," "nevertheless," "moreover."

—You can do it with phrases such as: "On the other hand," "Although this is what he said," "Returning to the budget," "In the case of," "Turning to the sewer problem," etc.

—You can do it by repeating key words from prior sentences or prior paragraphs to give the reader a bridge to step on.

—You can do it by introducing a new subject in a direct, not an offhand, manner. If you switch from one subject to another, avoid introducing the new subject in the form of a quote, or vague reference to some specific aspect of the new subject. Be direct and clear in letting the reader know that you are taking up a new subject, as in the following:

The City Council next took up the subject of roads.

* * *

Swanson's educational background makes him the best qualified candidate for the job.

* * *

The first witness called to the stand by the defense attorney was the defendant.

The following story, written in the inverted pyramid organization, makes use of several transitional devices. The transitional words, phrases, and sentences are underlined.

Quick police action Tuesday night led to the arrest of two Hometown men in connection with a jewelry store burglary, and led to the recovery of more than $5,000 in stolen merchandise.

The two suspects—Tony Angeles, 30, of 2100 Elm St. and Harold MacKinnon, 28, of 400 Pear Ave.—have been charged with grand theft, police Capt. Fred Silverman said.

The pair was arrested at MacKinnon's home where police were led when license plates on a car found near the scene of a jewelry store burglary showed the car registered to MacKinnon, Silverman said.

Police found about $3,000 in silverplate in the abandoned car Silverman said, and an additional $2,000 in gems in the MacKinnon home.

Police said the suspects admitted breaking into the Clark Jewelry Store, 800 North Main St. They said they had to abandon the car when it failed to start immediately and they heard police sirens approaching, Silverman said.

Police were brought to the scene of the burglary when an un-identified passerby called at 5 a.m. to report he thought a burglary might be under way.

Acting on the anonymous tip, police sped to the scene and found the window of the jewelry store jimmied open and the MacKinnon car parked in the alley behind the store.

A check of the license plate number led them to the MacKinnon home.

Angeles and MacKinnon will be arraigned in Circuit Court on Friday.

THE FACTS DETERMINE THE ORGANIZATION

The beginning writer must be cautioned that the facts at hand and the purpose of a piece largely determine the organization of the material. The examples cited in this chapter are just that: a few examples of the innumerable ways to organize material for a given purpose. The examples are not intended to be exhaustive or complete. They are just guides. They do not substitute for your job of analyzing the facts in a given situation and using them for your purpose. In other words, you cannot rely on stereotypic organizational forms to fall back on. You must think, analyze, arrange, organize for each piece you do. That is why writing is difficult. But it is also why it can be rewarding.

SUGGESTED EXERCISES

1. Cut an effective print advertisement out of a magazine or a newspaper. Rewrite it as a radio commercial (80 words for a 30 second commercial and/or 160 words for a 60 second commercial). Indicate use of music or sound effects to create an imagery created by the illustration in the print ad. Keep in mind the AIDA formula for advertisements as you reorganize the ad to be heard rather than read.

2. Tape a radio commercial, or obtain a copy from the station, and turn it into an ad for a newspaper or magazine. Use the illustration and headline to attract attention and arouse interest.

3. Create your own advertising campaign by visiting a local merchant, selecting a product to be advertised, getting as much information about the product as you can from the merchant and then creating advertisements for print and commercials for radio use. If you do a good job, the merchant might use your ads, especially in high school and community college newspapers or yearbooks.

4. Prepare an advertisement for your local newspaper and/or a commercial, 30 second or 60 second for a local radio station from the following facts:

PRODUCT: New type of shoe being introduced.

NAME: The Prince—Named for Prince Charles of England.

PRICE: $65 a pair

COLORS: Royal Blue, Windsor White, Regal Rust

OTHER BENEFITS: Lightweight. Slip on styling. Never need shining. Soft as (Provide your own metaphor or simile. Avoid such cliches as "walking on air.")

ADVERTISER: The Shoe Shoppe, 210 College Avenue West, Phone — 387-6446

5. Team up with a fellow student. Each of you select a well organized story from the newspaper. Do not show the stories to each other. Break down the stories, arrange the facts at random. Then exchange the rearranged fact sheets. Each of you write a story from your fact sheets. Then exchange the original stories and compare what each of you has written with the original stories.

6. Select a story or stories from the newspaper which are poorly organized. Rewrite them to improve the organization.

7. As a reporter for a newspaper, you cover the federal beat. When you call on Postmaster James T. Kellogg, he tells you he has a story for you. The following conversation ensues:

KELLOGG: Hometown will get a new branch post office next to Eastgate Mall (34th and Chestnut Streets).

YOU: When?

KELLOGG: Construction will start in six weeks. We already have the plans. Should be in use in eight months.

YOU: How much will it cost and how big will it be?

KELLOGG: It will have 18,000 square feet and cost $1.5 million.

YOU: What kind of architecture?

KELLOGG: It will fit in with the design of the mall. It will be joined to the mall by a covered passageway. It will be modern inside and fully air-conditioned.

YOU:	Who will build it?
KELLOGG:	Bids will be asked in a few days and contracts should be let within a month. The government is giving top priority to the construction because of the need in that section of the city.
YOU:	Will it create new jobs in the city?
KELLOGG:	Yes. About 50 new people will be employed. They will come from a pool of applicants who have already taken the Civil Service examinations.
YOU:	Will the new building have any unusual new equipment in it?
KELLOGG:	Glad you asked. Yes it will. The service will feature new computerized delivery slots.
YOU:	How will they work?
KELLOGG:	Well, every customer served out of this branch will have a coded card. When notified by phone that he has a package or letter that missed the delivery, he can come to the post office at any time of day and over the weekend, insert his card into a slot, and his package will be released down and through a door that will open just long enough to discharge the letter or package.
YOU:	How do you know such a system will work?
KELLOGG:	It has been tested in Knobnoster, Missouri, and we have been assured it does work.

Chapter V

WRITING TYPES: FROM FACTS TO FORM

Writing is creative, and each piece of writing is an individual work. However, as a writer you should be familiar with certain basic forms of stories, advertisements, promotions. In using these suggested forms and in reading the examples, always keep in mind that as facts change, stories and ads change. Writing changes with each assignment.

In math you learn that *two apples* added to *two apples* results in *four apples*. So long as you don't change the *two* and *two*, you can change the apples for *oranges*, *grapes*, or *pizzas* and the result is still *four*. That does not hold true with examples of stories or ads. In writing for the mass media if you alter *just one fact*, the result may be drastically changed. So *learn the forms*. And *note* the examples as *illustrations for the given set of facts only*.

The often used forms with which you should be aware include *advance* pieces about events that will take place in *the future, followup* pieces telling what happened at those events, or *combination* pieces such as stories about meetings or interviews that yield information about future events. *Not included*, because they are not written ahead of time, are *live broadcasts* of ongoing events such as sports competitions, interviews, panel discussions and on-site descriptions of breaking news stories.

To illustrate the close relationship of the various forms of information presented to the reader/listener/viewer, the forms described and the examples given in this chapter will all involve one major event. The examples will be about a typical university homecoming weekend which entails a variety of events and utilizes all of the forms—advance and follow-up news stories, feature stories, advertisements, commercials, and promotions. The basic events of the homecoming which will provide the information for most of the specific examples are:

—*A football game.*
—*A homecoming parade with floats and marching units.*
—*Crowning of a homecoming queen at a student pep rally.*
—*A leadership club dinner with a prominent speaker.*
—*An alumni breakfast.*
—*A Journalism School roast of prominent state and local politicians.*
—*Post game fraternity and sorority parties.*

PRINT NEWS FORMS

Basic print news story forms that would preclude, accompany and follow a typical homecoming weekend would include:

—An *advance story* announcing a meeting to coordinate the events.

—A *meeting story* to tell what took place at the meeting.

—A *speech story* following a leadership club dinner.

—A *sidebar news story* about a demonstration that took place at the Leadership Club dinner.

—A *roundup story* of all events for a wire service or distance newspaper.

—A *personality feature* about an outstanding graduate honored at the alumni breakfast.

—A *second day story* for a Monday paper about an incident that happened too late Saturday night to make the Sunday papers.

The Advance Story

The advance story is of great service to the reader/listener/viewer. It keeps him abreast of events in which he may have a great interest. He may want to attend the event detailed in the advance story. He may want to be made aware of the event so he can read about what happened if he can't attend himself. The advance should give complete details.

The advance story should be as individual as it can be, if not unique. Often the event you will be writing about will have some unique feature that will make it differ from all the other events that will be publicized. Use that unique angle to try to get some action and interest into a story that is basically passive. An advance tells about what is going to happen, and that is never as interesting as what did happen. Advance stories are usually short stories. You might tell about a planned meeting to coordinate homecoming activities, playing up the unique aspect of the meeting in this way..

Plans for the biggest ever homecoming weekend at Ourstate University will emerge from a meeting of city leaders, university administrators and student leaders Tuesday at 10 a.m. in city hall.

"We will coordinate traditional activities and make preliminary plans to make this year's homecoming the best since they started in 1932," OU Student President Laura Albertson said.

In addition to Albertson, attending the meeting will be Mayor Thomas Dwyer, Chamber of Commerce Executive Director Andrew McDougall, OU Student Dean Mary Cantrell, and OU Leadership Club President Barry Webster.

Each year OU homecoming weekend football game, parade, Leadership Club dinner and other activities bring more people to Ourtown than any other event. Homecoming Weekend will be Oct. 3, 4, and 5.

The Meeting Story

As a reporter, you will be expected to attend many and varied meetings and write stories about what occurs at the meetings. If the meetings are limited to one subject or action, your task as a writer is simplified. You analyze and organize the discussions and actions taken at each meeting and write a single story to fit the space available. However, if unrelated items are discussed and actions taken at a meeting, your problem is a bit more complex. You may have to write several stories. You or your editor may have to bypass some of the possible stories and concentrate only on one or more of the more important ones. You should rarely try to combine unrelated items in a single story. Such a story will probably be awkward and unsatisfactory. If there is plenty of time to write and enough space, you can write several stories. Local government reporters often write several stories generated at a single meeting of a city or county commission or board.

A meeting story should usually highlight important actions taken by those at the meeting—ordinances passed, votes taken, plans agreed to, items tabled (which usually means killed without a vote) or postponed, and items pointedly ignored. Disputes usually create news—citizen protests, arguments among participants in the meeting, controversial statements made by participants. Discussion sometimes produces interesting quotes.

Much of what happens at a meeting is not newsworthy. There is much dull discussion. Many actions and procedures are routine—the minutes, reports of subcommittees which have essentially done nothing, minor purchases and expenditures, votes on minor procedural matters.

As a reporter, you must listen carefully and must ask questions. Rarely will all of your questions be answered by the discussion at a meeting. You must ask questions at any time in an informal meeting and during recesses or at the conclusion of a formal meeting.

Typical of a meeting story would be one written about a meeting to coordinate plans for the homecoming weekend. It might read:

A speech by Jeffery Tower, former astronaut and now president of East-West airlines, and an expanded parade will highlight the 38th annual Ourstate University homecoming weekend.

Tower agreed to speak at the annual homecoming dinner of the Leadership Club at the university, it was announced at a meeting, to coordinate plans for homecoming weekend.

Tower, who retired from the space program in 1970 to become an airline executive, is a graduate of Ourstate University and its ROTC program. He served as a pilot in the U.S. Air Force for 12 years before joining NASA as an astronaut in 1964.

At the meeting in city hall, Mayor Thomas Dwyer also announced the city will contribute $1,000 from recreation funds to finance appearance in the homecoming parade of the Capital

Highsteppers Band, which won national recognition at last year's Western Bowl.

Five other high school bands from the state will march in the parade. The chamber of commerce will pay expenses for the additional bands, chamber executive director Andrew McDougall said.

"We are going to invite the five finalists from the band competition to be held in two weeks in Theirtown," McDougall said.

Laura Albertson, Ourstate University student government president, was named chairman of a homecoming planning committee. Her job will be to coordinate activities and planning in the five months before the Oct. 3-5 homecoming weekend. Other committee members are McDougall, Dwyer, Ourstate University Dean Mary Cantrell and OU Leadership Club president Barry Webster.

The newly formed committee discussed preliminary plans for the homecoming weekend and agreed to meet again May 18 in city hall to draft more detailed plans. Time of the meeting will be announced later.

The Speech Story

Like meetings, speeches are common events covered by reporters. Often the main activity at a meeting is a speech, so a meeting story is often a speech story. Speeches often contain little news, but they sometimes do provide news, or at least interesting viewpoints on subjects in the news.

There is not a lot of news produced by the best speeches. It is not unusual for a 30 minute speech to consist of 10 minutes of warming up the audience, 10 minutes of laying the groundwork for the theme of the speech, two minutes of good information, and eight minutes for questions. But don't despair, two minutes is sufficient time to give you all you need to write about. The question period can often produce newsworthy answers.

Writing the speech is a matter of condensation. You need to summarize in the space available the newsworthy points made in the speech. In addition to summarizing points made in the speech, you should tell the reader something about the circumstances in which the speech was made—the place and the occasion, presentation techniques and mannerisms of the speaker, the makeup and size of the audience, reactions of the audience, questions from the audience.

You will want to give direct quotes in the speech story, but not too many and none that are too long or cumbersome. Reserve direct quotes for expression of strong opinions, colorful statements, and descriptive or narrative passages. Routine explanations should be paraphrased.

Keeping in mind that each story is unique and that no formula fits all stories, a typical way to write a speech story would be to:

—*Summarize* the main point or points of the speech in the lead paragraph.

—*Expand and explain* the main point or points in paragraph 2 and/or 3.

—*Detail* the circumstances of the speech in paragraphs 3 or 4.

—*Detail* the circumstances of the speech in paragraphs 3 or 4 in what is often called a "bridle" paragraph.

—*Return* to the theme and give details in the following paragraphs.

—*Summarize* minor points made in the speech, or minor circumstances of the occasion in the closing paragraphs.

—*End* with a quote that may make a *suggestion*, issue a *warning*, cite *options*, or if the speech is a light one, *make a quip*.

A newspaper story of the Leadership Club dinner would probably be basically a speech story unless some other dramatic action was taken at the dinner. It might read like this:

Former astronaut Jeffery Tower hailed unfettered space walks from the space shuttle as an exciting breakthrough in U.S. space exploration.

Tower, who earlier had been critical of lack of support for the space program, told 350 people at the homecoming dinner sponsored by the Ourstate University Leadership Club "a new sense of enthusiasm has spurred NASA's daring new experiments."

Tower said, "The Russians had passed us in efforts and were approaching us in technology until this dramatic achievement." He called for a rededication to the space program.

Tower, now president of East-West Airlines, was the featured speaker at the 20th annual Leadership Club homecoming dinner in the student union ballroom. An alumnus of OU, Tower was named an honorary member of the Leadership Club. Tower quipped:

"I didn't make the Leadership Club as a student. I had to go to the moon to qualify. I knew you guys were spaced out, but this is ridiculous."

Also honored at the dinner was Gov. Fred Flint, former president of the Leadership Club. He was presented this year's Service to Society Award.

In addition to the governor, attending were most local officials, legislative leaders, members of the cabinet, and many from the state's congressional delegation.

When he thanked the club for his award, Gov. Flint glanced around the room and noted that everyone seemed to be at the dinner. He said "I'm glad to see that nobody essential to operation of the state is here."

Sidebar News Story

Often during coverage of a news story such as a speech or meeting, a second story will develop. If the secondary story is closely enough related to the main story, you should either include it in the main story or write a second story (a sidebar) that will run with the main story.

The decision whether to include the sidebar event in the main story or to write a separate sidebar story to run along with the main story is a subjective judgment made by you and your editor. But there are some guidelines in making that judgment. If the secondary story intrudes upon, interrupts, alters, or in any way affects directly the main story, you probably should include it in the main story. If, however, the secondary event does not disrupt the main story to the extent that the participants in the main story are aware of the secondary story, you probably should write a separate story. You do not want to distort the scope of importance of a secondary event so as to draw attention from the main story. However, you should not ignore a newsworthy event. The sidebar story is a good method to relate the minor event to the main event without distorting the main story.

Consider the example to be used to illustrate a sidebar story—a demonstration at the site of the Leadership Club dinner. If a large number of demonstrators gain access to the room where the dinner is being held and disrupt it, or make access to the dinner site difficult and uncomfortable for those attending, or keep them from leaving normally when the dinner breaks up, you have no choice. The demonstration would become a bigger story than the dinner and speech. You would have to write them as one story. However, if only a few demonstrators march outside the dinner site during the speech, and the guests are not aware a demonstration is going on, you would make a sidebar story of the demonstration. The following example illustrates the sidebar circumstances and approach:

A small group of demonstrators protesting the male only makeup of the Ourstate University Leadership Club was frustrated by poor planning and the elements Friday night.

The dozen demonstrators were in the wrong place at the right time, the right place at the wrong time, and ended up with egg mixed with water on their faces.

The group, eight men and four women, set up their picket lines in the lobby of the student union well before the annual homecoming dinner of the Leadership Club was to begin at 7 p.m. Friday.

But the guests entered the building through a door at the back directly off the parking lot and took back stairs to the ballroom. (Leadership Club president Larry Webster said the back-stairs route to the ballroom was used for convenience of guests only and not to avoid a confrontation.)

When the demonstrators realized what was happening, they hurried to the parking lot and began marching there, chanting such slogans as "Women are leaders, too," and "End male cronyism." But by that time, most of the guests were already in the building.

Then the rains came. A soaking shower hit at 9:30 p.m. just as the dinner was breaking up. Although the pickets continued their marching, they didn't get much attention. The pickets' signs were soaked and drooping, and exiting guests scrambled to their cars paying little heed to the demonstrators.

"It was really a fiasco," the leader of the group, nursing student Adele Hodgkins, said. "But we won't give up. We'll break that ridiculous rule. We'll have our day." •

Leadership Club officers have been warned by university administrators that if they fail to initiate women into the club in January, the club will lose its university charter. Webster said the Leadership Club, under pressure to admit women since the university became coeducational five years ago, will go off campus and become independent rather than change its membership rules.

The Roundup Story

Local newspapers and broadcasting outlets would write separate stories on all of the events making up homecoming. Trying to cover all aspects of so many separate events with one story would be futile. The story would be needlessly awkward. Separate stories would be preferred whenever possible.

However, there are occasions when a single story on the weekend might be desired by certain publishers. For example, newspapers or broadcast outlets in a distant part of the state might request correspondents to cover some aspects of the event because parents of students attending Ourstate University would be interested in such news. For the same reason, the wire services would want to cover the story for the newspapers and broadcasting outlets they serve in other parts of the state and region. But in both instances, news organizations might want to limit coverage to the football game for the sports pages and one *roundup story* covering everything else.

In *roundup stories*, some hard editing decisions must be made. The only really effective way to do a roundup story is to concentrate on one event, or more rarely two, and just give token coverage to everything else. In doing a roundup story for the homecoming, you would probably concentrate on the celebrity speaker and the demonstration, assuming nothing sensational happened at the rally, the parade, the alumni breakfast, the Journalism School skits, or the post game activities. It might read:

HOMETOWN—Former Astronaut Jeffery Tower, in a speech picketed by women's rights advocates, praised the United States space program's untethered space walks as a real breakthrough in space exploration.

Tower, who did not know that a dozen people were outside protesting the male-only membership policy of the Ourstate University Leadership Club, called for a rededication to the space program.

"The Russians had passed us in effort and were approaching us in technology until this dramatic achievement," Tower, now an airline executive, said.

Tower told an audience of 350 people, including many state leaders, that the space walks are "a great new start."

While Tower was speaking, 12 placard-carrying pickets were marching outside of the dinner site protesting the policy of his host, the Ourstate University Leadership Club. The organization has refused to admit women to membership despite the fact the university went coeducational five years ago and the current student body president, Laura Albertson, is a woman. The club may be forced off campus if it does not initiate women, a university representative said.

In other homecoming activities:

—Rex Adamson, 82, of Theirtown was honored at the alumni breakfast early Friday as an outstanding graduate of Ourstate University. A graduate of the class of 1921, Adamson is a retired architect.

—Elise Sandow of Bricker, N.C., was named homecoming queen at a pep rally Friday night. Attendants named were Eileen Relenko of Theirtown and Theresa Celli of Yourtown.

—Political figures were roasted at the annual skits of the Journalism College. Biggest target was Lt. Gov. Tom Tobert, depicted as knight Sir "Wantsalot" in search of the "Wholly Graft." Tobert was recently indicted for accepting illegal campaign contributions.

The Second Day Story

News stories sometimes happen at inconvenient times for newspaper deadlines. This is true of stories that occur late at night and miss the midnight to 1 a.m. deadline for morning papers. It is even more true for afternoon newspapers. Deadline for afternoon newspapers ranges from shortly after noon to not much later than 2 p.m. Anything happening after mid-afternoon must wait until the next day's editions. Because newspapers do not want to appear to be printing news late, stories that have missed the previous day's deadlines are written to play down the time element.

A common example of writing stories to play down the time element is the way sports stories are handled in afternoon newspapers. Most sports events are scheduled for late afternoon or early evening. Thus afternoon newspapers rarely have the results of the previous day's games ahead of morning newspapers. Sometimes a late game on the West Coast that goes beyond regulation time will finish too late for morning newspapers in the East to have the results, but such instances are rare. Afternoon newspapers solve the late news dilemma by writing stories to avoid emphasizing the time element. The newspaper might begin a story with a look at the game scheduled for the night of publication or a later time. Then the facts about yesterday's game will be introduced in a lower paragraph.

A story that happens too late Saturday to make the Sunday newspapers will not be published in a newspaper until Monday morning editions. There are no Sunday afternoon newspapers. So essentially such news is old news. Editors would probably not publish an event that took place late Saturday unless it was something readers would like to read even though it is two days old. And in writing such a "dated" story, you would de-emphasize the time element without misleading the reader. You could write a story for Monday about an incident that happened at homecoming late on Saturday night this way:

Hometown police are continuing their investigation into the apparent accidental death of a Hometown banker fatally injured while attending the Ourstate University homecoming weekend.

James Forrest, 43, a 1959 graduate of OU and recently appointed to the university's board of trustees, died Sunday afternoon in University Hospital of head injuries, police inspector Harry Grappo said.

Forrest was found unconscious outside the PPP fraternity house at 11:55 p.m. Saturday. Grappo said Forrest was lying at the edge of a swimming pool beneath a balcony of the guest room of the fraternity he had joined as a student in the late 1950's.

Grappo said Forrest probably fell from the guest room balcony and struck his head on the concrete rim of the pool. "We want to get a medical examiner's report and ask a few more questions before we close the investigation," Grappo said.

Forrest was last seen in the guest bedroom. Grappo said a fraternity member took Forrest to the guest room at 10:30 p.m. when the victim said he felt ill and wanted to lie down.

Etc.

The story would then give more details about the event, and, because Forrest was a prominent man, give details about his life, survivors and funeral arrangements. As the writer, you would have de-emphasized the time element by not mentioning until the third paragraph that the death occurred Saturday.

The Personality Profile

Feature stories come in diverse forms, but one recurring type feature that you, as a beginning writer, should be familiar with is the *personality profile*.

Whenever an interesting person is in the news, the opportunity presents itself to tell the reader more about that personality than would be possible within the news story itself. The *personality profile* explores the person in the news as an individual worth more attention than a brief mention in a news story.

The profile focuses on personality and character traits. The profile makes the person come alive to the reader, not unlike the delineation of a character in a work of fiction. But the profile is built on facts. The profile dwells on the subject's experiences and aspirations, his hopes and his fears, his accomplishments and his failures, his philosophy of life and his practice of that philosophy, his view of himself and others, and views of him as expressed by others. The profile is the person, or as close as you, the writer, can picture him.

If Rex Adamson, honored as outstanding alumnus, is vibrant and articulate when you talk to him, you might come up with a profile that could read:

Some people half his age might think that the modern college student is going to hell in a hatchback, but Rex Adamson, at age 82, disagrees.

Adamson, honored Friday as outstanding alumnus of Ourstate University, said, "These kids are just great, just great."

Adamson said today's college student is brighter, just as serious and much more sophisticated than were the students of 60 years ago.

"We were just babes in the woods," Adamson recalled, his alert eyes twinkling. "But we had fun. Yes we did. Only young people know how to have fun. We forget that when we get older."

Adamson remembered an incident that got him in trouble when he was an underclassman at OU. He and a fellow student captured a small wildcat in the wooded area that then surrounded the first dormitory buildings on campus.

"We sure got clawed up catching that cat.

We . . . it was Bobby Winkler . . . yes, Bobby and me trussed that cat up and let it loose in the closet of Professor Pearson's classroom."

Adamson paused, chuckling. He lifted a glass of water from the table next to his chair, his frail hands shaking slightly as he sipped.

"When Pearson opened the closet door next day to hang up his coat, that cat came squealing and clawing out of that closet . . up onto the desk . . and one leap he was through the transom.

I swear the scare nearly killed old Pearson," Adamson said, laughing.

An architect, Adamson headed his own firm in Theirtown until his retirement in 1968. A specialist in industrial architecture, he has designed buildings in cities throughout the United States and Europe. He has retained close ties to his alma mater. His firm endowed a chair in his name in the College of Fine Arts and Architecture.

Adamson has kept in tune with young people, according to his wife, Martha, seated across the room in their suite at the Ourtown Motel. "He always got along so well with our five children and the grandchildren and great-grandchildren all love him."

"It's true," Adamson said. "I bribe them.

No, I just listen. That's all it takes. Kids want someone to listen, that's all.

These young parents in their 40s and 50s don't understand that. They want to do all the talking. If they would just shut up and listen, they would be surprised at how quickly the generation gap would close up.

And I'm an expert on generations. I've been through about a hundred," Adamson said.

"Young people do foolish things. But so do adults. No age group has a patent on foolishness."

Turning to his wife, Adamson said, "Remember Ronnie's friend." He then told about his grandson's friend who had dropped out of school because the young man's parents insisted he prepare for medical school rather than study art.

"The parents just wouldn't listen to the boy. He loves art and hates medicine. They just wouldn't pay attention to him.

Now that is foolish," Adamson said, frowning. "Young people may not always know what they want to do, but they sure know what they don't want to do.

You end up with a family split. The boy hurts. The parents hurt. And it is so useless.

I've lived a lot longer than most people will live. And yet life is so short. It is a tragedy to waste any part of it. People should listen. They must listen."

Depending on what other material you as a writer might have from the interview and depending on how much space you have for the interview, you could end the profile on that philosophical statement, or go on with more anecdotes, quotes from Adamson and others, and descriptions. Each profile, in a way, takes its own form from the facts you have.

THE BROADCAST FORMS

The forms of news stories for broadcast differ somewhat from forms of stories for print, but not in any substantial way. The information to be given is the same. The value to the reader of the information is the same. Style of copy written for the ear rather than the eye differs in many superficial ways we have already seen. There are also some changes in form. Basically, news stories for broadcast will be:

—Shorter—Broadcast facilities do not have as much time as newspapers have space.

—More general—There is less time, but also the ear cannot absorb specifics as well as the eye can.

—More timely—Broadcasting is always on deadline. The present tense can be used often in broadcasting, rarely in print.

—Less informative—In broadcasting news, you are more likely to use titles ahead of, or in place of, names; avoid giving ages, addresses, telephone numbers, statistics, exact numbers (preferring to round them out); avoid pronouns; avoid direct quotes unless on tape.

—Clearer and more cleanly written—Copy for broadcast will be simpler in construction with more easily understood words and fewer cluttering clauses. Sentences will be simple declarative sentences for the most part and shorter than sentences in print stories.

—More informal—Broadcast stories are spoken directly to the listener on a one-on-one basis. They should sound conversational and contain contractions, more idioms, and even direct communications between the person delivering the news and the person receiving it. A news announcer can say, "Good evening, this is John Doe with tonight's news."

As noted earlier, television news stories and newscasts are highly technical productions beyond the scope of this book. Coverage here will be limited to three basic forms for radio news stories—the *advance*, the *follow-up story with taped inserts*, and the *follow-up story without taped inserts*.

The Advance Story

One form of advance story used extensively by radio stations is the *public service* announcement story done for non-profit organizations in fulfillment of FCC requirements for license renewal. Such stories often would not qualify for air time on news value alone. They include announcement of meetings and other activities of educational, service, and other nonprofit organizations. They are usually sent to the broadcast outlet by paid or volunteer public information officers for organizations. Typed neatly, often on post cards, they are read when time is available. One about a Homecoming activity might read like this:

STUDENT VOLUNTEERS ARE NEEDED TO HELP SET UP

AND COORDINATE THE O. U. HOMECOMING PARADE

SATURDAY. VOLUNTEERS SHOULD CALL THE STU-

DENT GOVERNMENT OFFICE — 3-2-6-4-9-5-5. VOLUN-

TEERS WILL BE ASKED TO ATTEND ORIENTATION MEET-

INGS WEDNESDAY AND THURSDAY EVENINGS AT 8

O'CLOCK. PARADE DUTY WILL BE FROM 6 O'CLOCK
SATURDAY MORNING UNTIL NOON. THAT NUMBER TO
CALL IS — 3-2-6-4-9-5-5.

That public service announcement would take about 20 seconds of air
time. It would be aired in open time between programs and commercial
announcements.

A Followup Story With Taped Inserts

Radio is a sound medium, and it tries to bring the sounds of events to its
listeners as well as a description of what is taking place. If a radio station in
Hometown could not broadcast the parade live, it would still want to have
on tape for later broadcast the sounds of the parade—the music of the
bands, the sounds of the crowd watching and quotes from both adults and
children watching or participating.

Just as many of the notes a print reporter makes at an event will not find
their way into a story, much of what is taped will not be aired. The tape will
be edited carefully to get the best sounds of the proceedings and the very
best quotes. Sometimes what seemed best on the scene will not do because
of poor tape reproduction. Interesting people sometimes do not tape well.
Their speech mannerisms, tone, lack of clear diction, or accent will not be
clear when played back. The editor should eliminate that unclear piece of
tape. It is frustrating to the listener not to be able to understand what is
being said. But the newscaster meshing his own observations and descriptions of the parade with the quality taped segments, might begin his
newscast like this:

GOOD EVENING. THIS IS DANNY DULCET WITH
WWXW NEWS AT SIX. HEADLINING THE NEWS TO-
NIGHT: HOMECOMING PARADE HAS CITY SWINGING.
THE COUNTY SCHOOL BOARD TO VOTE ON MERIT PAY
PLAN. FOUR HURT IN CRASH ON INTERSTATE. DETAILS
AFTER THESE MESSAGES

[CART A] (Cartridge A would be turned on, giving the first
commercials of the newscast . . . When commercials are
completed the newscast would resume.)
[CART B Fade in for 30 seconds and slowly fade out.]
(Cartridge B would be march music of the Capital Highsteppers
Band, recorded during the parade. As it faded the newscaster
would begin his first story of the evening's news.)

111

THAT ROUSING TUNE IS MUSIC IN THE CHAMPION-
SHIP FASHION OF THE CAPITAL HIGHSTEPPERS BAND.
IT HAD EVERYONE FROM SIX TO NINETY-SIX STOMPIN'
THEIR FEET TODAY ON UNIVERSITY AVENUE AT THE
ANNUAL OURSTATE HOMECOMING WEEKEND PARADE.
THE BAND WAS ONE OF MANY HIGHLIGHTS AT THE
PARADE WHICH ATTRACTED AN AUDIENCE ESTIMATED
BY POLICE AT 80 THOUSAND. UNIVERSITY AVENUE WAS
LINED BY YOUNG, OLD AND EVERYONE IN BETWEEN AS
THE TWO-HOUR PARADE WOUND ITS WAY FROM THE
UNIVERSITY TO COURTHOUSE SQUARE. MORE THAN 25
MARCHING UNITS FROM AROUND THE STATE DID
THEIR THING UNDER SUNNY SKIES. IN ADDITION THERE
WERE ANOTHER 22 FLOATS ENTERED BY CAMPUS
ORGANIZATIONS AND CIVIC GROUPS. DID THE CROWD
ENJOY THE PARADE? THE ONES WE TALKED TO DID.

[CART C] (Cartridge C would be switched on. It would
include comments from parade spectators, probably a cross
section of adults and children. Note that in leading into the
taped cartridge the newscaster *did not definitely say* he was
going to have comments on tape. He *did not* say, "Here are
some comments from spectators." He *said*, "The ones we talked
to did" (have a good time). Thus if there had been a mechanical
failure of the tape equipment, after only the slightest of pauses
the newscaster could relate what the people told him. The
listener would not even realize that anything was wrong. It is
harder to disguise a mechanical failure on television because the
screen usually goes blank. Assuming the tape worked correctly,
when the taped conversations ended, the newscaster would
return:)

PLANNERS OF TODAY'S PARADE WERE
DELIGHTED WITH THE RESULTS. MAYOR THOMAS
DWYER CALLED THE PARADE THE BEST IN THE HIS-
TORY OF THE HOMECOMING WEEKEND. STUDENT

GOVERNMENT VICE PRESIDENT HAROLD RUSH WAS PLEASED WITH THE EVENT:

[CART D] (Cartridge D would air comments of Rush taped earlier. Rush might announce the winners of prizes awarded to the participating groups in the parade. Then the story would be ended by the newscaster who would get to the next story using a transition from one to another:)

YES, IT WAS A GRAND PARADE, ENJOYED BY ALL. WELL, NOT QUITE ALL. MEMBERS OF THE COUNTY SCHOOL BOARD HAD TO MISS THE PARADE. THEY WERE AT AN EMERGENCY MEETING TRYING TO AGREE ON PLANS FOR A MERIT PAY HIKE . . . ETC.

The newscaster could then carry his listeners into the next story of the evening through a convenient transition device. But don't always expect or seek a transition to the next story. Don't make an artificial one. Such a transition strikes the reader as too contrived and will distract his or her attention rather than hold it, as you intended. If the transition is natural and not awkward, use it. If not, forget the transition and, after a pause, go directly to the next story.

Radio stations usually have fewer reporters than do newspapers serving the same audience. The preceding story, with taped inserts, would be the exception. Stories that come into the station by wire and many local stories are read in their entirety by newscasters. This story about an incident at the pep rally is written to be read by the newscaster:

ELISE SANDOW, CROWNED HOMECOMING QUEEN AT OURSTATE UNIVERSITY PEP RALLY FRIDAY NIGHT, HAD TO WAIT LONGER THAN SHE BARGAINED FOR TO HAVE HER MOMENT IN THE SPOTLIGHT. SHE HAD ALREADY WAITED A MONTH SINCE HER ELECTION BY THE STU-DENT BODY. AND FRIDAY NIGHT SHE WAITED FOR UNI-VERSITY PRESIDENT JAMES PIERCE TO SPEAK. THEN

(Weck - tuh - lish)

SHE WAITED FOR COACH SKIPPER WECHTERLITCH TO SPEAK AND THEN TO INTRODUCE THE 22 STARTING MEMBERS OF THE FOOTBALL TEAM. THEN SHE WAITED

FOR HER TWO ATTENDANTS TO BE INTRODUCED. THEN IT WAS HER TURN. AS SHE STEPPED FORWARD, THE SPOTLIGHT WENT OUT. AFTER TWO FRANTIC MINUTES, STAGEHANDS FOUND THE PROBLEM. AS THE SPOTLIGHT CAME BACK ON, THE HOMECOMING QUEEN RECEIVED THE BIGGEST HAND OF THE NIGHT.

(Note that when the writer of this newscast wrote the unusual name WECH-TERLITCH, the writer spelled the name phonetically above the correctly spelled name. As the announcer's eyes move ahead in the copy, he or she will see the correct pronunciation of the difficult name and will avoid faltering in reading the story.)

FORMS OF ADVERTISEMENTS

Advertising is a highly sophisticated business involving many diverse talents. Writing is just one of these. Effective advertisements in slick print magazines, on radio, and especially on television take the efforts of specialists in art, photography, marketing, public opinion and writing. This book will illustrate those advertisements you, the beginning writer, might be called upon to write—a *print ad* selling a *product*, a *print ad* promoting an *institution*, a *radio commercial* selling a *service*, and a *direct mail letter* offering a *service*.

Selling A Product

Advertisements selling products are usually, but not always, *hard sell* ads which try to get the reader/listener/viewer to purchase a product NOW. An ad that might appear in the newspaper or a homecoming weekend program could read like this:

(Headline)
OURSTATE UNIVERSITY ALUMNI . . .
your official chair is now . . .
REDUCED 30 PERCENT!
(The illustration running under or beside it would show the chair being offered.)
(The body of the ad would read:)
The beautiful Ourstate University armchair you have always wanted can be yours for *just $62.95.*

Tillman's Book Store offers black enameled or walnut finished chairs at *just 70 percent* of the regular $89.95 price.

This sale price is in effect for *Homecoming Weekend* only. The price returns to $89.95 Monday.

ADS CAN SELL A PRODUCT OR AN INSTITUTION. Lee Iacocca, Chrysler Corporation's Chairman, has been most effective as a spokesman for the "New Chrysler Corporation". Brooke Shields has also been an example of institutional advertising with her non-smoking commercials. (Courtesy Wide World of Photos/AP.)

Gleaming *black enamel.* Or *stained walnut.* With the embossed O.U. seal. *Just $62.95.*

It's the chair you want in your living room, family room or den.

We're right across the street from the Shea Library.

Drop in. Or phone. All credit cards honored.

(The logotype of the store with the address and phone number would be carried at the bottom of the ad.)

Selling An Institution

Advertisements promoting *institutions* are usually *soft sell ads* in that they do not urge the reader/listener/viewer to take any immediate action. Rather, institution advertising attempts to create in the reader/listener/viewer a good feeling about the institution being advertised. It attempts to leave the reader/listener/viewer thinking, "I'll have to buy that institution's product someday." Or, "I'll have to use that institution's service." Or, "I'll have to give that institution my support: financial, physical or spiritual." The purpose of the institutional ad is to create a favorable impression and create good will to be tapped immediately or, more likely, at some later date. An institutional ad that might be published during homecoming weekend that would aim to produce future, not immediate, response would be one about a local motel:

(The Headline)

We stress the *HOME* in *HOMECOMING.*

(The illustration would show a well-appointed room.)

(The body copy would read:)

Guests of the University Inn find they really haven't left home to attend Homecoming Weekend.

The *comfort* of home. The *convenience* of home. The *security* of home. Guests find them all when they stay at the *University Inn.*

Home at University Inn means:

—Blissful sleep in queen-size beds.

—Home Box Office movies on color television.

—Coffee in your room and the morning newspaper at the door.

—Security locks and security patrols.

HOMECOMING! We offer it all year at *University Inn.*

Selling A Service

Radio advertisements, or *commercials* as they are more commonly called, have the same purposes as do print advertisements. Commercials *sell products, offer services, promote institutions.* Commercials can take a *hard sell* tone or a *soft sell* tone. Commercials on *radio* are usually 6 to 8 lines of type for a 30-second time spot on the air, or 12 to 16 lines for a 60-second time spot. Seldom do radio commercials run more than 60 seconds. An example of a commercial for a service that might be aired during homecoming weekend would be this commercial that offers shuttle bus service to and from the homecoming weekend football game:

HOMECOMING SHOULD BE *HAPPY*. FOOTBALL SHOULD BE *FUN*. BUT A TRAFFIC TIE-UP IS A BUMMER TO BUMMER *BAAAD TRIP*. DON'T TRAVEL THAT ROAD. *PARK* YOUR CAR AT THE INTERSTATE MALL AND TAKE *A HOMETOWN TRANSIT COMPANY BUS* TO AND FROM THE O.U/T.U FOOTBALL GAME. IT'S *CAR TO GATE SERVICE* FOR *JUST $2* PER PERSON. *DON'T GET TENSE. STAY RELAXED. PARK YOUR CAR AND ENJOY!*

Modern Direct Mail Appeals

The direct mail sales or promotion letter is a form of advertisement young advertising and public relations writers may be called upon to produce. Modern computer programming and printing technology have added personal appeal and intimacy to the direct mail letter. The old, somewhat cold, style of address on such a letter "To Boxholder" has given way to a letter addressed specifically to an individual. In fact, computers can be programmed so they not only address the individual in the head of the letter, but refer to him by name throughout the letter. Assume the alumni association of Ourstate University has access to a computer into which the mailing list of alumni association members has been fed. The association could send the same letter addressed personally to each alumnus. It might read:

Dear George Graduate:
   We hope you have had as good a year as the football team. As you know, the team has won its first three games and is favored to win its next two games. The team should have a 5-0 record by HOMECOMING WEEKEND, Oct. 3-5. The game with Theirstate should be a monumental battle.
   You don't want to miss that!
   Well, you don't have to, Mr. Graduate. You and other members of the Graduate family can attend Homecoming Weekend at a cost that is a lot less than you may think.

The Alumni Association has come up with a package that will allow you and each member of your family to attend Homecoming for just $33.99 per person. *This includes:* FOOTBALL TICKETS, TWO NIGHTS AT THE VACATION INN, THE ALUMNI BREAKFAST, THE PARADE, A TOUR OF THE NEW SCIENCE BUILDING, AND BUS TRANSPORTATION TO AND FROM THE GAME.

You must admit, Mr. Graduate, that is a good deal.

Please fill out the enclosed reservation form and mail as soon as possible to:

> Ourstate University Alumni Association
> Old Main, Room 2064
> Hometown, Ourstate, 33333

Sincerely,

Peter Berryton

Peter Berryton
Executive Director

P.S. Send check or let us bill you.

SUGGESTED EXERCISES

1. Gather information for some event that is coming up—a speech, meeting, etc.—and write advances for the event. Write an advance story for print and one for radio. The event can be of citywide interest or of interest to a specific group. It might be easier if you pick a specific group such as your fraternity, club, church group or other group. Try to get the stories published and aired.

2. Do follow-up stories on a speech and a meeting. Again you might choose events of citywide interest. Or you can choose events of a more specialized nature. If you attend a meeting where many different subjects are discussed, or many different actions are taken, write about two or three of the items you consider the most newsworthy. Write your stories immediately after attending the speeches or meetings and before the local newspapers or radio stations have reported the events. Then when you read the newspaper accounts and/or hear the broadcast accounts, you can compare the professional coverage to your coverage of the events.

3. When you read or hear news coverage of some upcoming event, figure out what businesses or organizations might want to reach specific audiences taking part in that event. Try to get the cooperation of the business or organizations wanting to reach this audience and prepare print advertisements or broadcast commercials to reach the audience.

4. Contact officers of an organization you belong to or have knowledge of. Ascertain what mail message such an organization might want to send to its membership. Volunteer to gather the information needed, and write a direct mail letter to achieve the purpose of the organization's leadership whether it be to raise money, increase membership, promote a project, or sell a product or service.

Chapter VI

WORDS: MAKE THEM WORK FOR YOU

"Love words, and treat them with respect."

This is advice given student journalists by James Kilpatrick, nationally syndicated columnist.

Words are marvelous. They have the power to build a society or destroy a government. They ignite and inspire intellect or stifle the human spirit. They draw laughter from a confirmed pessimist or reduce a strong man to tears. Finding the right word at the right time is the constant challenge you face as a writer.

If you are fortunate, words fascinate you. If you have not been involved in a love affair with the language, you should resolve to become involved if you wish success in writing.

Ask yourself some questions:

Do you find such seemingly trivial pastimes as anagrams, crossword puzzles, and other word exercises fascinating?

Do you find yourself consulting a dictionary frequently to find out more about a word you run across?

Do you find the vocabulary quizzes in such magazines as *Reader's Digest* irresistible?

Do you read about semantics?

If you answer "yes" to most of these things, your interest in words is well established. If your answer is "no" and you still want to be a writer, begin now to develop such interests.

You can't treat words casually any more than a physician can be casual about medicine or an attorney about law. Words are the tools of professional writers. They have to know them. They have to appreciate them. They have to love them.

If you hope to be a successful writer you must love the language, appreciate the beauty and function of words, learn to make the words work for you. You can do all that by:

—Spelling *ALL* words correctly at *ALL* times.
—Using the appropriate words for your audience.
—Using only necessary words, avoiding unnecessary words.
—Using colorful words effectively.

There Are No Spelling Shortcuts

Spelling is the one aspect of writing which *leaves no room for personal preference or creativity.* Words are either spelled correctly or they are spelled incorrectly. Neither the public nor employer will tolerate personal idiosyncracies. Only one type of spelling is acceptable—correct spelling. Individuals and nonconformists have some jockeying room in other aspects of the writing process. Gathering information leaves room for different approaches. Writing styles can vary slightly from one writer to the other without upsetting the system. In some instances different words, different sentence structures, slightly varied paragraphing, or even different emphasis might not make all that much difference. Whatever style you use, regardless of word choice, however sentence structure differs, one thing remains exactly the same—words must always be spelled correctly! As a writer, you must accept this fact. If you don't, you should get into another line of work.

You Must Create A Spelling System for Yourself

The complaint journalism teachers hear most often from employers is that graduates cannot spell. "Why don't you teach them how to spell?" is the universal question. The answer possibly is that no one can teach students how to spell. All that can be taught is the necessity of spelling words correctly. Correct spelling is achieved as other journalistic demands are achieved— by diligent attention to detail. Spelling correctly is just a matter of accuracy, as are other areas of reporting and writing.

Some writers can spell almost any word correctly. They were the ones who were finalists in spelling bees in grade school. They have the knack. Other talented writers can never learn to spell well. But all writers can spell correctly.

Spelling is an individual problem. Each writer must find out where his or her deficiencies lie and work out methods of overcoming such deficiencies. Some may be able to look up words that are unfamiliar and forever after know how to spell them correctly. Others may look up the correct spelling of certain words hundreds of times and never be really certain. Spelling solution for the first type would be to make certain to diligently look up every word he or she has never seen before, knowing that having seen the word, he or she can spell it. The second type is doomed to looking up rarely used words every time they are used, and making a list of often-used words for quick reference without having to delve into the dictionary.

The Secret—Know Which Words to Check Out.

The writer must know which words or types of words are likely to cause problems. There are some types of words that cause everyone problems. The writer should identify these and look up such words always, or until certain he or she has them correct beyond doubt.

There are the *IE* and *EI* words. No one knows for certain why it is *IE* for *believe* or *EI* for *receive*, but it is. And if you can never get that straight, then look up all *IE* and *EI* words, or make a list of the ones used most often for easier reference.

There are the British spellings that may confuse you.

The British *colour* is American *color*.

The British *apologise* is the American *apologize*.

The British *aluminium* (which is also pronounced differently) is the American *aluminum*.

If you are confused and/or from Britain, look them up.

There are the prefixes and suffixes!

You drop the *E* from *tease* to make it *teasing*.

But . . .

You do not drop the *E* from *sure* to make it *surely*.

And usually prefixes do not change the spelling of the root word.

Necessary becomes *unnecessary*.

Patient becomes *impatient*.

Pleased becomes *displeased*.

And plurals can be so confusing.

If *penny* becomes *pennies*, why does *attorney* become *attorneys*?

If *radio* becomes *radios*, why does *zero* become *zeroes*?

There are rules to explain many of the reasons words are spelled a certain way. For example, in the plurals cited above:

The plural of *penny* is *pennies* because when *Y* follows a consonant *N* you use *ies*; *attorney* becomes *attorneys* because when the *Y* follows a vowel *E* you just add an *S* to the *Y*.

The *E* on *sure* is retained when you add the suffix *ly* to form a new word *surely* because if you dropped the *E* from *sure* you would have *surly* which is a different word. On the other hand, you can drop the *E* from *tease* when you add *ing* to make the word *teasing*, but there is no good reason to drop the *E*. Why not spell it *teaseing*?

And of course, there is the *IE/EI* rule:

I before *E* except after *C*.

Most people remember the *IE* rule because it is a bit of doggerel. But, of course, there are exceptions to the rule as in *leisure* and in *weird*. And that is the problem with the spelling rules technique. There are so many exceptions to the rules and the rules, if not weird, are not particularly logical. The rules do not work for most students.

For the less than one person in ten who can and will learn a whole series of rules with exceptions, the rules might help their spelling. For most students, who do not learn the rules and therefore cannot use them, some other method of making certain they spell words correctly must be employed.

Help for the poor speller is already at hand for the writer who will have a computer terminal and memory bank at his disposal, one who does his writing directly into a word processing system. Most systems used in newspapers, for example, are not actually programmed to correct misspelled words. But many of these systems have word lists of commonly misspelled words that a reporter can refer to by punching a key or two. Eventually, as the word processors get more flexible, they probably will be programmed to correct errors of spelling on commonly misspelled words.

But many of you will not have that luxury available to you in college or even on your first job. And you should not learn to rely on machines anyway. You should develop your own system for making certain you spell all words correctly.

Possible Plans

USING THE RULES—If you learn rules easily and can remember numerous exceptions, get yourself a spelling manual with all of the rules and exceptions, and lists of problem words. Studying that and applying it may be all you need to insure accurate spelling. But most of you will need to do more.

MAKE YOUR OWN LIST OF PROBLEM WORDS—Do not try to make a list of all the problem words you might ever use. Just list those that you use often. Keep the list relatively short. If the list is too long and cumbersome it becomes more trouble than using a dictionary. Those rarely used words not on your list, look up in the dictionary.

BEST LIST IS THE DICTIONARY—If you are a really poor speller, you will just have to leave yourself time when writing to look up a lot of words. You can't make up a practical list because it will be too long. Get a good dictionary and have it with you whenever you write. Use it as much as is necessary to make *certain* all spelling is correct. Eventually you will learn how to spell most of the words you use often. Some you may have to just keep looking up. Editors and teachers use dictionaries constantly to correct spelling of reporters and students. You must do the same thing.

Much of your misspelling comes about not because you do not know how to spell words, but because you make typographical errors. In the eyes of the reader there is no such thing as a typographical error—only a misspelled word. Sometimes proofreading entails such extreme methods as reading stories backward so you are forced to look at each word carefully and not dwell on the theme of the story. If you must do that, do it. There is no easy way to solve the spelling problem. There is only the reality that *YOU MUST SOLVE IT.*

USE FAMILIAR WORDS

In writing for the mass audience, you address the highly educated and the poorly educated; the articulate and the inarticulate; the well-read and the semi-literate. But mostly you address the average person who lies between these extremes. You do not address your piece to the person with a *sophisticated vocabulary nor do you aim at the lip reader. You focus on those* who are reasonably intelligent, with an average education and with an average vocabulary.

Remember this: If you employ the average vocabulary, both the average person and the highly sophisticated person will understand you; if you employ a sophisticated vocabulary, you will lose the average person. Therefore, it is wise to adopt this prudent policy when writing for the broad spectrum of readers/listeners/viewers. *Use the words that will be familiar to all. MAKE THE WORDS DIRECT.*

The direct word is usually the familiar one and the one that can best serve the journalist writing a news story or the advertiser preparing ad copy for print or broadcast media:

—*In a news story you would say "the accident victim died."* You would not say he "perished, passed away, succumbed."

—In an ad you would say the "hamburger tastes *good.*" You would probably not say it tastes "*scrumptious, delectible, or flavorful.*"

—In a feature story you would say the subject being interviewed *scowled,* not that he *looked disapproving,* had a *distasteful* look on her face, or *demurred answering with a grimace.*

Use the direct expression that the reader/listener/viewer will readily understand, the expression that says what needs to be said. A jurist in Florida scolded lawyers for using little understood Latin words when English words would do better. An Associated Press story quoted Florida Supreme Court Justice Arthur England as saying: "Lawyers should stop saying 'inter alia' when they mean 'among other things.' They should use clear English," he said. Lawyers should use *"this case"* instead of *"sub judice"* and *"for himself"* instead of *"pro se."* He said he was sick of hearing the phrase *"ex mero motu"* instead of *"on the court's own motion."*

"I'm reading along in a brief, following the lawyer's arguments and logic right down the line" England said, "and I'm about to agree with him and then I come to that phrase [*ex mero muto*] and all I can think of is a Japanese freighter sunk in World War II. That certainly will disrupt your concentration."

England also got the court to drop the habit of using *A.D.* after the date when he came on the court in 1975. Officials agreed that there wasn't much chance of anyone thinking the Florida Supreme Court took action in *1975 B.C.!*

If such an *august personage* (are those words that are familiar or should they be "*person in a high position?*") thinks that words should be more familiar, the average reader/listener/viewer will agree. Eliminate the pomposity, accentuate the clarity, and don't mess around with Mr. Confusion. Say it plainly.

Write For the Ear

Those of you who will be writing mainly for the ear rather than the eye should take special heed of the advice to make the words familiar and clear. The eye takes a photograph of a word and can make a reprint if the photograph doesn't develop right. The ear could make a recording, but unfortunately there is no tape deck in your listener's head. If the brain misses the ear's message, it's so long information. So be kind to your listener's ear. Make the message familiar for the brain; make it clear for the brain; make it easy for the listener. Tell the listener:

—The suspects were *jailed*, not *incarcerated*.

—The judge ordered the *picketing stopped*, not *enjoined the union from further disruption*.

—The returned hostage *grinned with happiness*, not *evinced effervescent joy*.

Newscaster Edwin Newman, in his book, A Civil Tongue, calls for clear, uncluttered writing, and gives some examples of what happens when writers forget to make it direct and clear. Citing a quote from a scholar that "our children have no viable *role models* to emulate," Newman bemoans the loss of the word *hero or heroine*. He reconstructs a conversation between George Washington and his father:

"Father, I cannot tell a lie. With my hatchet I chopped down the cherry tree."

"I'm proud of you, George. I was saying to your mother only last week that one day our son will be a *role model* for generations of Americans yet unborn."

Newman teed off on another broadcaster when he recalled the time *Howard Cosell* said he was "*Variously bounded and circumscribed by Senator Edward Kennedy and singer John Denver.*" Newman presumed that Cosell meant that the two celebrities were standing one on each side of him. But in defense of Cosell, an impressive, if not always clear vocabulary, is his trademark, and Howard's fans accept the affectation whether or not they can understand him.

Newman even makes fun of himself, citing Newman on a May, 1976, NBC broadcast saying: "Italy is in a *deteriorating economic situation.*" It's bad for the economy and writers.

Prefer the well-known word to the far-fetched. Say:

—*Fire* not *conflagration*.

—*Live* not *abide*.

—*Add* not *append*.

Prefer the concrete word to the abstract. Say:
—*Truck* not *vehicle*.
—*Briton* not *foreigner*.
—*Biologist* not *scientist*.
Prefer the single word to the phrase. Say:
—*Disagreed* not *differed in viewpoint*.
—*Allowed* not *gave permission to*.
—*With* not *accompanied by*.
Prefer the short word to the long. Say:
—*Burn* not *incinerate*.
—*Buggy* not *perambulator*.
—*Catch* not *apprehend*.
Prefer the Saxon word to the romantic word. Say:
—*Bedroom* not bed*chamber*.
—*Dream* not *reverie*.
—*Door* not *portal*.

Americans would probably say that Americanized English is simpler than the king's English of Britain. And in January, 1981 Lord Simon Glaisdale, one of Britain's most prominent attorneys, agreed. In the House of Lords, which has more tradition than power, Glaisdale proposed England abandon the difference in capital and small letters and eliminate the extra letters such as the U in labour, honour, etc. He also wants England to do away with irregular verbs so that it would be correct to say: "I was," "We was" and "They was." He said England should Americanize the language of Shakespeare. Lord Airedale of the opposition party argued against the proposal. He pointed out that while Americans simplified the spelling, they "undid the good work" by using long words instead of short ones. He said:

"An Englishman leaves his *flat* by the *lift* and gets into his *car* to go see a *film*. An American leaves his *apartment* by *elevator* and gets into his *automobile* to go see a *motion picture*."

Fun aside, perhaps there is a trend in America to complicate the language by preferring words other than the Anglo-Saxon variety that form the basis of the English language.

Keep The Big Word In Its Place

There is *only one good* reason to use an unfamiliar word—*that word gives the specific meaning you seek to convey*. When you do use an unfamiliar word, make certain it will be understood from the context in which you use it. The following passage containing the word *traumatic* would be understandable even to those unsure of the definition of traumatic.

The psychologist said that moving to a new town can be traumatic for children. They lose contact with friends and familiar surroundings and fear what faces them in a strange new home.

127

It might have been preferable to use *upsetting* in the passage above, but the more specific word, *traumatic*, will be understood by those readers who would not be able to define it.

Occasionally you might wish to use an unfamiliar word for stylistic effect to create humor, suspense, irony, satire. A writer might criticize a public figure in this satirical way:

> John Bigstar has been accused of being a *misanthrope*. Nonsense. He likes people. He prefers them charcoal-broiled, but *sauteed* will do. Besides he is not a loner as some claim. Everywhere he goes he takes along his *supercilious* ego.

Of course, satire is a sophisticated style of writing that is meant for a limited audience. Such an audience will understand the larger words.

But even in serious writing there is reason on occasion to use unfamiliar words which may seem to be synonyms for familiar words. Often the words have slightly different meanings which the writer wants to convey. Take a common word such as QUICK, for example. Think of the slightly different meanings the following synonyms have: *AGILE, BRISK, BUSTLING, LIVELY, PROMPT, RAPID, SPEEDY, SPRIGHTLY, SPRY, SWIFT*. Or take the word SHAKE. You might really mean *AGITATE, FLUTTER, JAR, JOLT, QUAKE, QUAVER, QUIVER, SHIVER, SHUDDER, SWAY, SWING, TOTTER, VIBRATE, WAVER*.

While there is only one good reason to use the less familiar word, there are several WRONG reasons for using big words. They are:

—To *show off* your large vocabulary.

—To *cloud* your *meaning*.

—To *cover* your *ignorance*.

—To *avoid* making a *direct statement*.

—To *mislead* your reader/listener/viewer.

Words Are Just Words—Not Brains

Immature writers try to illustrate their intelligence by using big words. They confuse words with ideas. A small idea can be couched in grandiose language. It becomes pomposity. A great idea can be expressed in familiar words. Parading a large vocabulary will not convince anyone your idea is profound. It is much more intelligent to express your thoughts in words that will reach your entire audience.

Mort Walker, author of the Beatle Bailey cartoon, illustrated the immature use of unfamiliar words when he had Lieutenant Fuzz ask Zero, "Where's your combat emplacement evacuator, Zero?"

> ZERO: "My what?"
>
> FUZZ: "Your shovel! Your shovel!"
>
> ZERO: "Oh."
>
> FUZZ: "If he'd just learn Army terminology, he'd sure make things a lot easier."

Don't be an immature Lieutenant Fuzz, even if you are given bureaucrat's help. Save the big words for the right time. Use the clear ones.

Familiarity Breeds Honesty

Some writers try to cloud the meaning of what they say by resorting to large, imprecise words. You've heard the politician do this when he does not want to be pinned down to a definite stand. It is easier to say nothing with big words than it is with small familiar words.

If you think this is not true, note the clarity of answers given by political figures on the Sunday interview shows. Everyone understands "yes" and "no." The man who wants to tell the truth will, as the expressions say, "Lay it on the line," "Let it all hang out," "Bare his guts," "Get to the bottom line," "Tell it like it is." Even those descriptions define honesty. There is not an unclear word there. They are basic, plain, clear, short. You, as a journalist, should be on that truth team. Don't fog up the truth by fogging up the language.

Don't Hide Behind A Big Word

When uncertain of his information, a speaker or writer will often try to hide the gaps by using unfamiliar, general words. You have undoubtedly tried to do this on occasion in answering essay questions on school exams. You did not fool the teacher and you will not fool your reader/listener/viewer.

Archie Bunker does such things all the time. He never hesitates to misquote the Bible, Shakespeare, or the U.S. Constitution rather than admit he doesn't know what he is talking about. Unless you are trying to get a laugh or actor Carroll O'Connor's job, don't do it. Go out and find out the answer in clear, familiar words.

Don't Be Evasive

It is a temptation to adopt large words when you want to avoid making a direct statement. *It is easier to be evasive with large words.* For example, if you must make a statement on a situation, you can say:

—It is *right.*

—It is *wrong.*

—It is *deplorable.*

With the first two responses you have committed yourself. You have retained your integrity, but if the situation does not involve any earnestly held principles, you may have alienated a friend, a source, your boss, your father-in-law, etc. With the third response, your commitment is hedged. It can be interpreted as agreement or disagreement. Such a response is perhaps appropriate for diplomats, salesmen and almost anyone to preserve social amenities, but such fence-straddling has no place in the mass media. You owe your reader/listener/viewer the *whole* truth.

Don't Mislead Your Reader

Some speakers and writers use unfamiliar words deliberately to mislead their audience. In covering an election for the U.S. Senate in a Southern state, several years ago, *Time* reported that one of the candidates included the following statement in a speech to rural, mostly unschooled voters:

"Are you aware that (his opponent) is known all over Washington as a shameless *extrovert?* Not only that, but this man is reliably reported to practice *nepotism* with his sister-in-law, and has a sister who was once a *thespian* in wicked New York. Worse of all, it is an established fact that Mr. (candidate) before his marriage habitually practiced *celibacy."*

These words are not particularly damning. Nepotism, or the hiring of one's relatives who may not be qualified for the job, is the only one that is at all negative. Being extroverted or friendly and outgoing, a thespian, an actor, and celibate, refraining from premarital sex, are admirable qualities. But when surrounded by certain adjectives and pronounced with the proper (or improper) inflection to an audience unsure of the meanings of the words, they are misleading and could be damaging. Perhaps that is acceptable politics, but it would be atrocious journalism. Use the familiar, direct honest word that will inform and not mislead your reader/listener/viewer.

USE THE APPROPRIATE WORD

One of the most difficult jobs the writer of the mass media has is keeping abreast of the acceptability and appropriateness of language in the media. Language changes constantly. Social customs change rapidly. Writers for the mass media are at the forefront of this change.

Yesterday's slang is accepted English today. Last year's vulgarity or profanity is this year's usage. Anything goes in *Playboy*, but the family newspaper and the broadcast media retain certain taboos. You have to analyze carefully the words you use in light of your audience and your medium. There are some general rules you can use in judging the appropriateness of language.

—*Avoid slang.*
—*Avoid provincialisms, or regional expressions.*
—*Avoid vulgarity, profanity, obscenity.*
—*Avoid clichés.*
—*Avoid jargon of a profession, trade or group.*
—*Use informal language with care.*
—*Use colorful language.*

Slang is Not "Cool"

Slang expressions are inappropriate for serious writing. You would never use slang in a news story unless you are directly quoting a source who uses slang:

INCORRECT: Thieves *ripped off* a convenience market here today of $134 in cash and an undertermined amount in merchandise.

CORRECT: The suspect was arraigned before magistrate James Cooper. He pleaded not guilty saying, "I know the *fuzz* said I *ripped off* the store. Man, I was *nowheres* near that store."

The slang expression is wrong in the first sentence, and *ripped off* should be changed to *robbed*. The slang expressions in the second instance are appropriate because they are the exact words of the witness. If you had chosen not to quote his exact words but to paraphrase the witness's statement, the second passage would read:

The suspect was arraigned before Magistrate James Cooper. He pleaded not guilty, saying he was not near the store at the time of the robbery.

With due care, slang can sometimes be used in a feature story or in an advertisement. An advertisement aimed at youthful readers might adopt youthful slang expressions.

TOUGH STUFF: Hang loose in our really tough jeans. These savvy pants come in stripes, solids, and prints. Denim, cotton, and polyester, they wash right up. Sizes for guys and gals from small to large.

You will notice in the above example that the slang is limited. Take note. Use it sparingly or it will lose its emphasis.

Avoid Provincialisms

In using provincialisms, expressions that are limited to a region of the country, or expressions of a specific age, social or ethnic group, you lose clarity. Those readers/listeners/viewers unfamiliar with the expression will be puzzled and improperly served. You should avoid expressions that are not likely to be universally used. Avoid such expressions as:

—*Poke*, meaning *bag*, as in *he had his clothes in a poke.*

—*Spell*, meaning a *time period*, as in *sit a spell.*

—*Bring* meaning *take*, as in *when you go fishing, bring enough bait.*

Of course, if you quote a person who uses provincialisms, you would reproduce his exact dialogue; but if you paraphrase what he says, you would write in standard English.

There are occasions when you would want to use provincialisms to flavor a piece. Southeastern Pennsylvania is the home of the Pennsylvania Dutch, descendants of early settlers from Germany. Many of these people, especially in the rural and small towns, have retained a dialect which involves a fractured diction as colorful and charming as it is incorrect. Commonplace are such expressions as:

—*Make out the light.*

—*She feels to school teach.*

—*To the store we went already.*

Despite the prevailing provincialisms, the local media in the Pennsylvania Dutch country use standard English. However, one advertiser makes good use of the provincialisms in selling his "Pennsylvania Dutch Noodles." His slogan is "Learn what good is."

You can use a provincialism under the rare and right conditions.

Avoid Vulgarity, Profanity, Obscenity

The swampiest ground you must tread in selection of words is in the area of vulgarity, profanity, and obscenity. The rules change constantly, and the writer is never quite certain where the boundaries lie. However, there are certain guidelines to keep in mind:

—*Vulgarisms are never appropriate.*
—*The audience determines what is acceptable.*
—*Avoid objectionable language unless it is essential to your purpose.*

Vulgar by definition means common. Vulgar expressions are expressions that are commonly spoken, but are not acceptable in professional writing. You should avoid them. The word "ain't" is a grammatically incorrect expression that is used by uneducated, indiscriminate people. Other examples of such grammatical vulgarisms are:

—Double negatives:
    INCORRECT — We *don't* expect *nobody* to show up.
    CORRECT — We *don't* expect *anybody* to show up.
    INCORRECT — *Irregardless* of the outcome, we will . . .
    CORRECT — *Regardless* of the outcome, we will . . .
—Incorrect verb forms:
    INCORRECT — We *was* glad to hear from you.
    CORRECT — We *were* glad to hear from you.
—Incorrect use of adverbs and adjectives:
    INCORRECT — Moving *slow*, she crossed the bridge safely.
    CORRECT — Moving *slowly*, she crossed the bridge safely.
    INCORRECT — She received a *goodly* amount in salary.
    CORRECT — She received a *good* salary.

These are just a few examples of vulgarisms that should not be transferred onto the printed page even though you may not have succeeded in eliminating them from your speech. There are many others. If you find that such nonstandard English expressions or words are getting into your writing, you must root them out. You can't go wrong using standard English. If you do vary from standard English, make certain you do it consciously and not accidently.

What Will the Audience Allow?

In that foggy and ever changing area of what does and does not violate the audience's standards of "decent" or "moral" language, the writer must write for the particular reader/listener/viewer of the material he or she is preparing.

The audience will determine the extent to which you can go in using language that is borderline. You are most restricted when you are writing for general circulation newspapers or radio and television outlets. The family newspaper and the family broadcast facility will permit an occasional "hell" or "damn," or sometimes something a bit stronger. But scatological or obscene words are permitted only in specialized publications—college and underground publications and practically never on radio or television unless it is a closed cable channel.

This can be a little restricting. For example, the Miami Herald as late as the late 1970s declined to print the common word for excrement in a serious scientific story about evidence of civilization under the Altantic Ocean. In telling that the evidence was based on the finding of excretory material from crabs, Dr. Jose Honnorez was quoted: "It's a very funny thing to think this whole thing was based on crab ___ ." The Miami Herald used a dash for the barnyard word for feces. When a scientist cannot use such words, no one else is likely to get by with it. There is more of a chance to print such words if you are writing about a scientific subject or some other subject in a serious way.

Make Certain the Controversial Language Is Essential

A good general rule to follow is to avoid using language that might be objectionable to a portion of your readers unless it is essential to your purpose. Why offend people by using profanity if it serves no purpose? Why use shocking language just to shock people? That's immature. Be sensitive to your readers. Don't be a hypocrite. If you would not use a word or expression in front of your mother or Aunt Harriet, or grandma, why inflict it on other mothers, aunts, or grandmothers, if it is not essential?

However don't hesitate to use specific essential words because of a misguided Victorianism. Modern mores permit you to use words that were taboo just a few years ago. As a writer you must keep aware of a changing society. Fortunately, you are not forced into the ridiculous situation of the writer of few years ago who could not use the word "rape." He would write a passage like this:

> The suspect beat the girl unmercifully, breaking her nose, cutting her mouth, knocking out two teeth and breaking her glasses, but he did not criminally assault her.

If the above paragraph does not describe a criminal assault, nothing does. But a few years ago *criminal assault* was a euphemism for rape.

Avoid Clichés

Writing is a difficult task. One of the rewards it offers is the pleasure of being creative or original. It is fun to arrange words in a way that has perhaps never been done before in expressing an idea, re-creating an event, reflecting emotions. For this reason, determine you will shun clichés, those stale expressions that everyone uses without thinking. The clichés were clever expressions by the first person who used them, but have become banal and meaningless by endless repetition.

Sometimes the words are horrible to begin with. They are clichés the first time they are written because of their poor taste. A couple of years ago, the car radio suddenly spewed forth the words:

DROP KICK ME, JESUS, THROUGH THE GOAL POSTS OF LIFE.

At first the driver thought a satirist had taken over the radio. But then he realized the words were meant to be taken seriously as a spiritual song.

Stale language indicates stale thinking. It also indicates a lack of pride on the part of the writer. Rather than trying to tread new ground, the user of clichés is willing to walk in the path cleared by someone else. Don't let that be you. If you cannot think up a good original expression to say what you have to say, say it in clear, standard English. The following passage in a sports story illustrates the way a mentally lazy writer without pride might write:

The slugging third-sacker took a hefty swing at the smoking three-two pitch from the portside flinger and poled it into the left field stands, clearing the bags.

This is an exaggerated example, but not by much. Beginning writers often think they are being clever by trotting out all the clichés. There is nothing wrong with writing this straight:

Third baseman Jones hit the fast ball into the left field stands, scoring the first home run of the game. Smith, Hayes, and Conners scored ahead of Jones.

The example above may not seem exciting, but it tells the story without stealing stale figures of speech from some more creative writer from the past. If you can come up with original imagery, fine. If not, play it straight.

Just in case you do not realize what a cliché is, here are a few examples no self-respecting writer would use:

A blunt instrument; a tower of strength; a paragon of virtue; an acid test; blissful ignorance; olive branches; the naked truth; a square peg in a round hole; a sight for sore eyes; rack and ruin; to hell in a hand basket; shadow of a doubt; diamond in the rough; the king of beasts; a heart of gold; and comfortable as an old shoe.

Writing cliches may be to you as comfortable as a new shoe or it may seem like old times, or to your eagle nose it may seem like you smell a squirrel. Either way, swear off using clichés. If everyone did, there would be no more clichés, and that would be a week of reckoning.

You can make clichés work for you. Because they are so familiar to you, they will come to your mind when you are searching for a way to express an idea or comparison. Don't use them, but you may be able to change them around a bit and make them fresh. For example, if you are trying to describe something that is green, the first thing that will come to mind is:

As green as grass.

You don't want to use it, because it is trite, but play around with it a bit and maybe you can use it in a fresh form:

As green as grass ought to be.

As green as artificial grass.

As green as the grass on the other side of the fence.
Etc.

But don't use these, because they are no longer fresh. Think up your own variation.

Avoid Jargon

As a writer you should be wary of picking up the specialized language of a profession, trade or group. If you write regularly about the specialty, you might forget that your readers have not become as familiar with the words as you have. A court reporter soon becomes familiar with the definitions of an *injunction* (court order to someone to stop doing something he is doing and refrain from doing it in the future) or *writ of mandamus* (a court order to force the performance of some public duty) or plea of *nolo-contendere* (a defendant's plea that she will not contest a charge but will not plead either innocent or guilty).

The same trap awaits writers of science and medicine stories, police, sports labor stories, etc. It is even true on college campuses. The expression *Greek* is understood by college students to mean a member of a fraternity or sorority. *Greek* is used in that context in college newspapers. But to most readers, a *Greek* is a citizen of or native of Greece. This should be remembered when you move from writing for the campus publications to writing for general circulation publications.

The writer of advertisements should understand this also. The writer should make certain the words chosen in advertising a product or service are clearly understood by the consumer. The writer especially needs to be careful if his or her knowledge of the language of a product or field is wide. The writer may understand, but should not use the words if the reader/listener/viewer will not understand.

That does not mean that everyone must know the language, but your reader/listener/viewer must. When you write for a specialized audience, you can use some "in language," but no more than necessary.

Be Informal With Care

Most expository writing for the print media—stories, features, columns—while avoiding stuffiness or pretentiousness, tends to use formal standard wording and construction. It usually features the:

—*Formal identifications,* such as a representative, Jones, Miss, Mr. or Mrs. Smith, Sen. Kennedy, Gov. Brown, President Reagan, and E. Ronald Kirk, laborer.

—*Third person,* rather than the informal second or first person. It is Jones, not you or I.

—*Complete sentences,* not fragments or disjointed phrases and clauses.

—*Correct word,* not slang or common idioms.

However, in writing for radio or television and in writing advertisements for any medium, you are permitted a lot more leeway in your choice of words. Under certain circumstances when writing ads or continuity and sometimes even news copy for broadcast, you can use the more informal:

—*Contractions.*

—*Slang.*

—*First names.*

—*Sentence fragments.*

—*Spoken idioms.*

The main thing to remember is that you should always be certain that whatever words you use are acceptable to your audience for the purpose you intend them. You have to know your audience and what it will consider acceptable.

AVOID UNNECESSARY WORDS

The most prevalent disease of writing is probably using unnecessary words. Wordiness robs your writing of exactness and readability. But every writer is a victim, every written piece, an example. Every piece can be improved by tighter writing. While tighter writing is desirable for the general writer, it is essential for those writing for the mass media.

It is simple enough. If they are not terse, writers will not be published. Space in newspapers and magazines and time on radio and television are expensive. Editors and producers must make every word count. They demand no less from writers.

Incentives to keep it short do not apply as strongly to the amateur writer. In fact, the pressure is often to make it longer. Think about some of the influences in your writing experiences that may have made lengthy writing seem desirable.

Remember when you stretched 50 words' worth of experience and knowledge into a 500 word essay because that was the minimum allowed by the teacher? Didn't you get an impression that the term paper would receive a better grade if it was puffed up by excessive verbiage?

How many times have you listened to the professor, politician or preacher spend 50 minutes delivering 10 minutes' worth of specific wisdom, statesmanship or salvation?

Even your parents added to your problem when they pressured you into longer letters to grandma after Christmas when all you had to say was "thanks."

It is an oversimplification to assume that these nice people sabotaged your writing technique. You carry most of the guilt for your natural laziness in using words to replace thought and factual research. But the problem is there. You should recognize it and determine to overcome it.

There are basic human traits that push all writers into wordiness. You should constantly guard against them. Keep this in mind:

—*It is faster to write long.* There is a story about the reporter who was told by an editor to write a story in 100 words. The reporter said, "Can I write 200 words? It is too close to deadline. I haven't time to write 100 words." The reporter was right. It does take longer to keep it short and specific and still express the essential facts and ideas.

—*It is easier to write long.* Writing effectively in as short a space as possible requires intensive thought, rigid discipline, good organization and, most important, rewriting.

There are three ways to reduce wordiness:

—*Eliminate unnecessary words.*

—*Eliminate unnecessary phrases or reduce them to words.*

—*Eliminate unnecessary clauses or reduce them to phrases.*

Useless Words

Many words creep into your writing to clutter it and serve no useful purpose:

—*Useless articles.* Often you can eliminate the articles *a, an,* and *the,* when they serve no useful purpose. But make certain the eliminated articles will not make the phrasing awkward or confusing. Note in the following example the underlined articles are not needed, whereas those in capital letters are:

The city commissioners met today in THE auditorium at City
Hall for a discussion of the new taxes. The citizen participation
was not as large as THE commission expected.

—*Useless adjectives.* Many useless adjectives clutter your writing. They usually occur when you try to make an inadequate adjective serve by giving it a helper. One of the most common is the word *very.* It is a meaningless word. For example, if you want to say something is bigger than *big,* it does no good to say *very big.* Perhaps you can say it is *immense, huge, gigantic, vast, gargantuan,* or *immeasurable.* Better yet, give the dimensions. Ralph Sampson is a *seven-foot* basketball player, not a *very tall* one.

Other useless adjectives are: *rather* pretty, *slightly* depressed, *nearly* finished, *somewhat* tired. The list goes on *almost* endlessly.

—*Redundant words* containing useless repetitions telling your reader the obvious. Eliminate the redundant words that make your writing stodgy. *Young* boy (all boys are young); *brave* hero (aren't they all?); *totally* destroyed (destruction is total); continue *on* (how else could you continue?); raise *up* (can you raise down?)

—*Unnecessary relative pronouns.* The words *who, which* and *that* can be eliminated as in the following example:

The patrolman said *that* the suspect *who is* being questioned
has denied ownership of the burglar tools *which* police found in
his car.

—*Two imprecise words where one specific word would do.* Often you can find one word to replace two inexact ones.

A *severe* and *strict* father can be a *stern* father.

A *pale, waxy* face can be *ashen.*

A *tall, slender* man can be *lanky.*

—*Opinion words.* Eliminate from your writing opinion words that add no meaning:

He will give an *interesting* speech. (Let the listener decide whether it is interesting.)

Good seats are still available for the game. (Acceptable if it is an ad or someone is quoted, but a news story should eliminate the *good.*)

The *sad* news of the mayor's defeat in the election spread quickly throughout the city. (Maybe only the mayor and his family are sad. Obviously, a majority voted against him.)

—*Repetitious words.* Eliminate the underlined words which repeat something already expressed:

The important legislation is vital to the economy.

The subject of taxes will be the theme of the seminar.

A winning jump of 12 feet won the pole vault.

Eliminate Phrases or Reduce Them to Single Words

To make your copy tighter you can often eliminate meaningless phrases that creep into your writing.

—*"Think time" phrases.* When we speak extemporaneously, we often use phrases to fill time while we are thinking of the right thing to say. Such phrases as:

As a matter of fact . . . .

It's interesting, but . . . .

The idea is that . . . .

Etc. . .

There is no need to carry over such expressions into your writing. You don't have to write while you are thinking what to say, or you can easily edit the phrase out of your writing.

—*Phrases that emphasize the obvious.* Eliminate phrases that tell the reader things he already knows.

The collision occurred at the intersection of Main Street and First Avenue. (It's obvious that Main and First come together only at the intersection).

The sum of $300. (Everyone knows $300 is a sum).

He teachs the subject of history. (It is no news that history is a subject.)

In the three examples cited, the phrase underlined can be left out of your copy.

—*Weak verbal phrasing.* Use direct verbs in your writing rather than verbal forms ending in "ing."

WORDY—He *will be running* for reelection.
BETTER—He *will run* for re-election.

WORDY—The club *is planning* a picnic July 4.
BETTER—The club *plans* a picnic July 4.

WORDY—The street department hopes to end the traffic bottleneck by *the repaving of* Elm Street.
BETTER—The street department hopes to end the traffic bottleneck by *repaving* Elm Street.

You can tighten up your writing by reducing a phrase to a word.
—*Appositives.*

WORDY—*James, who is 10,* sustained a broken right arm in a fall from his bicycle.
BETTER—James, 10, sustained a broken right arm in a fall from his bicycle.

WORDY—The amendments, *eight in number,* were voted down.
BETTER—The *eight* amendments were voted down.

WORDY—Acme Television sets, *which are self-tuning,* are sold only at Media Shops, Inc.
BETTER—*Self-tuning* Acme Television sets are sold only at Media Shops, Inc.

—*Bureaucratic wordiness.* Your writing has probably been infiltrated by a widespread tendency to use space-consuming phrases instead of the obvious word. It might be called "bureaucratic" because the worst offenders are bureaucrats who rarely use one word when they can use more. Such expressions as "at that point in time" when a simple "then" would have sufficed were introduced into the language during the infamous Watergate hearings. Unfortunately, while Watergate has faded, the pompous phrases are still around. Do not be guilty of continuing such bastardization of the language. Other examples are:

Done away with—ended
For the reason that—because
In regard to—about
Holding a meeting—meeting
Brought to a conclusion—ended
In the neighborhood of—about
Placed into operation—started
Got under way—began

There are many others. Such expressions become second nature to you. Unless you are conscious of them, you will not avoid them. Scan your writing for such wordiness. Edit it out.

Eliminate Unnecessary Clauses or Reduce Them

Don't write a long clause to express an idea when it can be expressed just as well in fewer words.

WORDY—*It is the responsibility of each taxpayer to* see that his return is filed by April 15.
BETTER—*Each taxpayer* must file his return by April 15.

WORDY—The defendants, *who were all named in the one indictment,* were tried together.
BETTER—The defendents, *all named in one indictment,* were tried together.

WORDY—The Monongahela River and the Allegheny River, *which come together in Pittsburgh,* form the Ohio River.
BETTER—The Monongahela River and the Allegheny River *unite in Pittsburgh to form* the Ohio River.

There are many other reasons for wordiness not covered above. For example:

—*Euphemisms.* Many people have infected the language with expressions meant to make things appear less stark than they are. Some of these expressions are well intentioned, some laudable, some silly. You must judge which serve useful purposes in your writing. Examples:

Passed away—died
Displaced person—refugee
Sanitary engineer—janitor
Culturally deprived—poor or needy
Senior citizen—aged
Previously owned car—used car

Euphemisms are futile and often wordy attempts to make realities sound less harsh than they are. As Gertrude Stein might have said, "A weed is a weed is a weed."

—*False Courtesy.* In trying to be courteous, writers can often be guilty of wordiness.

If you will be so kind—please
At your convenience—anytime
With deep appreciation—thanks

—*Unnecessary question.* In writing a news story, avoid writing the question asked of a source if the question is apparent from the answer.

WORDY—Asked when the newly appointed city manager would begin his work, the mayor said, "City Manager Jones will begin his duties Jan. 1."

BETTER—"City Manager Jones will begin his duties Jan. 1," the mayor said.

Some Specifics "Hints"

Understand that wordiness means eliminating those words that add nothing to your piece. It *does not* mean eliminating essential facts, legitimate stylistic adornments, or color from your writing. Comedian Bob Newhart once did a skit in which he portrayed Abraham Lincoln's press agent. He told Lincoln he had looked over the draft of the address to be delivered at Gettysburg and he had some suggestions to make. He said that "Four score and seven" was too wordy. "Make it 87," he told Lincoln. The bit went on from there and massacred one of history's great pieces of prose. It was hilarious because it was outrageous. In trying to achieve conciseness, *avoid butchering* copy. Just eliminate the useless verbiage.

USE COLORFUL WORDS EFFECTIVELY

Make your writing as bright as you can within the limits of good taste and normal restraint. Straight informational news stories are usually best presented briefly, clearly and without fancy literary fringes. Feature stories, advertisements, descriptive stories, and promotional pieces can be improved with a judicious use of imagery and other literary touches.

—*Use similes:*

As cool as a mother-in-law's kiss.

—*Use descriptive metaphors:*

From the air at night, the city was a huge, black velvet jeweler's tray, its multi-hued lights, little gems dancing and twinkling.

—*Use juxtaposition for a humorous touch:*

The *new* city hall is ready for business. The *new* offices have been painted; the *new* furniture is in place; the *new* equipment installed. The *old* staff moves in Monday.

—*Use alliteration,* but with great caution. Spiro Agnew, with his "nattering nabobs of negativism," and similar efforts did more to destroy alliteration as a stylistic gimmick than Simple Simon and Peter Piper. However, if you use two, or at the most three words in a tasteful way, the device can still work as in these advertising phrases:

Sizzler Steak

Fine Furniture

Bestform Bra

—*Use exaggeration,* especially in satire or to express the intensity of a reaction.

As Johnny accepted the debate prize amid the applause of his classmates, his smile was a yard wide and he grew ten feet taller.

—Use colorful verbs:
> The high jumper *soared* 7 feet, 2 inches.
> The angry senator *scorched* the newsmen in a fiery response.
> Give up mere walking; *float* along in Super-Soft slippers.

—Use extended metaphors:

An extended metaphor is one which is used more than once in slightly different forms. For example, during President Reagan's tenure as president, writers will undoubtedly trade on his former career as an actor for metaphoric color. There will be mention of his *"performance"* good or bad in his *"starring role in the Potomac drama, comedy, or follies."* Writers will wonder when time comes for his second term if the public will want a *"Reagan sequel,"* or if the end of his first term will bring a *"curtain call,"* or if he will take his *"show back to California."* Nancy Reagan will be referred to as the president's *"leading lady"* or his *"co-star."* Writers will call the voting public the president's *"audience"* or the *"ones in the balcony seats,"* or the *"critics* in the aisle seats." As you can see, an extended metaphor carried to its extreme can become a bit nauseating, but limited to maybe three references in one piece, and handled with taste, it can make the piece more colorful and more readable.

In using colorful language, also use restraint. Good taste demands that. But to achieve good taste, you don't have to be dull. If a colorful word or approach will help the reader visualize the scene you describe, or feel the emotion you wish to evoke, or understand the situation better, by all means be colorful.

SUGGESTED EXERCISES

1. Replace the unfamiliar words underlined in the following sentences with familiar and appropriate words.

a. The country's economic stagnation will probably not deteriorate further in the months ahead, the secretary said.

b. The country is probably at the nadir of its precipitous business decline, he added.

c. Steps designed to gain the optimum results will begin soon, the secretary surmised.

d. There may well be an amelioration of the tax burden, he further opined.

e. In the crash, Miss Jones suffered facial contusions and abrasions on her arms, a hospital spokesman declared.

f. The fired workers will not receive remuneration for the week in which their larcenous activities occurred.

g. The suspects have been incarcerated in the county jail to await disposition of their cases, police recounted.

h. Police added that the perpetrators would not be accorded their release until the stolen money had been fully recompensated.

i. Under the rule, the proprietor of a gun business wanting to sell guns to Indians had to show that the merchandise was not being retailed for an extralegal purpose.

j. He suggested that the health authority promulgate fees on a regional basis to be integrated gradually commencing with Medicare and Medicaid.

2. Replace the inappropriate words underlined in the following sentences with more appropriate words.

a. Joseph Pulitzer was a notorious publisher in New York City.

b. He waived his right to be represented by an attorney.

c. The whole sorority jetted to Bermuda for Easter break.

d. A Rhodes scholar, she is an unintelligent writer.

e. John was tried in the honor court violation.

f. Murl's philosophy is different than mine.

g. The accident was at the corner of Main and First Streets.

h. Fast automobiles require the best quality gasoline.

i. She continued on to the heart of her speech.

j. After a long illness, his father passed away.

k. The new record by the "objectionables" is not cool.

l. She bought a splint basket of peaches.

m. Her new carpet was as green as grass.

n. Ajax Company officials said they would seek an injunction against striking workers.

o. Why did the party list include everyone accept Oscar Obnoxious?

p. Henry agreed with the contract offer.

q. Let's split the bill among the two of us.

r. The dog set on the floor beside the desk.

s. The hungry (and dumb) snake swallowed it's own tail.

t. Jean complained because she had less jelly beans than Joe had.

3. Find a piece of writing—a feature story or an ad—that seems to be written in a dull way. Rewrite it trying to replace dull nouns, verbs and modifiers with more colorful ones without changing the tone or purpose of the piece.

4. Make a list of words you think you might have trouble spelling. Have a friend read the list to you and you spell each word. Have your friend mark those you spell incorrectly. Add to the list and keep it handy to your desk. It might make looking up your "trouble" words easier for you. If the list remains short, you might be able to learn to spell your troublesome words.

5. The following passages were taken from various publications meant to inform people of plans, programs, procedures. All are wordy and inexact. Most of them can be rewritten more clearly and much more to the point in fewer words, often half what the writer used. Rewrite these passages. Omit no essentials, but cut each considerably and make each more exact and more direct:

a. Regardless of the steps the student may have completed, if he has not checked in all materials by the close of regular registration, it will be necessary to obtain a new set of registration materials and start registration from the beginning during the late registration period. A registration started in the regular registration period cannot be finished in the late registration period.

b. Correspondence study courses are not limited to those persons residing within the geographic limits of the state of Florida or even the continental limits of the United States. Many courses listed in this catalog are available to all English-speaking persons the world over. Out of state fees are listed under the appropriate regulations in this catalog. Overseas service is particularly helpful to military personnel, embassy personnel, and United States citizens residing temporarily abroad, but may also be utilized by citizens of other countries.

c. Any full-time, permanent employee of the Board of Regents and the institutions under its jurisdiction who meets the academic requirements of the university may during any quarter register without charge for one course not to exceed six hours, two graduate courses not to exceed nine hours where one is a thesis course, or six hours of thesis only. However, a non-faculty employee may enroll for a course held during working hours only upon certification by the department chairman that the course will contribute to the efficiency of the employee. The time lost while attending classes in such instances must be made up.

d. One of the most important and difficult tasks facing journalists today is reporting and explaining the actions of government as its functions grow more complex. Before a journalist can report government activities, he must understand the men and process through which government functions. The Washington Journalism Center, situated at the seat of the national government and in close touch with the men who make and cover the news in Washington, provides a unique opportunity for students and journalists.

e. The recruiting and holding of able young talent for journalism careers is one of the principal objectives of Sigma Delta Chi. The importance of helping to provide a continuing source of qualified personnel for the nation's newsrooms was recognized by the society when the McKinsey Plan of reorganization was adopted in 1960 and recruiting was declared to be one of the "working" objectives of Sigma Delta Chi.

Chapter VII

SENTENCES:
MAKE THEM CLEAR AND EFFECTIVE

The sentence is the basic structure of any composition. If a writer can express a message in effective sentences, he or she has gone far toward gaining the confidence, attention, interest and understanding of the reader/listener/viewer. Effective sentences are particularly critical in writing for the mass media audience. The casual attention and limited involvement of the reader/listener/viewer of the mass media story or advertisement means that nothing but effective sentences will suffice. Of course, any writer who is being read is writing effective sentences. But with fiction, essays, scientific writing, philosophy, history, etc., the material and the intense involvement of the reader/listener/viewer can overcome sentences that may be less effective than those necessary for mass media consumption. There are certain qualities that all sentences must have:

—*Unity.*
—*Coherence.*
—*Proper emphasis.*

UNITY

If you remember your high school grammar, you will recall that a sentence has *unity* if it expresses just one basic thought and includes only that which amplifies, restricts or reflects that thought. For example, take a sentence that might come from a biographical story about an individual:

Jones attended public schools in Chicago and earned his bachelor of arts degree and law degree at the University of Illinois.

This sentence shows *unity* because it is all about Mr. Jones' education.

Using the same subject matter to illustrate a sentence where the *unity* has been destroyed:

A veteran of World War II, Mr. Jones was active in Illinois politics, having served in the legislature and as lieutenant governor.

Unity is destroyed because Mr. Jones' war service has no direct bearing on his political service and should not be mentioned in the same sentence.

COHERENCE

A sentence has *coherence* if all parts of the sentence are logically related to all other parts of the sentence. A coherent sentence should be immediately clear to the reader/listener/viewer. It should not leave him or her puzzled or confused. An example of a coherent sentence:

> Jones, founder of the Jones, Jones, Swanson and Smith Law Company, was active in the firm until two years ago when he retired.

This sentence is clear and all of the parts clearly relate to the other parts. There is no chance to confuse the thought of the sentence or misunderstand the information provided. Using the same information, the sentence below shows how *coherence* could be destroyed:

> Active in the company until his retirement two years ago, Jones was founder of the Jones, Jones, Swanson and Smith Law Firm.

The version directly above is *not coherent*. You refer to "the company" before you have mentioned what company you are talking about. This would make the reader/listener/viewer pause, thinking he had missed something. Anything that makes the reader/listener/viewer lose concentration on the message diminishes his understanding of it and frustrates the writer's purpose.

PROPER EMPHASIS

In constructing sentences, you draw attention of the reader/listener/viewer in two ways. You can show *emphasis* by where in the sentence you place a specific bit of information. You can also show *emphasis* by structuring the sentence to make the part you want to emphasize stand out.

Emphasis By Placement

The most emphatic parts of any sentence are the *beginning* and the *end*. The least emphatic place is the *middle* of the sentence. In the following sentence you can see that the most important parts of the message (underlined) are at the beginning and at the end:

> The evacuation order remained in effect while the cars were placed back on the tracks in case there was another release of gas.

Another example taken from an advertisement:

> She chose an Ace disposer, according to Mrs. Jones, because of the faithful service her old Ace dishwasher is giving her.

Emphasis By Sentence Structure

In structuring sentences, you can give material the most *emphasis* by having the material stand alone in a simple sentence:

> Brown is a Harvard-educated economist.

You can *reduce emphasis* by making the thought one of two independent coordinate clauses in a compound sentence:

> Brown is a Harvard-educated economist and he is a member of the U.S. Senate.

You can *further reduce emphasis* of the thought by making it a dependent clause in a complex sentence.

> Brown, who is an economist educated at Harvard, is a member of the U.S. Senate.

You can *reduce emphasis* of the thought *even further* by making it a phrase.

> Brown, a Harvard-educated economist, is a member of the U.S. Senate.

You can give the thought the *least emphasis* by changing it slightly, but not significantly, and reducing it to a word:

> Economist John V. Brown is a member of the U.S. Senate.

To sum up then, you need to give a lot of thought to the material you emphasize. Sophisticated writing calls for a variety of grammatical structures that permit you to give the proper weight to each item of information so that information will be in proper perspective for the reader/listener/viewer. You are guiding him or her by the weight you give a particular piece of information. In the examples above, you were telling the reader/listener/viewer that the fact Mr. Brown was a Harvard-educated economist was *important enough* to have its own sentence, *unimportant enough* to be reduced to a word, or somewhere in between.

While some readers of this volume might find this discussion of *proper emphasis* and proper use of independent and dependent clauses, phrases and words somewhat elementary, there is evidence that many beginning writers in college have never fully understood these relationships. And even for those who understand, a review of the basics of your trade cannot hurt. In addition to achieving the *unity, coherence* and *proper emphasis* necessary for effective sentences in any context, sentences for news and feature stories and advertisements for the print and broadcast media have other demands the writer must consider. Sentences for mass media must also be:

—*Shorter on the average* than sentences for other types of writing.
—*Varied in length.*
—*Varied in structure.*
—*Parallel in organization.*
—*Repetitious on occasion.*
—*Active in voice preferably.*
—*Clear of traditional sentence faults.*

MAKE SENTENCES SHORT

Author Robert Gunning in *The Technique of Clear Writing* stated bluntly, "I know of no author addressing a general audience who averages much more than 20 words per sentence and still succeeds in getting published."

Gunning studied sentence length of writers throughout history. He documented the fact that there has been a steady decline in the average sentence length since several hundred years ago when reading was limited to only a few learned men. As the masses learned to read, writers shortened sentences to insure an audience. Gunning pointed out that John Milton's 17th century writing averaged 61 words per sentence. Now you know why you had so much difficulty comprehending *Paradise Lost*. Actually, of course, short sentences will not insure acceptance by readers/listeners/viewers of your efforts, but it is one factor you can do something about.

As you read newspapers and magazines, take note of sentence length. You will note some of the writing characterized by overlong sentences, but much of the best will have sentences that are short on the average.

A quick check of several stories in a typical newspaper will probably show that the average sentence length varies from a low of about 17 words to a high of about 25. Typical, easily understood news stories examined had an average of 18.2 words per sentence. That is a good average to aim for in a news story. In feature stories and in interpretive stories, sentence averages might go just a bit higher and still be efficient. In broadcast stories, the average should not be any higher than 15 to 16 words per sentence. Remember, the ear is not as keen for detail as the eye. Advertising writing is characterized by extremely short sentences. It is not unusual for the average sentence length for a printed advertisement to be only 10 words. You probably should not go much higher than 12 for display ads. To recap what the average sentence length for the various forms of mass communications should be:

—*News stories:* About 18 words per sentence.
—*Feature stories:* Not much more than 20 words per sentence.
—*Broadcast news stories:* About 15 words per sentence.
—*Advertisements:* About 10 words per sentence.

VARY THE SENTENCE LENGTH

Remember what an average is, it is an arbitrary figure that has no particular relationship to the individual elements that are averaged. It is just a measurement. Don't set out to write all 18-word sentences. Your writing should be characterized by a majority of sentences fairly close to the average, some that are considerably shorter, and some that are much longer.

To test your sentence length, take a sample of your writing at least 150 words long. Count the words in each sentence. Total these and divide by the number of sentences in the sample. If the result is above the words-per-sentence maximum, go back to the typewriter and rewrite.

A typical news story of 15 sentences had five sentences considerably shorter than the average, which was 18.2 words per sentence. It had six sentences considerably higher than the average, and it had four sentences close to the average. The length and order of the sentences were: 28 words, 26, 26, 4, 28, 20, 31, 20, 4, 26, 16, 9, 28, 8, 9. The order is not important, nor is the length of the individual sentences. It is the variety of the lengths and the ebb and flow of the rhythm that makes the composition read smoothly, and it is the *AVERAGE LENGTH* that makes the piece more easily understood.

Obviously you do not set out to write certain length sentences. You write your piece, trying to keep it clear and give proper space and emphasis to the important facts, and organize it logically. Then, when you are done, you use the sentence profile to analyze your work and determine where it can be improved.

VARY THE STRUCTURE OF SENTENCES

Mature writing makes full use of the various constructions possible in sentences. Most of your sentences for mass media readers/listeners/viewers will be *SIMPLE DECLARATIVE* sentences. But you will also use:

—*Compound sentences.*
—*Complex sentences.*
—*Compound-complex sentences.*
—*Interrogative sentences.*
—*Imperative sentences.*
—*Periodic sentences.*
—*Sentence fragments.*
—*Sentences with something before the subject.*

Simple Declarative Sentences

The *simple declarative sentence* is a thing of beauty. (The preceding sentence is a simple declarative sentence.) In mass media writing you will use a preponderance of such sentences. But be wary that you do not overdo a good thing. A series of such sentences can become choppy and monotonous.

> Helen had nothing to do. It was a rainy Saturday. She thought she would like to go to a movie. She called her friend, Harriet. Harriet was busy cleaning up her room. She couldn't go to the movies. Helen hung up the phone. She decided to do her homework.

As you can see, such dependence on the simple form makes for immature writing. Occasionally a skilled writer can use such a staccato technique to create a mood, but the beginning student should avoid the practice. Vary the structure with a more mature organization of ideas expressed:

> With nothing to do on a rainy Saturday, Helen decided to attend a movie. She called her friend, Harriet. Busy cleaning up her room, however, Harriet couldn't go to the movie. Hanging up the phone, Helen decided to do her homework.

Compound Sentences

A *compound sentence* is needed in writing stories or advertisements when you want to express two ideas so equal in importance that you must give them equal weight and so closely related that they should be in the same sentence. For example, you might be writing a story about two men who are vying for the same political office and you might want to contrast their views on a particular issue. You could use a compound sentence to say:

Jones said the budget should be balanced immediately, but Smith said a balanced budget must wait the completion of some essential programs.

In an advertisement, you might want to emphasize equally two benefits the buyer is offered in the ad. A compound sentence would achieve that equal treatment:

Our new TEENY TRAVELER sedan is tailored for your lifestyle, and it will fit neatly into your budget.

Complex Sentences

A *complex sentence* is needed in writing stories or advertisements when you have two ideas which are closely enough related that they should be in the same sentence, but are *NOT* of equal weight. Using the same political story as above, you might want to say:

Jones, *who previously served in the Florida legislature,* announced his candidacy for the U.S. House of Representatives Monday.

The dependent clause italicized in the above example indicates to the reader/listener/viewer the lesser weight the writer has given that particular piece of information.

Compound-Complex Sentences

The *compound-complex sentence* is rarely used in writing for the media because it is a complicated structure. The information it contains can usually be given in more than one sentence. It would almost never be used in advertisements, or even in stories for broadcast outlets. However, in a print news story or editorial you might occasionally see a *compound-complex sentence* to indicate a close, yet unequal, relationship of certain facts to other facts. This might be acceptable in your political story.

Jones, who switched to the Republican party last year, filed for the 2nd Congressional seat Friday; and Smith, a life-long Democrat, filed for the same seat Monday.

Interrogative Sentences

Asking a *question* can often be an effective way to communicate. Don't you agree? And doesn't that previous sentence (and this one) answer the question? Not used often in news stories, questions can be used effectively in editorials and advertisements:

—A *feature story* might ask the question: "Has her change from housewife to businesswoman brought happiness to . . .?"

—An *editorial* might say to the reader/listener/viewer: "Have you ever calculated just how much an inefficiently run city government costs you, the taxpayer?"

—An *advertisement* for a television set might ask: "Do you like a clear, crisp picture?" "Do you want dependable service?" "Do you want the very best in viewing enjoyment?"

In all of the examples cited, the pieces would go on to provide answers to the questions. The questions could come anywhere in the piece. They might serve as the lead, or they might provide transition in the middle of the piece. But questions can and should be used effectively in writing for the mass media.

Imperative Sentence

The *imperative sentence* might be called the bossy sentence. It tells the reader/listener/viewer what to do. It is a teaching sentence, used throughout this volume when the author tells you what you should do to improve your writing. It also has a broad use in writing for mass media. It is used by:

—The *feature writer* of how-to-do-it articles as in a recipe on the cooking page:
   After you have cleaned and stuffed the turkey, put it in the oven
   and roast for five hours at 350 degrees.
—The *editorial writer:*
   Go to the polls Tuesday and vote for the man you think will best
   handle the problems of the country. But make certain you vote for
   the man who understands those problems.
—The *advertisement writer:*
   Don't miss out on this great entertainment treat.
   Call now and reserve your ticket. That number is 368-4000.
   Pick up the phone. Call now.

Periodic Sentences

In your writing, mix *loose and periodic sentences.* The emphasis on a loose sentence is at the beginning, and the sentence can be cut off at various points without losing meaning as in this sentence:
   Mayor Jones will not run for re-election if by the end of his term
   he has accomplished his goals and if a suitable candidate appears
   to replace him.

As you can see, the above "loose" sentence could have been stopped at two different places without destroying the sense of the sentence. If you want to add some suspense to the sentence, and perhaps heighten the emphasis on the main thought, you could invert the sentence, making it periodic in this way:
   If by the end of his term he has attained his goals and if a
   suitable candidate appears to replace him, Mayor Jones will not
   run for re-election.

Sentence Fragments

Sentence fragments, or incomplete sentences, can be used to create variety in your sentence structure, but they must be used with care. Advertising writers probably make the widest use of sentence fragments. An advertisement might read:

Pure power. Unleased when you step on the accelerator of the Acme sedan. Comfort. Miles slip by as you relax in the deep foam buckets. Class. Look over the chrome dashboard. Economy. Thirty miles per gallon.

Sentence fragments can also be effective in news stories as a change of pace. Use them cautiously in descriptive passages in trying to recreate sense impressions for the reader. A reporter might describe a loaded school bus in this way:

Grinning faces everywhere. And noise. It rolls from the front of the bus to the rear. Then, reinforced, sweeps once again to the front. On the left, a girl is crying. And noise. It swells. The smell of peanut butter sandwiches. An apple rolls down the aisle. And the noise. Can 30 children generate such a crescendo?

Sentence fragments should be used with care and avoided in straight expository writing. But don't be afraid of them when the occasion calls for them.

VARY SENTENCE BEGINNINGS

While the usual construction of a sentence calls for the subject to come first, the verb second, and the object or complement last, begin a certain percentage of your sentences with something before the subject. Although this would be done rarely in the lead of your piece, in the body of the piece the technique could be used about a third of the time.

Principle ways to do this are:

—Begin with a *verbal:*

Grinning, the commissioner admitted his suggestion was not to be taken seriously.

—Begin with a *verbal phrase:*

Agreeing with the mayor's recommendation, city council passed the tax increase.

—Begin with a *prepositional phrase:*

In less than ten minutes firemen were at the scene of the blazing house.

—Begin with a *subordinate clause:*

Because of the crime wave, policemen were put on a six-day week.

—Begin with a *coordinate conjunction.* But do so only if the meaning will be clear because of the preceding sentence. (The two preceding sentences furnish the example.)

IMPROVE SENTENCE QUALITY

Insure the quality of your writing in part by correct and skillful use of sentences. In addition to what we have discussed in this chapter there are

certain other things you can do to make certain your sentences are efficient—
clear, smooth flowing and effective. They include:
—Preferring the *active voice* over the passive.
—Using *repetition* effectively.
—Using *parallel construction* consistently.

USE THE ACTIVE VOICE

Writing for the mass media should come alive. It should carry the reader
along smoothly and swiftly. It should be descriptive and colorful. It should
depict action and movement. It can best be done by relying heavily on the
active voice. Description and color can be provided most effectively by action
verbs. In the following passage note how much more effective the active voice
is:

PASSIVE VOICE—The boy *was rescued* from the burning
house by the brave city fireman.

ACTIVE VOICE—A city fireman *fought* his way through the
flames and *carried* the boy from the burning house.

The active voice can be used effectively in advertisement to symbolize
action and give movement to the copy. An ad for the Air Force uses active
verbs thusly:

Graduating soon? If you're under 29—*make your move*—as an
Air Force Officer. *Move up fast* . . . *do important work* . . .
experience a challenge . . . *talk* with an Air Force recruiter today .
. . *Call* toll free . . .*Send* in the service card . . .

You should use the *passive* voice *occasionally* for variety in your writing
and usually if the receiver of the action is more important than the doer. For
example, if something happens to a prominent person, you would tell of the
event in the passive voice to give proper emphasis to the person acted upon.
Note use of the *active voice* in the following example where a non-prominent
person is involved:

A careening automobile leaped over the curb, crashed through
the fence and struck down a local man who was mowing his lawn
today.

Now assume the person injured in the accident is a person of prominence.
Your sentence might make note of that prominence by giving the emphasis to
the receiver of the action by using the *passive voice*:

State Sen. Joseph Brown was seriously injured today when an
automobile jumped the curb, smashed through a fence and struck
him as he was mowing his lawn.

USE REPETITION FOR ADDED EMPHASIS

Occasionally you will find it effective to *repeat phrases or words* to achieve
strong emphasis in a particular situation. Advertising writers use repetition in

independent clauses or short sentences to achieve their points. An advertisement might repeat a clause in this way:

A savings account at First National Bank brings you peace of mind: *it provides* funds for an emergency at any time; *it provides* a place to save for your child's education; *it provides* security for your retirement years.

Repetition can be a useful tool for a news writer on occasion, especially one writing news to be broadcast. A newsman might try to add emphasis to a sentence using repetition in the following way:

The mayor made it clear to union representatives *he will not* approve a pay raise, *he will not* approve a pension fund increase and *he will not* approve other fringe benefits while the strike continues.

The repetition might indicate the forcefulness with which the source made the remarks better than could any other method.

USE PARALLEL CONSTRUCTION

One way to make your sentences clearer to your reader is to make certain you use *parallel structure*. This means you put similar ideas within your sentences in the same grammatical construction. If an idea is expressed in a phrase, other ideas of equal weight should be expressed in a phrase. If one idea is expressed in a gerund or an infinitive, other ideas of equal weight should be expressed in similar constructions. Suppose you were writing a story about a switch from use of oil to use of coal by the city's power company. If you wrote about the benefits of the move in this way, it would be non-parallel, awkward and unclear:

Saving taxpayers money, Mayor Dwyer said the switch to coal would provide unlimited electricity during the power shortage, and employee retraining is minimal.

How much better your story would read if you listed the benefits in parallel construction in one of the following ways:

All Active Voice Verbs

Mayor Dwyer said the switch to coal would save taxpayers money, provide unlimited electricity during power shortage and require minimal employee retraining.

Multiple Subject

Taxpayer savings, unlimited electricity during the power shortage and minimal employee retraining would result from the switch to coal, Mayor Dwyer said.

Prepositional Phrases

The switch to coal is being made to save taxpayers money, to provide unlimited electricity during the power shortage and to require minimal employee retraining, Mayor Dwyer said.

Demands of *parallel construction* also dictate that you keep various parts of your sentence in the same *person, voice, tense, mood, number.*

In the following sentences, note there is a switch in person in the first example, with the corrected version following:

WRONG—As *one* enters the exhibition hall, *you* see hundreds of paintings along the walls. (First person becomes second.)

BETTER—As *you* enter the exhibition hall, *you* see hundreds of paintings along the walls. (All second person.)

In the next version, note the switch in voice in the first example, with corrected version following:

WRONG—Firemen *sped* to the fire scene, and the blaze *was extinguished* within minutes. (Active voice becomes passive.)

BETTER—Firemen *sped* to the scene and *extinguished* the blaze within minutes. (Active voice remains active.)

In the following sentences, note the switch in tense in the first example, followed by the corrected version:

WRONG—The first two batters *struck out,* and the rout of the visiting team *begins.* (Past tense becomes present.)

BETTER—The first two batters *struck out* and the rout of the visiting team *began.* (Past tense stays past.)

In the following sentences, note the switch from imperative to indicative mood in the first example, followed by the corrected version:

WRONG—*Keep* your thermostat turned down to save fuel, and *you should caulk* window cracks. (Mood changes.)

BETTER—*Keep* your thermostat turned down to save fuel and *caulk* window cracks. (Mood stays same.)

And finally, note the change in number in the first example, followed by the corrected version:

WRONG—*Every homeowner* should file for homestead exemption by April 1 or *they* will lose *their* homestead exemption. (Singular becomes plural.)

BETTER—*Every homeowner* should file for homestead exemption by April 1 or *he* will lose *his* homestead exemption.

LEARN TO AVOID SENTENCE TRAPS

This book is not intended to replace a complete writing manual, with comprehensive coverage of punctuation, grammar, word usage, correct sentence usage, and all of the errors that can mar writing. It is intended to be used along with a writing handbook of general rules and practices. This book concentrates on writing for mass media specifically, with some review of writing problems in general. With that understanding you should be aware of certain *sentence faults* which are common among inexperienced writers and which can mar the efforts of more experienced writers on occasion. Such *sentence traps* include:

—*Lack of agreement between the subject and verb.*
—*Lack of agreement between the pronoun and its antecedent.*
—*Vague pronoun reference.*
—*Misplaced modifiers.*
—*Comma splices.*
—*Dangling constructions.*

Subject-Verb Agreement

Often, when words stand between the subject and the verb, beginning writers become confused and fail to observe the grammatical rule that a verb must agree with the subject of a sentence *in number*. The following sentence is an example of such an error:

> The *police squad,* including two detectives and two patrolmen, *are* near a solution to the robbery Capt. Walker said.

Of course the word "squad" is the subject of the sentence. It is a collective noun and takes the singular verb. The sentence should have read:

> The police *squad,* including two detectives and two patrolmen, *is* near a solution to the robbery, Capt. Walker said.

Pronoun-Antecedent Agreement

Whenever you use a pronoun that refers to antecedents used earlier in the sentence, make certain that *the pronoun agrees in number with the antecedent* to which it refers. An example of failure to do this follows:

> The tax assessor said *each* of the homeowners must file an appeal if *they* are not satisfied with *their* assessment.

Of course it should read:

> The tax assessor said *each* of the homeowners must file an appeal if *he* is not satisfied with *his* assessment.

Vague Pronoun Reference

Beginning writers sometimes fail to make certain that the *pronoun* used clearly refers to a *noun* used elsewhere in the sentence or in the previous sentence. You would be wise to exert care in editing your copy. One of the most common errors is using a pronoun that refers only to an implied noun, as in this sentence:

> At the police station, *they* questioned the suspect about the burglary.

If you will analyze that sentence carefully, you will see that the policemen who did the questioning were only implied. The pronoun *"they"* refers to *nothing* in the sentence.

Don't be afraid to *repeat the noun*. If the pronoun is too far from its antecedent, you create a problem for the reader. While it may seem monotonous to repeat words, it is better to be repetitious than unclear.

Sometimes a sentence will be constructed so that there are two possible nouns to which a pronoun might refer. Make certain the reader/listener/viewer will clearly understand the sentence even if you have to rewrite it. An example of a pronoun that could refer to either of two nouns:

> Mayor Dwyer met with the union president, Walter Smith, to discuss *his* latest contract proposal.

The reader/listener/viewer would have no way of knowing from this sentence whether Mayor Dwyer or negotiator Smith made a new proposal. A sentence recast to eliminate the confusion might read:

> Mayor Dwyer met with the union president, Walter Smith, to discuss the union's new contract proposal.

Or . . .

> Mayor Dwyer met with union president, Walter Smith, to discuss the latest contract proposal made by the city.

Misplaced Modifiers

Humor in your writing brightens it up and makes the reader happy. It is a quality to be desired. But the humor should be provided intentionally. You do not want the reader to laugh at your serious passages. The following sentence might provide a laugh for the reader, but at the writer's expense:

> In discussing the plight of the refugees made homeless by the flood, Red Cross officials said volunteers are needed to prepare hot meals in the worst way.

Obviously the writer did not mean to imply that poor cooks are wanted, but that the need for volunteers is acute. He could rewrite to eliminate the *misplaced modifier:*

> In discussing the plight of the refugees made homeless by the flood, Red Cross officials said there is an acute need for volunteers to prepare hot meals.

It is not unusual for *misplaced modifiers* to creep into the writing of even experienced authors. As a beginner, you must be extremely cautious. Rewrite when you have time, and always read your copy carefully to catch such errors.

Comma Splices

You must take care not to join sentences or independent clauses with a comma. This structure would be incorrect:

> The commissioner was unable to answer, he did not have the budget figures with him.

You could correct it by making it two sentences:

> The commissioner was unable to answer. He did not have the budget figures with him.

You could make the last part of the sentence a dependent clause used after the main clause or before:

> The commissioner was unable to answer because he did not have the budget figures with him.

> Because he did not have the budget figures with him, the commissioner was unable to answer.

Or you could join the two dependent clauses with a semicolon:

> The commissioner was unable to answer; he did not have the budget figures with him.

Dangling Constructions

An easy trap to fall into in your writing is to write a phrase or clause, usually introductory, that does not directly modify anything in the sentence, or seems to modify an unrelated word. This can be unclear to the reader as well as ungrammatical, and, worse, it can be unintentionally funny, as in this incorrectly written ad:

> Filled with gas, you can drive the Ajax sedan 350 miles before you have to look for a filling station.

Of course, the ad does not mean that you must have indigestion to achieve economical operation, but that is what it seems to say. By rephrasing such a sentence, avoid the unintentional humor. Rework the sentence to make certain *the car is filled with gas and not the driver:*

> Filled with gas, the Ajax sedan will carry you 350 miles between filling stations.

To avoid such errors and others, make certain you analyze your sentences carefully. Learn what is correct and write to be effective and correct.

SUGGESTED EXERCISES

1. Take a news story from the paper, one that you think is well written and is at least 150 words long. Do a complete sentence analysis of the story in the following steps.

   a. *Do a sentence length profile.* Count the number of words in the story. Then count the number of sentences. Divide the number of sentences into the number of words to get a sentence average. Analyze how many sentences are considerably longer than the average, how many are considerably shorter than the average, and how many are within five words of the average. Analyze the order of the sentences and determine if the length and the order contribute to the quality of the piece.

   b. *Do a sentence structure analysis.* Determine how many and which sentences are *simple declarative sentences,* which are *compound, complex, compound/complex, interrogative, imperative, periodic, sentence fragments,* or have something before the subject. Try to determine how the sentence structure contributed to the quality of the story.

c. *Do a quality analysis.* Determine the percentage of active verbs, as opposed to passive verbs, whether repetition was used effectively, and if parallel construction was maintained at all times.

d. *Determine if the piece had any other sentence faults.*

2. Do an analysis of an advertisement, following the same procedure as outlined in Exercise No. 1.

3. Make the same analysis of a poorly written piece to determine how it could be improved. Then rewrite the piece trying to correct the shortcomings.

4. Make the same analysis of an original piece you have written. Then rewrite it seeing if you can improve the sentences and the overall piece.

5. Correct the following sentences which contain examples of the more common sentence faults. Determine what is wrong and correct it.

   a. The team decided they would honor the coach.

   b. Hoping for a job, the employment agency gave him the news there were no openings.

   c. Most of her knitting was practical. The afghan for example.

   d. Neither the owner nor the dogs was happy.

   e. Television is a means of relaxation and many people need it.

   f. If one wants a job done right, you must do it yourself.

   g. John, along with the other members of the debate team, were honored for the victory.

   h. Janie finally learned to ride her bicycle after trying for several days on Friday.

   i. When Mary finally caught the teacher's eye she quickly looked away.

   j. The blood transfusion stabilized the patient, the doctor left.

   k. He entered the room. He saw John was there. He moved across the room. He spoke to John. He got angry with John. He left the room.

   l. The new television news show is interesting, lively, and informs the viewer.

   m. She was trying out for cheerleader, being hired right away.

   n. The nationwide problem of forced utility cutoffs have not been felt in Yourtown, said a utility representative.

   o. The police commissioner said the city needs 20 new patrolmen to enforce the law desperately.

Chapter VIII

PARAGRAPHS:
KEEP THEM SHORT AND EFFICIENT

Someone discussing human anatomy with Abraham Lincoln is said to have asked the future president how long he thought a man's legs ought to be. Lincoln, whose own long frame probably prompted the question, is reported to have replied, "Just long enough to reach from the ground to his hips."

The same thing could probably be said about a paragraph. It ought to be long enough to reach from the paragraph ahead of it to the paragraph that follows it. That is not as witty as Lincoln's answer, but it probably is about as good a definition. Paragraphs, like legs, can vary greatly in length and in other qualities.

A more traditional definition of a paragraph is that a paragraph is a unit of composition made up of a topic sentence and other sentences that relate to the topic sentence. The topic sentence expresses the main idea of the paragraph. The other sentences expand on the idea, limit it, explain it, but are always related to the idea expressed in the topic sentence. The number of sentences in a paragraph can vary from one, common in a newspaper story, to a dozen or more, quite unusual in writing for the mass media but common in essays, academic treatises, some fiction, and other literary forms. Short paragraphs are preferred in news stories, feature stories, and advertisements in print for reasons of:

—*Appearance.*
—*Efficiency.*

SHORT PARAGRAPHS LOOK BETTER IN PRINT

Short paragraphs *look better* in newspaper and magazine stories and advertisements. They break up the long gray masses of type and make the stories and ads look more inviting to the reader. Newspaper and magazine columns are often quite narrow, ranging from less than two inches wide to rarely more than three inches. Such narrow columns of type provide great flexibility for editors in laying out their pages, but make paragraphs run longer than they would were the columns wider.

Short paragraphs permit the printer to provide relief from the dull gray print by putting space between the paragraphs. In addition, the paragraph indentation provides a natural break in the lines of type. When you are reading the newspaper, take note of how the short paragraphs break up the monotony of solid print.

SHORT PARAGRAPHS MAKE IT EASIER FOR THE EDITOR

Short paragraphs make it much easier for editors and production people to function. Short paragraphs facilitate:
—*Editing stories for publication.*
—*Changing stories between editions.*
—*Making corrections in stories.*
—*Laying out pages.*

Short Paragraphs Facilitate Editing

In *editing stories,* editors often must make wholesale changes in the copy to make it more readable and more effective. Editing often involves moving certain information to other sections of the piece. Because it is easier to move entire paragraphs in this sort of reorganization, it is convenient if the paragraphs are short.

In *cutting stories* to fit a designated space, it is easier to cut paragraphs than sentences within paragraphs. Where editors are using modern electronic terminals, of course, all editing steps are simplified. But even on a video display terminal, where a story is on a screen rather than on paper, it is easier to add, delete or move paragraphs than it is sentences.

When combining stories from two sources, merging paragraphs is easier than merging sentences.

Changing Stories Between Editions

When stories substantially change from one edition to another, a newspaper editor has to make quick additions, deletions, and changes. If paragraphs in the original story are short, it is much easier to merge the new information with the old information that will remain in the story.

And it is also easier to kill dated information not wanted in the new version of the story. All changes must be in complete paragraphs. The paste-up worker cannot paste a new sentence into an old paragraph and have everything come out even because the sentence might begin any place on a line and end any place. He must have a whole new paragraph to work with. Even on the new electronic systems it is quicker to cut out and/or add entire paragraphs.

Short Paragraphs Facilitate Making Corrections

The same things as above apply if it is necessary to make a correction in a story or an advertisement. If something is deleted, the entire paragraph has to be reset. If something is added, the same is true. When corrections are made on page proofs, the stories or ads are already pasted up on the page, ready to be photographed and be made into a plate for the press. There is less danger of a mistake being made if the entire paragraph in which an error exists is replaced. In the old letterpress system of printing, where each line was a separate piece of lead, simple corrections were often made into worse errors when the corrected line was placed in the story but the wrong line removed.

Then there were two copies of one line—the one containing the error and the corrected one—but an entire line was missing. The story made no sense. That is not likely to happen when the whole paragraph is replaced either in letterpress printing or the more modern, more widely used photo-offset printing.

Short Paragraphs Help in Layout

Short paragraphs in newspaper stories are extremely helpful in laying out a story on a page. They can help when the story is a bit too short to fill the allotted space. The paste-up worker can cut the story apart at the paragraphs and leave a bit of extra space between each paragraph so the story fills the space. Obviously, more paragraphs mean less space between each paragraph, and the reader will be less aware that an adjustment was made.

Shorter paragraphs can also help in layout when the story is too long. As mentioned earlier it is much easier to cut out entire paragraphs without having to reset type than to cut out a portion of a paragraph.

HOW LONG SHOULD PARAGRAPHS BE?

It is difficult to give any stringent rules as to the ideal length of paragraphs. Generally, *newspaper story paragraphs* should average about three type-written lines, and rarely be longer than five lines. *Magazine stories,* often set in wider columns and read under different circumstances, can be somewhat longer. However, they are usually shorter than paragraphs in more formal writing. *Advertising paragraphs* vary in length from extremely short in certain display ads to average in institutional ads. The length of *paragraphs for broadcast* stories or commercials is not a critical matter. The public will not see the copy unless it is in a television visual, in which case print rules apply. But a short-to-medium broadcast news item is often written in one long paragraph. The same is true of commercials. Often an 80-word commercial for a 30-second spot or a 160-word commercial for a 60-second spot will be written as one paragraph. But the length of broadcast paragraphs is just not as important a consideration as is the length of paragraphs for print material. If the broadcast writer feels frequent paragraphing will help the announcer in the delivery of the material, he can make frequent paragraphs.

A random analysis of newspaper stories, magazine articles and print advertisements confirms earlier observations about the number of sentences making up paragraphs in the various print forms. A survey of 10 newspaper stories, 10 magazine articles and 10 print advertisements shows the following:

In the *newspaper stories,* 90 of the paragraphs, or 58.8 percent, were made up of one sentence; 34 of the paragraphs, or 22.2 percent, were made up of *two sentences;* 18 of the paragraphs or 12.3 percent were made of *three sentences;* and 11 of the paragraphs, or less than 7 percent, were made up of *4 or more sentences.*

In the *magazine articles,* the preponderance of short sentences was not so apparent, but 61 percent of the paragraphs were made up of fewer than four sentences. The figures were 22 of the paragraphs, or 11 percent, had *one sentence;* 56 of the paragraphs, or 29 percent, had *two sentences;* 40 of the paragraphs, or 21 percent, had *three sentences.* But magazine articles definitely had more longer paragraphs: 32 of the paragraphs, or 17 percent, had *four sentences* and 42 of the paragraphs, or 22 percent, had *five or more sentences.*

You must remember that what has been quoted above are averages. There were wide variations within the divisions, but the averages make a good guide in writing the various forms.

MASS MEDIA PARAGRAPHS MUST BE TRUE PARAGRAPHS

In your reading you might have developed the idea that paragraphs in writing for newspapers and broadcasting have no standards. That could be understandable when you might read a news story in which all of the paragraphs are single sentences or an ad in which a sentence fragment forms a paragraph of its own. Nevertheless there are rules for paragraphs written for the mass media. They must pass the same test for integrity as sentences. They must have:

—*Unity.*
—*Coherence.*
—*Proper Emphasis.*

Unity

The *unity* of a paragraph is insured in the same way that the unity of a sentence is insured—the writer puts nothing in the paragraph that does not relate to the main idea of the paragraph. Of course that leaves a lot of leeway. A topic sentence could be so broad that you could write a paragraph several pages long and not destroy the unity. You could write a topic sentence such as this:

"You can protect your good health by taking the following steps. . . "

. . . and go on and write a book about preventive medicine in one paragraph. Of course, that is a bit of an exaggeration. You would undoubtedly break the book up, logically, into chapters, and the chapters into paragraphs without destroying unity. The thing about *unity* is that *anything* you insert into the paragraph that doesn't belong will destroy the unity. But you can break up large paragraphs into smaller paragraphs without destroying unity. This serves as a compelling reason why you should make *smaller paragraphs* in stories and advertisements for print media. In the following examples, note how information written in one long, formalized paragraph can be logically broken up into several short paragraphs.

Two local men were injured when an automobile smashed into a tree on the Lake Road early today. Victims of the accident were identified by police as John P. Jones, 36, 3402 W. Main St., and Fred Simpson, 29, 2936 S. 32nd St. Taken to Lakeview Hospital, the men were listed in fair condition. Jones received a broken left leg, and Simpson a concussion. Jones, the driver, was charged with operating a vehicle without a proper license.

The paragraph above is a logical paragraph. Everything in the paragraph applies to the opening topic sentence. But a newspaper reporter would probably write the story this way:

Two local men were injured when an automobile smashed into a tree on the Lake Road early today, police said.

Victims of the accident were identified by police as John P. Jones, 36, 3402 W. Main St., and Fred Simpson, 29, 2936 S. 32nd St.

Taken to Lakeview Hospital, the men were listed in fair condition. Jones received a broken left leg, and Simpson, a concussion, a hospital representative said.

Jones, driver of the car, was charged with operating a vehicle without a proper license, police said.

In the second example, you can see that the one paragraph becomes four. Nevertheless, *unity is preserved.* The first paragraph gives the general information about the accident. The second paragraph identifies the participants; the third dwells only on the injuries; and the fourth discusses the police action in the case. There are *logical divisions* and *legitimate paragraphs.*

Coherence

Coherence is maintained in paragraphs just as it is in sentences, by organizing things in the proper order so the reader/listener/viewer gets the message clearly, quickly and effortlessly. This means the order of the sentences in a paragraph will be logical. The following paragraph illustrates a *logical, coherent* paragraph:

The mayor said the new library will be built as quickly as possible. Contracts will be let next week. He said it is hoped that work will begin in a month, and the building completed by the end of the year. Dedication is tentatively planned for early next January.

If that same information had been handled in the following way, it still would be logical and coherent.

The major said dedication of the planned new library is scheduled for early next January. The building should be completed late this year, he said. Work is expected to start next month after contracts are let next week, the mayor said. Work will be completed as soon as possible.

The second example is still *coherent.* While the time order was reversed, it remained consistent from *then to now.* The first example was organized in a time frame of from *now to then.* But if you interfere with logical organization, whatever that organization may be, you lose coherence. The way *not* to write the paragraph would be:

Contracts for the new library will be let next week, the mayor said. The building will be completed by the end of the year. Work is expected to start next month, the mayor said. Dedication is tentatively set for next January. The work will be done as soon as possible.

The example is poor. You have the reader/listener/viewer jumping all around in time. He will be confused and lost. You have *destroyed the coherence* of the paragraph.

Proper Emphasis

Emphasis in paragraphs, like emphasis in sentences, is closely related to the structure of the paragraphs. Just as the emphasis in a *loose sentence* is at the beginning and the emphasis in a *periodic sentence* is at the end, the emphasis in a *deductive paragraph* is at the *beginning* of the paragraph and the emphasis in an *inductive paragraph* is at the *end* of the paragraph. The forms of paragraphs most widely used in writing for the mass media are:

—*The deductive paragraph.*
—*The inductive paragraph.*
—*The complex deductive paragraph.*

The Deductive Paragraph

In the *deductive paragraph* the topic sentence is at the beginning of the paragraph and the emphasis is at the beginning. The topic sentence usually makes a general statement, and the sentences following give specific information that develops the general statement. An example of the use of a deductive paragraph would be the following biographical information that might appear in a news or feature story about an individual:

He served in World War II. A pilot in the U.S. Army Air Corps, he flew 25 combat missions over Europe. He won the Distinguished Flying Cross and the Air Medal with five Oak Leaf Clusters. He was discharged in 1945.

Or an advertisement might have this deductive paragraph:

The Acme Empress Necklace is a masterpiece of the jeweler's art. Its diamonds dazzle. Its style entrances. Its silver setting enchants.

The deductive paragraph would be used extensively in news stories. Like the inverted pyramid news story form, it goes from the general to the specific.

The Inductive Paragraph

The *inductive paragraph* is the reverse of the deductive paragraph. The topic sentence of the inductive paragraph is at the end of the paragraph. And the paragraph is organized with specific sentences leading to the general statement and the strongest emphasis at the end. An example of an inductive paragraph in an advertisement:

It gets great mileage. It costs a pittance. It looks like a million. It drives like a dream. It is the Ajax Jackel, built with care for you.

While the inductive paragraph would not be used as often in news stories as would the deductive paragraph, it might be used in a sociological story as follows:

They come from the slums of Haiti. They escape from the tyranny in Cuba. They flee from the hunger in rural Mexico. They are the new immigrants to the United States who are seeking the opportunities that brought all but the native Indians to these shores.

The inductive paragraph also lends itself to persuasive writing. It could be used in an editorial in this way:

Do you want candidates who are honest? Do you want public officials who care? Do you want to get rid of the hacks in government? You can, but only if you will take the time and interest to vote.

The Complex Deductive Paragraph

Just as in the compound sentence, equal treatment is given to two ideas equal in value, the *complex deductive paragraph* can give equal value to two parts of an idea in two topic sentences within a paragraph. The complex deductive paragraph begins with more than one general sentence and then goes on to specifics. An example of such an organization in a news story:

The merit pay plan will be adopted by the university. It will involve some workers but some will be exempt. Staff people will come under the new plan; however, faculty and administrators will not. There are 6,000 staff employees and 4,000 faculty and administrative personnel.

Paragraph Emphasis Through Typography

While paragraphs for news and feature stories and advertisements for print media achieve emphasis in the traditional way by the organizational plan of the paragraphs, there are also ways paragraph emphasis can be achieved typographically. They include:

—*The use of all capital letters.*
—*The use of larger type.*
—*The use of italics.*
—*The use of underlining.*
—*The use of indented paragraphs.*
—*The use of bullets (●), arrows (→), or checkmarks (✓).*

—The use of very short paragraphs.
—The use of color.

Some of these methods are used in news stories, but more are used in advertisements, promotion letters and direct mail advertisements, brochures, etc.

Most of these typographical emphasis techniques have been used throughout this book. They can be illustrated while discussing them.

THE INCLUSION OF AN ALL-CAPS PARAGRAPH IN A STRING OF PARAGRAPHS SET IN CAPS AND SMALL LETTERS WOULD INDEED GIVE THAT PARAGRAPH A CERTAIN EMPHASIS.

Using larger type in a paragraph than the type in other paragraphs surrounding it will, of course, give emphasis to that paragraph.

So will the use of italic letters in a long paragraph or a short paragraph like this one.

Underlining part of a paragraph or the whole paragraph and/or indenting it will make it stand apart from those that are not underlined or indented.

The use of bullets, arrows, or check marks will:
— Make the paragraph stand out.
— Make the paragraph shorter.
— Provide more white space in the story.

A very short paragraph stands out.

Setting a paragraph or part of a paragraph in color will call attention to it. Adding a postcript in handwriting will add a dash of emphasis.

Public relations writers probably make the most effective use of "emphasizing by paragraphs." The methods discussed above are excellent for many publications prepared by public relations writers. Effective use of paragraphs can improve brochures, promotion letters, annual reports, posters, print and T.V. visuals, training and educational materials and convention and showroom displays.

The main message that beginning writers need to get about making paragraphs more effective is that they should be shorter than paragraphs in other sorts of writing. But they should be true paragraphs, with *unity, coherence,* and proper *emphasis.*

SUGGESTED EXERCISES

1. Analyze paragraphs from several news stories in the newspaper you read for unity, coherence, and emphasis. Determine if the lengths of the paragraphs are similar to the lengths suggested in this chapter and if the paragraphs are effective.

2. Do the same thing with advertisements and feature articles.

3. Look through the circulars and promotion materials you and members of your family get in the mail. Note the use of typographical differences, color and handwriting to add emphasis to the message in the promotion. Using those same techniques, do a promotion or direct mail advertisement for an organization in which you are active—a school organization, church group, civic group. If the directors of the organization like your effort, try to *get them to use the piece.*

4. Find a piece of expository writing that utilizes paragraphs that are long and contain several sentences. It could be from a textbook, how-to-do-it brochure, an academic work, or any factual informational source. Then rewrite the piece, breaking the paragraphs up into many shorter ones without destroying the smooth flow of the writing or using any paragraphs that lack unity, coherence, or proper emphasis.

Chapter IX

SPECIFICS: THEY ENHANCE INTEREST

Students often complain that their studies are not "relevant." They mean the information being presented does not seem to relate to themselves, their friends or family, or any part of their lives, experience, or future. In truth, everything one can study is in some way related to him. Everything one can read or hear is in some way related to the reader/listener/viewer. The problem is one of failure to communicate. The writer or teacher has failed to present the material in such a way that the reader/listener/viewer can relate it to his or her own life. Such failure often occurs because writers are presenting abstract ideas or theories in such a way that no one can recognize how the information bears on life. The challenge of the communicator is to present information in such a way that the reader/listener/viewer will relate to it. Communication can most easily be achieved by using specifics to establish a relationship between the audience and the information to be conveyed. The theory, inasmuch as it is possible, should be accompanied by applications which are concrete enough to relate to the reader/listener/viewer's general knowledge. Failure to use specifics is a universal problem for those writing for a mass audience, and only those who recognize the problem will be successful in being read or listened to. Writers who have recognized this include:

—*Arthur Brisbane*, the editor of Hearst newspapers early in the century who drew readers to a story by changing the headline from "Rome had Poor Sanitary Conditions" to "Pity the Poor Romans, They Had no Toilets." "Sanitary conditions" is an abstract term; "toilet" is specific.

—*Ernie Pyle*, a popular war correspondent of World War II, who told of the war by writing the individual stories of hundreds of soldiers in the lines, one at a time. Stories of huge armies moving and vast fronts were too general to the readers. They couldn't relate. But the story of Pfc. Joe Brown, 19, from Sioux Falls, S.D., was specific. The reader could relate to Joe.

—*The writers of the most popular best-seller ever*, the Bible, who told stories and parables, sang psalms, discussed a great variety of people by name. The reader can relate to this.

—*The novelist* who has characters drinking Jack Daniels, not just whiskey, wearing Calvin Kleins, not just slacks, smoking Parliaments, not just a cigarette, driving a Jaguar, not just a car.

—*Writers of advertisements* who create specific personalities to sell their products—Mrs. Olson, Mr. Wimple, Dominick the monk, Rosie the waitress.

—*The sports writer* who in writing a 300-word story might have 100 specific facts—names, scores, past scores, records, top performers, future performers, attendance figures, etc.

You, as the writers mentioned, would do well to make a conscious effort to use as many specifics as you can in a piece for the mass media. You can do so by:

—*Using the exact word.*
—*Giving the reader the information in human terms.*
—*Using good direct quotes when possible.*

FIND THE EXACT WORD

The beauty of language is that there is usually a word to fit the situation that confronts the writer. Chances are that the word is stored in your brain if you just let it come out. If not, quick reference to a dictionary of synonyms will produce the exact word needed.

You use the *exact word* to serve the reader/listener/viewer. You use the exact word to insure accuracy, clarity, and understanding. This is the minimum you owe the audience and the source of your information. If you use specific names, addresses, ages, and identifications, you have done a professional job.

Take names, for instance. The specific name should be used for a great variety of reasons.

—You would be surprised how many *John Swansons* there might be in a given circulation area of a newspaper or broadcasting facility. You'll help narrow it down if you say this is *John Cameron Swanson*, if that is the name he goes by. And why shouldn't you use the name he goes by? Would you say you read a poem by Edgar Poe? No! You would say Edgar Allen Poe. Doesn't *John Cameron Swanson* deserve the same accuracy?

—You might think it is an affectation for a person to call himself or herself *J. Cameron Swanson*, but that is his or her privilege. Nobody ever saw J. Edgar Hoover, late FBI director, ever referred to as Edgar Hoover. *J. Cameron Swanson* deserves the same courtesy.

A name is a very personal thing. If someone wants to make his name a bit more exclusive, Engelbert Humperdink has that right. By using the specific name, you enhance the chance that readers/listeners/viewers will recognize the person referred to.

Addresses—These are also important to the reader/listener/viewer. Along with the exact name, an address quickly helps the reader determine if the name and address coincide with the person he or she may know. It also helps eliminate persons with the same names but different addresses.

Ages—The reader/listener/viewer needs the subject's age to determine if the person being discussed is the one known. If it is *J. Cameron Swanson*, 48,

MARINE LEAVING LEBANON. Specifics are helpful for understanding larger, more complex situations. Here, a photo showing a marine loaded and obviously "moving out" graphically symbolizes an entire troops' exodus. Remember, this is not limited to photos, your words can accomplish the same thing through specific examples. (Courtesy Wide World of Photos/AP.)

of 1000 North Main St., it is the father; if it is *J. Cameron Swanson*, 21, of the same address, it is probably the daughter.

Use Specific Nouns

If you think of writing as creating scenes or pictures for your reader/listener/viewer, you will see the importance of using specific words. People can only visualize concrete words from their own experience. Use concrete nouns to place the reader/listener/viewer at the scene you are describing:

GENERAL—One *person* was hurt when his car crashed into a tree.
SPECIFIC—*John Brown* was hurt when his car hit a tree.

GENERAL—The *building* was leveled by the fire.
SPECIFIC—The *two-story motel* was leveled by the fire.

GENERAL—The *weather* was unbearable.
SPECIFIC—The *heat and humidity* were unbearable.

Use Specific and Colorful Verbs

GENERAL—The dancer *walked* across the stage.
SPECIFIC—The dancer *wriggled* across the stage.

GENERAL—The tailback *ran* into the end zone.
SPECIFIC—The tailback *sprinted* into the end zone.

GENERAL—The squirrel *climbed* the tree.
SPECIFIC—The squirrel *scampered* up the tree.

Use Specific and Colorful Adjectives

GENERAL—The *tall* center scored 36 points.
SPECIFIC—The *6-foot-10* center scored 36 points.

GENERAL—The *handicapped* woman made her way across the *busy* intersection as the traffic officer halted all traffic.
SPECIFIC—The *blind* woman crossed the *six-lane highway* as the traffic officer halted *30 cars and two buses*.

GENERAL—He wore a *soiled* tie.
SPECIFIC—He wore a *gravy-stained* tie.

Use Specific Adverbs

GENERAL—She smiled *disapprovingly* at the suggestion.
MORE SPECIFIC—She smiled *icily* at the suggestion.

GENERAL—He reacted *quickly* to the warning.
MORE SPECIFIC—He reacted *instantly* to the warning.

GENERAL—The fog drifted *slowly* across the moor.
MORE SPECIFIC—The fog drifted *lazily* across the moor.

Give Specific Details

Readers love details. Novelists know this. You can observe and learn from them. Admittedly, the novelist has more room to give details, but within the limits of your space, give what details you can.

Miscellaneous—Was it a *compact car* involved in the accident? Or better yet, make it a *Volkswagen Rabbit*. Was the speaker tall or short, sloppy or well dressed, bald or with curly hair?

Ads—In ads, tell the reader/listener/viewer the specific colors of your product; not *blue*, but *aqua*, or *navy;* not *red* but *cerise* or *burgundy;* not *green*, but *nile* or *olive*. Tell the reader/listener/viewer the engine in your car generates *156 horsepower*, that it gets *24.9 miles per gallon of gasoline*, that the car has a wheelbase of *109.5 inches.*

Think about the last murder mystery you read. The detective did not take a drink of *whiskey*. He took a drink of *Vat 69*. He did not get into his *car*. He got into his *Ferrari Special*. He did not shoot his *gun*. He shot his *Smith and Wesson snub-nose .38*. The author knew these details would make the story more vivid to you, the reader. The same holds true in your writing. You'll be writing non-fiction, but you can be just as specific.

Use the Word With the Specific Meaning You Want to Convey

Finding the word to convey the exact meaning you wish to convey is not always easy. The meaning of a word can change depending on the context in which it is used. It might be acceptable in an informal situation, but not otherwise. For example, a *policeman* might refer to himself as a *cop* among other policemen and in an informal setting. But if a reporter referred to a police officer as a *cop*, he or she might be criticized. *Police Officer* would be the correct formal usage. Some words are *factual* and would mean the same thing to everyone. *Police Officer* is a *factual* word. It is the *accepted term* for an *officer of the law. Cop* is a *slang* word, which may be as much a *value* word as a *factual* one, depending on the way it is used and by whom. When the *police officer* says proudly, "I am a cop," he or she is placing a value judgment of *"desirable"* on the word. When a lawbreaker snarls, "He's a cop," the lawbreaker also is putting a value judgment on the word—only the value is *negative* or *"undesirable."* So the reporter, who is attempting to be objective, should say "police officer."

Another clear-cut example of seeming synonyms actually having different meanings is the widespread practice of beginning writers mistakenly trying to avoid saying *"said"* too often and falling into the trap of using words with opinion, or at least diverse meanings as substitutes. Most people *"say"* things for publication. But young, inexperienced writers have them *stating, declaring, claiming, adding, denying, affirming, avowing, averring.* All of these words have meanings that are slightly different from "said," and those differences may not be *factual* or may add *opinion.* The word "claim," for example, has an implication that it might not be true or that it remains to be proven. To "avow" means broadly to swear to. To "add" means that the person said what is quoted immediately after what had been reported earlier, and such is often not true. So you see that by being careless with synonyms you can step into a quagmire of inaccuracy or misrepresentation.

Use Words For Their Connotation Not Denotation

Usage and acceptance by the public give words their meaning. They often mean different things to the public than they did when they were coined. An example is the word "dame," used for woman. Women of high social caste in England are called "dames," but in America the word "dame" has a tough, or socially undesirable connotation. So a word may *denote* one thing yet have a different *connotation.* Or words may seem synonymous but have different *connotations. Examples:*

Being *drunk* is dreadful. Being *inebriated* is not so bad.
Being *skinny* is not desirable. Being *lean* is okay.
Being *stubborn* is deplorable. Being *hardheaded* is practical.
Being *intelligent* is good. Being a *grind* is socially unwise.
Being *inquisitive* is a virtue. Being *nosy* or *prying* is a vice.

The list is almost endless, and the best cure is careful and diligent use of a dictionary. However, the writing and editing committee of the Associated Press Managing Editors Association has published a list of the 50 most common errors in newspaper writing. Most of them are based on using words incorrectly, often because the *connotation* of the words *differs* from the *true meaning* the writer really wanted to express. Although the list is not complete, it is a good place to start understanding how easy it is to get into trouble if you fail to use the exact word you need.

A LIST OF 50 COMMON ERRORS IN NEWSPAPER WRITING
AS PREPARED BY THE WRITING AND EDITING COMMITTEE
OF THE ASSOCIATED PRESS MANAGING EDITORS ASSOCIATION

1. *Affect, effect.* Generally, AFFECT is the verb; EFFECT is the noun. "The letter did not AFFECT the outcome." "The letter had a significant EFFECT." But EFFECT is also a verb meaning to bring about. Thus: "It is almost impossible to EFFECT change."
2. *Afterward, afterwards.* Use AFTERWARD. The dictionary allows use of AFTERWARDS only as a second form. The same thinking applies to TOWARD and TOWARDS. Use TOWARD.

3. *All right.* That's the way to spell it. The dictionary may list ALRIGHT as a legitimate word but it is not acceptable in standard usage, Random House says.
4. *Allude, elude.* You ALLUDE to (or mention) a book. You ELUDE (or escape) a pursuer.
5. *Annual.* Don't use first with it. If it's the first time, it can't be annual.
6. *Averse, adverse:* If you don't like something you are AVERSE (or opposed) to it. ADVERSE is an adjective: ADVERSE (bad) weather, ADVERSE conditions.
7. *Block, bloc:* A BLOC is a coalition of persons or a group with the same purpose or goal. Don't call it a BLOCK, which has some 40 dictionary definitions.
8. *Compose, comprise.* Remember that the parts COMPOSE the whole and the whole is COMPRISED of the parts. You COMPOSE things by putting them together. Once the parts are put together, the object COMPRISES or is COMPRISED of the parts.
9. *Couple of.* You need the OF. It's never "a couple tomatoes."
10. *Demolish, destroy.* They mean to do away with completely. You can't partially demolish or destroy something, nor is there any need to say TOTALLY destroyed.
11. *Drown.* Don't say someone was DROWNED unless an assailant held the victim's head under water. Just say the victim DROWNED.
12. *Different from.* Things and people are different FROM each other. Don't write that they are different THAN each other.
13. *Due to, owing to, because of:* We prefer the last.
Wrong: The game was canceled DUE TO rain.
Stilted: Owing to rain, the game was canceled.
Right: The game was cancelled BECAUSE OF rain.
14. *Ecology, environment.* They are not synonymous. ECOLOGY is the science of the relationship between organisms and their ENVIRON-MENT.
Right: The laboratory is studying the ECOLOGY of man and the desert.
Right: There is much interest in animal ECOLOGY these days.
Wrong: Even so simple an undertaking as maintaining a lawn affects ECOLOGY.
Right: Even so simple an undertaking as maintaining a lawn affects our ENVIRONMENT.
15. *Either:* It means one or the other, not both.
Wrong: There were lions on EITHER side of the door.
Right: There were lions on EACH side of the door.
16. *Fliers, flyers:* Airmen are FLIERS. Handbills are FLYERS.
17. *Flout, flaunt.* They aren't the same word; they mean completely different things and they're very commonly confused. FLOUT means to mock, to scoff or to show disdain for; FLAUNT means to display ostentatiously.

18. *Funeral service.* A redundant expression. A funeral IS a service.
19. *Head up.* People don't HEAD UP committees. They HEAD them.
20. *Hopefully.* One of the most commonly misused words, in spite of what the dictionary may say. HOPEFULLY should describe the way the subject FEELS.

    For instance: Hopefully, I shall present the plan to the president. (This means I will be hopeful when I do it.)

    But it is something else again when you attribute hope to a nonperson. You may write: Hopefully, the war will end soon. This means you hope the war will end soon, but it is not what you are writing. What you mean is: I hope the war will end soon.
21. *Imply and infer.* The speaker implies. The hearer infers.
22. *In advance of, prior to.* Use before; it sounds more natural.
23. *It's, its.* ITS is the possessive; IT'S is the contraction of IT IS.

    Wrong: What is IT'S name?

    Right: What is ITS name? ITS name is Fido.

    Right: IT'S the first time he's scored tonight.

    Right: IT'S my coat.
24. *Lay, lie.* Lay is the action word; lie is the state of being.

    Wrong: The body will LAY in state until Wednesday.

    Right: The body will LIE in state until Wednesday.

    Right: The prosecutor tried to LAY the blame on him. However, the past tense of LIE is LAY.

    Right: The body LAY in state from Tuesday until Wednesday.

    Wrong: The body LAID in state from Tuesday until Wednesday. The past participle and the plain past tense of LAY is LAID.

    Right: He LAID the pencil on the pad.

    Right: He HAD LAID the pencil on the pad.

    Right: The hen LAID an egg.
25. *Leave, let:* LEAVE ALONE means to depart from or cause to be in solitude. LET ALONE means to be undisturbed.

    Wrong: The man had pulled a gun on her but Mr. Jones intervened and talked him into LEAVING HER ALONE.

    Right: The man had pulled a gun on her but Mr. Jones intervened and talked him into LETTING HER ALONE.

    Right: When I entered the room I saw that Jim and Mary were sleeping so I decided to LEAVE THEM ALONE.
26. *Less, fewer.* If you can separate items into the quantities being compared, use FEWER. If not, use LESS.

    Wrong: The Rams are inferior to the Vikings because they have LESS good linemen.

    Right: The Rams are inferior to the Vikings because they have FEWER good linemen.

    Right: The Rams are inferior to the Vikings because they have LESS experience.

27. *Like, as.* Don't use LIKE for AS or AS IF. In general, use LIKE to compare the nouns and pronouns; use AS when comparing with phrases and clauses that contain a verb.
Wrong: Jim blocks a linebacker LIKE he should.
Right: Jim blocks the linebacker AS he should.
Right: Jim blocks LIKE a pro.
28. *Marshall, marshal.* Generally, the first form is correct only when the word is a proper noun: John MARSHALL. The second form is the verb form. Marilyn will MARSHAL her forces. And the second form is the one to use for a title. FIRE MARSHAL, Stan Anderson, FIELD MARSHAL Erwin Rommel.
29. *Mean, average, median.* Use MEAN as synonymous with AVERAGE. Each word refers to the sum of all components divided by the number of components. MEDIAN is the number that has as many components above it as below it.
30. *Nouns.* There's a growing trend toward using them as verbs. Resist it. HOST, HEADQUARTERS and AUTHOR, for instance, are nouns, even though the dictionary may acknowledge they can be used as verbs. If you do, you'll come up with a monstrosity such as: "Headquartered at his country home, John Doe hosted a party to celebrate the book he had authored."
31. *Oral, verbal.* Use ORAL when use of the mouth is central to the thought; the word emphasizes the idea of human utterance. VERBAL may apply to spoken or written words; it connotes the process of reducing ideas to writing. Usually it's a VERBAL contract, not an ORAL one, if it's in writing.
32. *Over and more than.* They aren't interchangeable. OVER refers to spatial relationships. The plane flew OVER the city. MORE THAN is used with figures. In the crowd were MORE THAN 1,000 fans.
33. *Parallel construction.* Thoughts in series in the same sentence require parallel construction.
Wrong: The union delivered demands for an increase of 10 percent in wages and to cut the work week to 30 hours.
Right: The union delivered demands for an increase of 10 percent in wages and for a reduction in the work week to 30 hours.
34. *Peddle, pedal.* When selling something, you PEDDLE it. When riding a bicycle or similar form of locomotion, you PEDAL it.
35. *Pretense, pretext.* They're different, but it's a tough distinction. A PRETEXT is that which is put forward to conceal a truth.

He was discharged for tardiness, but this was only a PRETEXT for general incompetence.

A PRETENSE is a "false show"; an overt act intended to conceal personal feelings.

My profuse complaints were all PRETENSE.

36. *Principle, principal.* A guiding rule or basic truth is a PRINCIPLE. The first, dominant or leading thing, is PRINCIPAL. PRINCIPLE is a noun; PRINCIPAL may be a noun or an adjective.
Right: It's the PRINCIPLE of the thing.
Right: Liberty and justice are two PRINCIPLES on which our nation was founded.
Right: Hitting and fielding are the PRINCIPAL activities in baseball.
Right: Robert Jamieson is the school PRINCIPAL.

37. *Redundancies to avoid:*
Easter Sunday. Make it EASTER.
Incumbent Congressman. CONGRESSMAN.
Owns his own home. OWNS HIS HOME.
The company will close down. THE COMPANY WILL CLOSE.
Jones, Smith, Johnson and Reid were all convicted. JONES, SMITH, JOHNSON AND REID WERE CONVICTED.
Jewish rabbi. Just RABBI.
During the winter months. DURING THE WINTER.
Both Reid and Jones were denied pardons. REID AND JONES WERE DENIED PARDONS.
I am currently tired. I AM TIRED.
Autopsy to determine the cause of death. AUTOPSY.

38. *Refute.* The word connotes success in argument and almost always implies an editorial judgment.
Wrong: Father Bury REFUTED the arguments of the proabortion faction.
Right: Father Bury DISPUTED or DISAGREED WITH the arguments of the proabortion faction.

39. *Reluctant, reticent.* If he doesn't want to act, he is RELUCTANT. If he doesn't want to speak, he is RETICENT.

40. *Say, said.* The most serviceable words in the journalist's language are the forms of the verb TO SAY. Let a person SAY something, rather than declare or admit or point out. And never let him grin, smile, groan or giggle something.

41. *Slang.* Don't try to use "with it" slang. Usually a term is on the way out by the time we get it in print.
Wrong: The police cleared the demonstrators with a sunrise bust.

42. *SPELLING.* It's basic. If reporters can't spell and copy editors can't spell, we're in trouble. Some ripe ones for the top of your list:
It's CONSENSUS, not concensus.
It's RESTAURATEUR, not restauranteur.
It's DIETITIAN, not dietician.

43. *Temperatures.* They may get higher or lower, but they don't get warmer or cooler.
Wrong: Temperatures are expected to warm up in the area Friday.
Right: Temperatures are expected to rise in the area Friday.

44. *That, which.* THAT tends to restrict the reader's thought and direct it the way you want it to go. WHICH is nonrestrictive, introducing a bit of subsidiary information.

For instance: The lawnmower that is in the garage needs sharpening. (Meaning: We have more than one lawnmower. The one in the garage needs sharpening.)

—The lawnmower, which is in the garage, needs sharpening. (Meaning: Our lawnmower needs sharpening. It's in the garage.)

—The statue that graces our entry hall is on loan from the museum. (Meaning: Of all the statues around here, the one in the entry hall is on loan.)

—The statue, which graces our entry hall, is on loan. (Meaning: our statue is on loan. It happens to be in the entry hall.)

Note that "which" clauses take commas, signaling they are not essential to the meaning of the sentence.

45. *Under way, not underway.* But don't say something got under way. Say it STARTED or BEGAN.

46. *Unique.* Something that is unique is the only one of its kind. It can't be very unique or quite unique or somewhat unique or rather unique. Don't use it unless you really mean unique.

47. *Up.* Don't use it as a verb.
Wrong: The manager said he would UP the price next week.
Right: The manager said he would RAISE the price next week.

48. *Whom, who.* A tough one, but generally you're safe to use WHOM to refer to someone who has been the object of an action. WHO is the word when the somebody has been the actor.

—A 19-year-old woman, to WHOM the room was rented, left the window open.

—A 19-year-old woman, WHO rented the room, left the window open.

49. *Who's, whose.* Though it incorporates an apostrophe, WHO'S is not a possessive. It's a contraction for WHO IS. WHOSE is the possessive.
Wrong: I don't know WHO'S coat it is.
Right: I don't know WHOSE coat it is.
Right: Find out WHO'S there.

50. *Would.* Be careful about using WOULD when constructing a conditional past tense.
Wrong: If Soderholm WOULD NOT HAVE HAD an injured foot, Thompson wouldn't have been in the lineup.
Right: If Soderholm HAD NOT had an injured foot, Thompson wouldn't have been in the lineup.

WRITE IN SPECIFIC HUMAN TERMS

In writing you must try to produce in the minds of the readers/listeners/viewers the information, emotions and pictures as you see them. The closer you can keep to specific information, feelings, actions and descriptions, the clearer the picture will be. People find it difficult to relate to abstractions and generalities. There are several steps you can take to make your writing more specific.

—*Write about specific people with a problem rather than problems without people.*

—*Draw on the cultural interests of the audience.*

—*Cite examples, case histories, anecdotes.*

Write About Individual People

Many newspaper stories are about momentous events involving complex problems, huge institutions, and thousands of people. One of the best ways to make a story understandable is to tell how the situation affects individuals. The crime problem can best be understood by telling how it affects a victim of crime, an individual criminal, or a police officer. It is difficult for the reader/listener/viewer to relate to the information that 200 citizens were attacked and robbed over a given period. However, if you discuss the case of one person, giving the specific details, the reader/listener/viewer can readily understand and better appreciate the overall problem. For example, you might want to get into a story on muggings in this way:

James Brown will be 55 next Tuesday. He had planned to spend his birthday with his daughter and grandchildren in Neartown as he has done for the past four years since his wife died. But he won't make it this year.

Brown of 2366 North Pear St. is in Hometown Hospital in a coma. He has been in a coma for the past three weeks since he was beaten and robbed by unknown assailants while walking home from his night shift job at Hometown Telephone Co.

Brown is one of 86 persons beaten and robbed in this city during the past six months.

You could then give more statistics and other angles about the problem, perhaps even cite other individual cases, and give more about Mr. Brown's experience. The same technique can be used in stories about:

—*Inflation.* Select families from various income levels and show how inflation has affected each of them.

—*Welfare.* Select a family on welfare and tell why it is on welfare, how it fares, etc.

—*Disaster victims*—The devastation of a flood or tornado becomes much more real to the public when the effects on individuals and families are told in print or electronic news stories. General statistics do not have the same impact.

STORIES ABOUT SPECIFIC PEOPLE ENHANCE INTEREST. Writing about how life's complex situations affect one person brings a story closer to the reader. Two sisters who reduce the larger problems of life into everyday terms are shown on their 65th birthdays last year. Abigail Van Buren (Dear Abby) and Ann Landers deal with problems of human behavior in hundreds of newspapers throughout the country on a daily basis. (Courtesy Wide World of Photos)

The examples above merely introduce the possibilities. Myriad situations can be made more readable by citing specific people involved.

The technique is useful in advertising as well as news stories for print or broadcast media. You could take the following approach in an advertisement about life insurance:

Gary Larson is a happy young man. He has a fine home, a loving wife, Nancy, and three great kids, Gary, Jr., 10, Jeff, 8, and Nancy, 5. Gary makes good money as a cost accountant and has a bright future.

But Gary's happiness was clouded by a nagging thought: What would become of his home, his wife, his children and his plans for their future if anything happened to him?

Gary contacted his Security Insurance Co. agent who worked out a plan to free Gary from his worry. If anything happens to him, his house will be paid for, income assured so his wife can raise the children and send them to college.

Gary sleeps better now that his family is secure.

How about you? Maybe you ought to see a Security agent.

The advertising writer made a point by telling of a specific individual. The reader/listener/viewer can identify with that individual.

Draw On The Reader's Cultural Background

People feel comfortable with things that are familiar to them. If they visit strange places, most of them will still seek out that which is familiar. The traveler to Europe will try to find an American hamburger. He or she will be delighted to find a Hilton Hotel, Holiday Inn, or Howard Johnson's. And when two American strangers meet in a foreign setting, they react like lifelong friends.

You can make use of these human tendencies in your writing. In making comparisons or references, draw on factors in the popular culture with which your reader/listener/viewer is familiar and comfortable. Such factors can include popular books, movies, songs, nursery rhymes, or advertising slogans. Writers often make reference to familiar quotations, plays of Shakespeare, and other literary data in common usage.

Over the past several years there has been a series of movies on the subject of possession of a human by the spirit of the devil. The first of these was The Exorcist. When this type of picture was at its height of popularity, a commerical on television extolled the virtues of eliminating bugs from your house by using "Pest-orcist."

A news writer could quote Shakespeare in a news story in this way.

"To be or not to be . . ." is the question Shakespeare's indecisive Hamlet could not answer. Whether there is to be or not to be a new industrial park on Pearl Street seems as perplexing to the city zoning commission.

For the fourth week, the commission last night failed to take action on a proposed zoning variance to clear the way for construction of the $2 million development.

Of course, if a business was fortunate enough to have been mentioned by a literary figure, the business could run an ad such as this one that appeared in an English publication for *Annabelinda Dress Designers:*

"She by my lady's advice desires a new dress of the new silk striped stuff very pretty. So I went to Annabelinda presently, and bought her a very fine rich one—the best I did see there and much better than she desires or expects." —Samuel Pepys Diary, 1660.

You could even call on a universally recognized nursery rhyme to give that comfortable feeling to a reader/listener/viewer and lure him or her into reading or listening to a news story:

Mother Hubbard with her bare cupboard would be right at home today. With high prices compounded by shortages of staples, the modern housewife is finding it harder and harder to keep her shelves stocked.

Cite Examples, Case Histories, Anecdotes

As a professional writer, you will find yourself at a disadvantage. The reader/listener/viewer owes you nothing; you owe him or her everything. He or she doesn't have to pay full attention to what you write; and doesn't have to accept what you say; and doesn't have to believe you. It is up to you to show what you say is true. You can't do it with general statements. You must *cite examples, give case histories, give anecdotes* to prove what you say.

A broadcast commercial might give examples to back up a general statement in this way:

Super-Grow Fertilizer will increase the yield from your tobacco field. John Grove of Decatur, Ga., reports his tobacco crop yield 20 percent higher since he switched to Super-Grow; William Grant of Sumter, S.C., reports his increase since switching to Super-Grow is 28 percent; and Silas Potter of Winston-Salem reports a 33 percent increased yield from using Super-Grow. Shouldn't you switch to Super-Grow?

A print or broadcast editorial might make its point more strongly if it details a case history the reader/listener/viewer can identify with:

Overhaul of regulations governing private pension plans in this country is long overdue. In an era where consumer rights are a growing concern, private pension plans continue to victimize unsuspecting Americans.

Take the case of William and Margaret Johnson.

Johnson is 62. For the past 18 years he has worked as a bookkeeper for a company in Neartown. He went to work for the firm when he was 44 after his own business went bankrupt.

The pay wasn't too good, but once burned, Johnson was reluctant to strike out on his own. In his new job he came under a company-paid pension plan that would provide a dignified retirement for his wife and himself, so he hung on.

William and Margaret Johnson lived frugally. They looked forward to retirement at 65 when they could travel and enjoy life.

Three months ago, the Johnson retirement plans evaporated. The company was sold. The new owners made some changes. Johnson was fired. He found he was not eligible for a pension because he had not been with the company 20 years. He got two weeks' pay with his termination notice.

William Johnson is looking for a job, and having a hard time finding one at 62. He can't afford to take his Social Security benefits at a reduced rate now, and even at 65, will be hard pressed to survive let alone retire in dignity.

The story of William and Margaret Johnson is just one of the horror stories that illustrate the shocking inadequacy of pension regulations.

The editorial writer could then detail the shortcomings of pension regulations and offer suggestions for improvement. By showing how the problem affects one family, the writer has brought the problem into specific focus for the reader/listener/viewer.

Another specific tool you should adopt is the use of anecdotes. They work beautifully in establishing personality and character when you do a feature story about a person. It does you no good to merely tell the reader/listener/viewer that the subject of your profile has a certain personality quality of character trait. You have to prove it. Anecdotes show the personality or character in action. The reader/listener/viewer can arrive at his own judgment. Study profile stories in magazines. You will note that most of them rely on anecdotes. Often the writer of a profile will lead off with an anecdote, sprinkle others throughout his piece, and end with another anecdote.

Let's say you were doing a story about a professor who really was absent-minded. You might start this way:

Professor Amos Pickett was irritated when his wife did not meet his plane last month when he returned from a three-day physics conference in Atlanta. He had been a bit out of sorts since he had failed to find his return ticket and had to buy a one-way ticket in Atlanta.

He was about to call his wife when a neighbor, Fred Samples, offered to drive him home. His wife was working in the yard as Samples pulled up to the Pickett home.

"What happened to your car, Amos?" she asked.

"My car? Oh, my God, I did drive to Atlanta, didn't I?"

Leaving his car in a motel parking lot in Atlanta is perhaps the most dramatic illustration that Amos Pickett's concentration on his work leaves little room for incidentals.

The writer could then discuss the dedication of his subject, citing other examples of his single-mindedness (absent-mindedness, if you will).

Use Direct Quotes

Quoting *the exact words* of the subject of a story or the source can add specificity to your writing, but only if the quotes are terse, colorful, descriptive and lively. Most direct quotations are not. The writer has the job of editing carefully to make certain the direct words are superior to a rewritten paraphrase.

The decision often depends on the medium. In television you obviously want to put the subject or source on camera and mike for a realistic presentation. But even then you should do a lot of editing. The same applies to radio. You want to have the subject on tape if possible. But again you should edit sharply to retain only those quotes which will enlighten the listener and not bore him.

When you are writing for print media—newspapers or magazines—there is less pressure to use direct quotes. But they are still desirable when they are interesting, to the point, descriptive. Use quotes when they:

—*Express strong opinions.*

—*Tell of a person's experiences in his own words.*

—*Are shocking or bizarre.*

—*Are humorous, sad, angry, or express some other emotion strongly.*

—*Give information as concisely, clearly, and in as interesting a way as you could by paraphrasing the words.*

—*Add immediacy, accuracy, objectivity, authenticity to a story.*

Some examples of the use of such quotes:

—*Expressing a strong opinion.* The Iranian hostage who, when asked upon his return to the United States if he would return to Iran, answered, "Yeah, in a B-52." The B-52, of course, is an Air Force bomber.

—*Telling of their own experiences:* Many of the hostages gave graphic descriptions of their fears, dashed hopes, anger and frustration. There were repetitions of such expressions as "they kept me blindfolded," "they kept threatening to shoot me," "they kept me in the hole," "they kept my hands tied," "they made me sleep on the floor," "they awakened me in the middle of the night and moved me to another room," "I thought I was going to die."

—*Making a shocking and bizarre statement:* The regent of a state university who complained of low morals on campus by saying that "dormitories have been turned into taxpayers' whorehouses."

—Making an emotional statement, humorous, sad or angry: Asked how he felt when lack of support forced him to withdraw from the race for the presidency, Congressman Morris Udall said, "It hurts too much to laugh, and I'm too big to cry." Or the statement made by Winston Churchill to a female member of Parliament who accused him of being drunk in the chamber: "Yes, Madam, I am drunk. But you are ugly. Tomorrow, I will be sober."

—Giving information as well as the reporter could paraphrase it: Describing the experience with a "walking catfish," a rare species of amphibious fish that have migrated from Southeast Asia to the west coast of Florida, a Clearwater (Florida) fishing enthusiast said she heard what she thought was a snake in the grass near where she was fishing. "It wasn't a snake. It was my fish. He jumped out of the pail like a fish, but he ran off like a snake." (From a story in the St. Petersburg Times, April 22, 1984.)

—Adding immediacy to a story: Stories about speeches, meetings, debates, etc. should have quotes to indicate that things are said even when the quotes are not world shaking. For example, a story on an immigration bill paraphrased Democratic Majority Leader Thomas (Tip) O'Neill that the bill had little support other than from the Judiciary Committee members who drafted it. The story added, "I haven't seen anybody out there who is truly interested in it," O'Neill said. "The Hispanics say it's the most devastating thing that could happen to them."

—Adding accuracy to a story that might be of interest to certain groups or to researchers: Direct quotes in a story interrupted by ellipses (three dots . . .) to indicate something was being left out of the quotes, indicated the strength of feeling of the speaker and gave notice to researchers to look in the Congressional Record for additional quotes that did not make the story. In discussing Sen. Jesse Helms' moves to block a proposed holiday in honor of Martin Luther King, Rep. Edward Markey, D-Mass., said in opposing Helms' stand: "We have listened to this venom for three centuries. . . and we have had enough."

—Adding authenticity and authority to a story: In quoting such an authority figure as the president, you might want to use a direct quote merely to add authenticity. In discussing a proposal on arms reduction made by President Reagan, a story paraphrased much of the information, but directly quoted the president as saying, "We want to reduce the weapons of war, pure and simple." That may not have been a priceless piece of prose, but reproducing the exact words of a world leader on a particular occasion added authenticity.

When Not To Use Quotes

Do not use direct quotes to give statistics, biographical facts, or background material which is routine and a matter of record: You can do that much more efficiently by putting such information in your own words. Never switch from one source to another by going right into a direct or indirect quote. The reader will not know you have switched from quoting one person to another. Tell him first with a transitional phrase as in the following:

Management indicated it is ready to sign a new contract on the basis of an offer made to strikers at the Acme Bottling Co. Tuesday. Company president Phillip Jones said, "We feel the offer is a fair one. It matches the rise in the cost of living and is all we can give."

Union spokesmen for the 300 strikers were not optimistic. "The offer is just not enough," negotiator Jack Burns said. "We have fallen behind in recent years and must catch up."

Without the italicized introductory sentence, the reader initially would think Jones was still speaking. Let your reader know when you are about to quote someone new.

Do not put anything in quotation marks that is not in the exact words of the speaker quoted: Quotation marks indicate that the reporter has not altered the speaker's quotes at all. The only exception for altering something within quotation marks is to correct an inadvertent grammatical error the speaker might have made. You can change a present tense verb to past tense if that is what the speaker meant. If the person speaking has made several errors because of an unfamiliarity with the language or total lack of knowledge of formal English, stick to a paraphrase. Do not needlessly make a person appear ridiculous or semi-literate.

Do not place attribution haphazardly in a direct quote: Do not write, "We are going to raise taxes," said the mayor, "because city workers must have a raise." Get the attribution out of the middle of the quote. Place it at the end or at the beginning.

Do not attribute a direct quote to more than one person: Do not write, "The parade was great," all who attended said.

Do not attribute a direct quote, or even a paraphrase, *to an institution:* Do not say, "She is in critical condition," said the hospital. Quote an official or representative of the hospital.

Do not follow a paraphrase with a direct quote that says the same thing: Do not write:

Union President Charles Wells said that if the company does not increase its pay offer by Friday, the Union will strike.

"We will strike on Friday if the company doesn't give us more money," said union president Charles Wells.

SUGGESTED EXERCISES

1. In the following sentences indicate where and how the writer could have been more direct and exact in word choice:

   a. The town turned out in record numbers to pay respect to its most elderly citizen who passed away from a malignancy.

   b. One of the best fishing places in the world is where the Indian River and the Spanish River come together at a junction near a third river, the Mexican.

   c. A sheriff's deputy, acting as spokesman, said the widow of the dead man will be evicted from her living quarters unless she comes across with the rent by 10 a.m. day after tomorrow.

   d. Grand Jury will meet in the month of August to consider several urgent pieces of business.

   e. James, who is 26 years old, will pursue a course of study at Harvard University. He will major in the field of biology.

   f. The teacher opened each class by starting the roll call.

   g. Jensen, who lives in the 1200 block of Main Street, was arrested by policemen while committing a misdemeanor by disturbing the peace.

   h. The city commissioners will take up the traffic problems at the Monday night meeting in the city hall where the citizens will have the opportunity to air the complaints they have for the commissioners.

   i. The judge detailed, item for item, the events that led to the imposition of the injunction ordering the union to halt all picketing endeavors.

   j. Hospital spokesmen said the victim sustained abrasions, contusions and lacerations on her body in addition to her head area.

2. Study profiles in such magazines as *Reader's Digest, New Yorker, People, Saturday Evening Post, Playboy,* other similar magazines and note how often the profiles begin with anecdotes, have other anecdotes sprinkled throughout, and end with another anecdote or with a specific quote. Do a profile of an interesting personality you know using an anecdote as a lead, include at least two other anecdotes, and end with an anecdote or a good quote. Also try to use at least three figures of speech—similes or

metaphors. Give yourself added credit if you can effectively use an extended metaphor.

3. Clip some stories out of the newspaper, stories that can be rewritten and made more readable. You might try meeting announcements or meeting followup stories that have been written dully. In rewriting them try to utilize something from the popular culture to help relate them more closely to the reader. Use literary allusions, songs, ad slogans, popular sayings.

Chapter X

GATHERING INFORMATION: KNOW YOUR SOURCES

It often comes as a shock to beginning students of writing for the mass media that they must go farther than their imaginations or personal experiences for material. This is understandable. Until they begin studying advertising, broadcasting, journalism, or public relations, their writing has centered on their own experience, inventiveness, or knowledge. In English classes, too often their writing has been limited to essays on their experiences or opinions, short stories carved from their imaginations, or essay test answers based on their required readings in school. Some of the luckier students, those who had teachers rooted in reality and those who worked on their school newspapers or yearbooks, have already learned to deal in facts. Others must learn quickly that writers of pieces for the mass media deal in facts.

Gathering facts, far from being a minor aspect of writing, is almost an equal partner in most efforts. News reporters for print or broadcast outlets, for example, must be skilled in gathering information. Often the reporting aspects of a reporter's job are more important than the writing. Given the choice between someone who is an excellent reporter and an average writer and someone who is an excellent writer but a poor reporter, most editors will take the good reporter. The average writing can be sharpened in editing if the facts are there, but if essential facts are missing, no amount of rewriting will result in a good story. The *facts* are the *story*. The *writing* is the *package*.

Although today most reporters write as well as gather facts, many newspapers in big cities employ "leg" reporters who never write anything. They call in their information to rewrite which does the writing. Not too many years ago there were reporters in large cities who could not even type. This is rare now, but every reporter will at times call the facts of a story into a newspaper or broadcast station to be written by another.

It is not just the reporter who must gather facts. Facts are also essential for the advertisement writer, the editorial writer and the public relations writer. Facts or opinions of people other than the advertiser will be more likely to move the modern well-informed consumer than unsupported statements. Editorial writers too had better marshal facts and expert opinion if they hope to mold opinions or motivate actions. Unsupported personal opinions will do little more than bore the reader. Public relations writers, who may be asked to write everything from news releases to ads, brochures, annual reports and speeches, had better be up to their keyboards in facts.

Facts to be used in news stories and feature stories for print or broadcast and advertisements for print or broadcast can come from only two basic sources:

—People, or primary sources.
—Printed materials, or secondary sources.

PEOPLE MAKE THE BEST SOURCES

In journalism, as opposed to academic writing, writers are much more likely to get most of their information from people involved in the story, feature, or advertisement. The types of people news reporters, ad writers or public relations writers might talk to either by phone or in person are almost endless. However, here are a few examples:

Public Officials—Presidents, governors, mayors, legislators, educators, city and county councilmen or commissioners, law enforcement officials from all levels of government, appointed department heads, auditors, inspectors, political party leaders and public information officers for all of these.

Private Officials—Corporation officers at all levels, union officials, directors of social and professional associations, civic and social leaders, business leaders, private school educators, directors of advertising, owners of wholesale and retail outlets and public information officers for all of them.

Expert Sources—Jurists and lawyers, economists and other social scientists, meteorologists and other physical scientists, physicians and other authorities on health, religious leaders and other philosophers, athletic directors and head coaches, marketing and sales specialists, educators, other specialists in all walks of life and their public information directors.

Participants—Pickets, strikers and strike breakers; protestors, demonstrators, rioters; lawbreakers, victims of lawbreakers, victims of accidents, and bystander victims; athletes, sports officials and judges, coaches, trainers; entertainers; speakers, panel members, hosts, emcees; sellers, buyers, consumers; all participants in any activity that is either newsworthy or advertised.

Witnesses—The writer as witness, the expert witness, the involved witness, the casual witness, spectators, audience members, viewers and listeners.

Confidential Sources—Reporters all have confidential sources in both public and private organizations where officials and executives are reluctant to talk about a newsworthy situation. These sources are often subordinates—assistants, secretaries, minor associates—who, for reasons both noble and otherwise, are willing to talk to reporters anonymously. They will be discussed elsewhere in this book.

The General Public—Members of the public at large should be used as sources when the writer is trying to determine public opinion, as in a poll, seeking reaction of the general public to a story of significance, trying to determine desires for a proposed new product or acceptance of one already on the market, trying to determine what mass media consumers like in news, features and advertising.

As a general rule a writer should talk to as many sources as possible before writing a news story, feature, print or broadcast advertisement. More sources and more viewpoints can only result in a more accurate, more objective, more complete and more interesting piece. However, there will be occasions when the press of deadline will force the reporter to use a system of priorities in trying to reach various sources. In contacting sources, the reporter should observe the following general rules:

—*Talk to people as close to the story as possible.*
—*Talk to people who have clear authority to speak.*
—*Talk to witnesses who are trained to observe.*
—*Rely on cooperative expert sources.*

Get Close to The Story

The reporter should always get close to the core of any story or advertising assignment by contacting the source closest to the information. In news this means talking to the *participants*. In advertising it means talking to the *merchant* advertising, the *buyer* who decided to invest in a particular item at a particular time, and the *salespeople* who will be dealing with the *consumers*.

Take a specific news situation that might arise. When a reporter arrives at the scene of a news situation, whether by accident or on assignment, he or she should immediately locate participants and talk to them. With any luck the response will be more fortunate than the legendary reporter on the way to lunch who spotted a man falling from the third floor roof of a building. The reporter braked to a stop, got out of his car, ran to where the man was lying on the grass, and said:

"What happened?"

The dazed victim looked up at the reporter and said, "I don't know. I just got here!"

All seriousness aside, as Steve Allen might say, the more likely situation might demand quick decisions be made when a reporter arrives at the scene of a fire. He might be confronted with several sources, and must make instant decisions as to which he should approach first. Let's assume the following situation.

—A woman, wrapped in a blanket, is lying on the sidewalk in front of a house. Smoke is coming from broken windows on the second floor.
—Firefighters are on ladders pouring water into the second floor room of the house.
—The fire chief is directing the firefighting from the porch.
—A policewoman is keeping both automobile and pedestrian traffic moving.

—A man, about the same age as the woman lying on the sidewalk, is sitting on the porch comforting a young child.

—Several neighbors or passers-by are standing back from the house and front yard watching the proceedings.

Who should the reporter talk to first?

Assuming the woman lying on the sidewalk is a victim of the fire, the reporter should talk to her first. Why? She may know better than anyone else what happened, and assuming an ambulance may be on the way to take her to a hospital, the reporter may only have a short time to talk to her.

Should the reporter ask the policewoman if he may talk to the victim?

Definitely not, because the policewoman, if asked to make a decision, will play it safe and say, "No." She might try to stop the reporter from talking to the victim if he doesn't ask, but then she might not.

To whom should the reporter talk next; the possible husband and child of the victim, the fire chief, the policewoman or witnesses in the crowd?

The husband, because he may be a participant and is more likely to know what happened, and he probably will accompany his wife to the hospital and be out of contact. The witnesses probably are unreliable, and the fire chief and the policewoman will be around for a while to give what they know.

And so it would go with similar situations. Contacting participants by phone or in person in a news event can gain a reporter a good story, an exclusive angle no one else has, or a time advantage over competitors. An alert wire service reporter in Detroit once called the home of Walter Reuther, a founding father of the CIO labor confederation and president of the United Automobile Workers, when the police radio reported a shooting in Reuther's neighborhood. Reuther himself answered the phone and told the reporter that, yes, he had been wounded by a shotgun blast through a window of his home. While he waited for the ambulance to arrive, he talked to the reporter who became the only reporter to have talked to Reuther before he landed in the hospital. Reuther did recover. There have been many instances of quick-dialing reporters getting interviews with victims, criminals and others who were making news at the time of the interview.

Getting news from participants is why correspondents covering the president go along wherever the president goes, if not on the president's plane then on a follow-up one. It is why sports writers fly with the visiting teams to the sites of athletic contests, and it is why they want to get into the locker rooms with note pads, recorders and cameras as soon as the game ends.

Go to the Top

The best source, if he can be reached, is usually the person at the top. He or she is the most authoritative spokesman both because he or she does have the authority to talk and the public will more readily accept his or her word. Any reader/listener/viewer will place more stock in a statement by the man or woman in charge. The person at the top is in a position to know what policy is and in a position to feel free to discuss policy. Subordinates sometimes do not know the full situation and are less willing to discuss a situation that is at all controversial. That is understandable. Why should they go out on a limb their superior may saw off later? The moral is clear: The writer should go first to the highest source available in seeking information.

Seek Out the Trained Witnesses

The reliability of witnesses varies considerably, as does their acceptance by the reader/listener/viewer. The writer should try to reach the trained uninvolved witness—the police officer, the fireman, the social worker, the sports official, the doctor, the nurse, the scientist, the researcher, the merchandiser, etc. Such witnesses are more likely to give accurate, unemotional, and knowledgeable answers to questions. And such witnesses will satisfy the desire of the reader/listener/viewer for quality sources.

Although trained witnesses are preferred in most instances, there are times when the writer wants to quote a variety of witnesses of an event. You may want to show viewpoints of several witnesses, trained or not, involved or not, emotional or not. Of course, if the trained witnesses are in any way involved in the news event, their statements become suspect. Then a variety of viewpoints, including and perhaps even limited to untrained witnesses, is preferred. Statements from a variety of witnesses are always good. Witnesses who are knowledgeable, uninvolved, unemotional and most likely to be accurate are the best witnesses.

Build A Stable Of Experts

All reporters should attempt to cultivate a variety of potential sources who are experts in a particular field. These should be people to whom a writer can turn for background information needed to place a particular news event in proper perspective. Examples of such experts would be physicians, lawyers, economists, urban or rural sociologists, labor relations consultants, realtors or land use planners, architects, military leaders, historians, policemen, fire officials, experts on various religions, educators, etc.

Such a list of available sources is not easy to build. Sources have to trust writers not to misquote them or misrepresent them by oversimplification. That trust comes slowly, and can be lost instantly. The reporter must accurately represent statements made by such sources or they will not continue to cooperate. Losing such sources makes the reporter's job much more difficult. He then has to find new sources or write stories lacking special insights expert sources could have provided.

INTERVIEWING IS AN INVALUABLE ART

Knowing who has information that will assist in writing a story or advertisement is to the writer like knowing that a bank has money. The information can't be used or the money spent until it has been obtained. Sometimes it takes as much persuasive skill to draw information from a source as it does to talk money out of a banker. Thus the art of interviewing is one that all writers must learn.

Informal Interviewing

Much of the interviewing done by reporters is the informal questioning that is involved in all stories. The questions are often obvious and routine. Reporters are seeking basic facts—names, ages, addresses, sites of events, times of events, explanation of how and why something is newsworthy. There often is little time for planning, and fortunately the obvious questions come readily to mind. Sometimes such questioning is live, at the scene of a news story, but often the information is obtained by telephone.

The Live Informal Interview

The reporter may conduct an informal interview alone with the source, or along with other reporters. If alone, the reporter has full opportunity to ask those questions he or she wants answered. In a group, the reporter will have to share the question time available with others. That can work well when other reporters come up with the right questions. It can be painful when incompetent reporters waste the time of the source and the other reporters. You may have to contact the source again either in person or by phone to get the answers you want. Such impromptu news conferences can be challenging, especially if the source is not eager to talk at all. Reporters sometimes have to ask questions under difficult conditions such as:

—While police are rushing a crime suspect from jail to a court appearance.

—While a union negotiator is hurrying from a conference room into a hotel suite to confer with his colleagues.

—While a president, governor, or mayor is hustling from his office to his car.

Reporters have to ask the really vital questions in the time available and hope the source will give some sort of answer that can add to a news story. Planning does not help much. Reporters must fall back on experience and instinct.

INTERVIEWING IS AN ART THAT ALL WRITERS MUST LEARN. It can be done live or over the phone and both fulfill different purposes. Telephone interviewing greatly expands the writer's reach and saves valuable time with fast-breaking stories. (Courtesy Wide World of Photos)

Interviewing by Telephone

Much informal interviewing is done by telephone. Many reporters never leave the office to cover major stories. They get information by telephone. The telephone, of course, extends the reach of the reporters tremendously. You can call anywhere on earth for all intents and purposes. News organizations have large phone bills because a phone call is cheaper than sending someone to the distant scene of a story. But most phone reporting is again of the routine informational type of informal questioning. In a fast breaking story being covered by telephone, you do not have much more preparation time than in live questioning situations, but you usually do not need a lot of preparation. Questions are obvious and routine. In interviewing by telephone, whether the interview is informal and brief (or more rarely extended and formalized), there are some rules you should follow:

—**Be Accurate:** It is dangerously easy to get information incorrect if the quality of the telephone transmission is poor. If you have difficulty in understanding what a source is saying, make every effort possible to double check. Ask the source to repeat the information more slowly. Ask him or her to spell names phonetically, if necessary. Repeat information back to the source for verification. If, when all this is done, you are not certain about the information, try to verify it in some other way before using it in a story. Just get it right.

—**Call back when necessary:** Don't hesitate to call a source back to verify information or to get more information that you forgot to get on the original call. The source will appreciate your thoroughness.

—**Get Permission to Tape Telephone Calls:** You may want to tape a telephone conversation with a source, either to play back if you are writing a story for radio or television, or just for your own convenience if you are writing for print. But you should never tape a source on the telephone without letting the source know you are making a tape. It is unethical. If you have the permission of the source, there is no reason you cannot tape a telephone conversation if it suits your purposes.

Formal Interviews Should Be Done Live

The rare occasion might arise when you would need to conduct a formal and extended interview by telephone. Once, for example, the late eccentric recluse Howard Hughes, who had not been seen for years, wanted to prove to the world he was alive without appearing in person. Reporters interviewed him by telephone and determined by their questions and his answers that they were, indeed, talking to the real Howard Hughes. But most extended and formal interviews are conducted live. The writer has ample time to set a convenient place and adequate time for the interview. He or she has time to adequately prepare questions for the interview. There are two basic types of formalized interviews:

—The informational interview.
—The personality profile interview.

Informational Interview

The emphasis on an informational interview is on the material a source has to give to the interviewer, not on the source himself. The informational interview is by far the more common type of interview. The profile interview is just a fraction of total interviews. In planning to conduct the informational interview, the interviewer should take certain steps. He should:

—Learn as much as possible about the subject matter.
—Learn as much as possible about the person to be interviewed.
—Prepare a list of questions to ask.

Knowing the Interviewee

No interview can be really productive if the interviewer does not know the person being interviewed. A relationship has to be established quickly between the questioner and the questioned. The person being interviewed cannot respond warmly if the questioner is not aware of what is of prime importance to the interviewee. Even Johnny Carson, probably the highest paid interviewer in the world, can, in his words, bomb occasionally. French actress Catherine Deneuve appeared on his show one night prepared to discuss her latest film. When Johnny mentioned that he had not seen the film, Deneuve iced up rapidly with typical French hauteur.

Interviewers less skilled than Johnny Carson had better beware of similar mistakes. If the interviewee has written a book, let the interviewer be aware of it. If the interviewee has won an award, let not that milestone be ignored. The interviewer should know about the source's job, triumphs, experience, expertise, and other interests.

Preparing Questions

The interviewer should never begin a scheduled interview without a list of prepared questions to ask. No one can rely on trying to think up questions as he or she goes along. He or she could run dry and be unable to think of what to ask next. The interview will then either end abruptly or drift off into idle conversation which will yield little for a story or ad.

Taking into consideration the particular knowledge the source has to offer and the purpose of the piece to be written or aired, the interviewer should carefully draft a list of questions the reader/listener/viewer would like answered in the piece. Suppose, for example, that the writer is about to interview a transportation specialist who has recommended that the city establish a bus system to provide for mass transit needs. He or she could prepare the following list of questions:

—How will the system be financed?
—How much will be subsidized by the city? The county? The state? The federal government?

—How much will fares be?

—How many people will use the system now? Five years from now? Ten years from now?

—How many buses will be needed? How many drivers? How many other employees?

—Will the system be operated by the city or a private company?

—How many routes will there be? What sections will they serve? How often will they run?

—Will they operate seven days a week? Will they operate only on business days?

—What was the decision based on? Was a study of needs made? A survey of potential riders? What were the results of the survey?

—When will the system be in operation?

—Has bus service been successful in similar communities?

—How will the city convince citizens to ride the bus instead of driving their cars?

—Will downtown parking be restricted to force people to use buses?

This list is not complete. No list of questions ever is. The writer should, if there is time, set the list aside for a day, or even a couple of hours. Then, when he or she returns to the list, he or she probably will have thought of some more questions to add. Even then the list will not be complete.

Conducting the Interview

Conducting the interview involves use of psychology, gentleness, aggression, persistence, cajolery, and tact at various times. At all times it requires detachment, patience, and quiet toughness. As an interviewer, you cannot allow yourself to be intimidated by a source regardless of the circumstances. You should not become involved with or influenced by the emotions of the interviewee. You should remain professional and never sound judgmental. Conducting an interview requires skill. In conducting an interview, you should:

—*Gain the confidence of the source.*

—*Put the source at ease.*

—*Be flexible in questioning the source.*

—*Be persistent and firm in seeking answers.*

—*Be patient and let the source talk.*

—*Take effective notes.*

—*Use a tape recorder ethically and without fanfare.*

Gaining Confidence of the Source

The interviewer gains the confidence of the source by being professional. The interviewer:

Arrives on time for the interview, dressed appropriately. Cutoff jeans and a slogan tee shirt might be fine for interviewing a surfer at the beach, but they look pretty silly in a business office.

Knows the subject at hand. Early in the preinterview discussion, the interviewer should make it apparent he or she is well versed in the subject matter of the interview. He or she should also demonstrate genuine and serious interest in the subject matter.

Keeps questions objective. The interviewer should word questions so that no inference of bias could be projected. If the questioner has to ask embarrassing, controversial and provocative questions, they can be stated clearly and with no inference of approval, disapproval or any other judgment factor.

Putting the Interviewee at Ease

While the interviewer should not waste the source's time at an interview appointment, a few minutes putting the source at ease is not time wasted. The interviewer can:

Massage the source's ego. Tell the source how much he or she enjoyed the source's book, lecture, an article about the source.

Divert source's attention to pleasant areas. The interviewer can get the source's attention momentarily on family, hobby, diversion. A glance around the source's office, if that is where the interview is being held, will yield conversation gambits—family photos, college documents, a bronzed golf ball for that hole-in-one, a commendation from the Boy Scouts to a volunteer, etc. If the interview is being held somewhere other than the source's office, the interviewer's prior research should provide similar conversation tips. If both are fans of the same sports team or TV shows they can talk about last week's game or show.

Speak softly and don't argue. The interviewer should take advice from former President Theodore Roosevelt who based his foreign policy on the premise of speaking softly but carrying a big stick. The questioner can do the same. He or she should ask provocative questions but ask them in a soft voice and without hostility. Some beginning interviewers feel they should debate the source. Argument is usually counterproductive. It is likely only to provoke hostility and non-cooperation. It is the opinion of the source that is important, not the opinion of the questioner.

Ask the easy questions first. Unless there is a time factor that dictates otherwise, the interviewer should ask the non-controversial questions first. This puts the source at ease and overcomes inhibitions. After the questioner has won the confidence of the source and has the source committed to the interview, he or she can ease into the tough questions at the end. By that time the source might be convinced the interviewer is interested in a rounded story and does not want to "hang" the source. The person being questioned is much more likely to be open and frank about the controversial questions at that time than if the questions are thrown out right away. Of course, delaying such questions only applies to an arranged interview where there is plenty of time. If the interviewer has time only for a question or two, as at a general press conference, he or she must throw the "zingers" when possible.

Being Flexible with Questions

Interviews always have a way of turning up information the questioner did not think about or had no way of knowing would arise. Often the source will volunteer information the interviewer is not prepared for. When that happens, do not be bound by a list of questions. The interviewer should follow any promising leads that arise. When that unexpected line of questioning runs dry, the interviewer can return to his list of questions. Sometimes the source gets off the subject at hand. Then, the interviewer should politely direct the conversation back to the original topic.

When they outline their story or begin to write a piece, many interviewers find they have forgotten to ask some vital questions. The interviewer should not hesitate to contact the source again to get the information needed. Usually, the source is happy to cooperate because he or she, too, wants the story to be accurate and complete.

Being Persistent and Firm

The interviewer must be persistent in an interview to get information essential to a story and information the source may be reluctant to give. One can do this by:

Asking specific questions. The interviewer can make it more difficult for the source to give an evasive answer if questions are asked for specific information. Instead of "Did you *know about* the mayor's proposal?" try "Did you *get* the letter outlining the mayor's proposal?" or "You did *read* the letter outlining the mayor's proposal?" If the source has to lie to be evasive, he or she might prefer to be truthful.

Repeating the question. If the response of the source is evasive or incomplete, the interviewer can sometimes get an answer by repeating the question, or at least asking for clarification of the answer.

Rephrasing the question. Sometimes the interviewer can receive a more satisfactory answer by rephrasing the question to make it more difficult to evade.

Return to the question. Sometimes the interviewer can be successful by dropping a question for the moment and returning to it later.

Using information he or she already has. Sometimes an interviewer can use information he or she already has to loosen up a source. For example, if the interviewer is questioning a union official on labor negotiations, he or she can tell the source what he or she already has been told by a management source or a mediator. This information could convince the union spokesman to publicize the union's side of the dispute.

Persuade the source the answer is to his or her advantage. Often an interviewer can convince the source that answering a question he or she has been reluctant to answer could be to his or her advantage. The interviewer could say a straight answer would make the source appear more frank before the public; that the answer will probably surface anyway from some other source and the first source will appear to have been trying to cover up; or that a story saying the source declined to answer will cast suspicion perhaps worse than a frank answer.

Quote source's own words. The interviewer can cite previous statements on the subject that the source may have made. This might convince the source to talk if his or her stand has changed.

All of these methods should be used calmly and professionally. They often work. However, there is no way anyone can bat 1,000. Sometimes nothing works. Sometimes the writer has to seek answers to the questions from other sources or by other means.

Being Patient

Sometimes a little patience can elicit information from a shy, taciturn, or reluctant source. The interviewer can:

Utilize the "pregnant pause" to an advantage. Beginning interviewers are often as nervous as their sources and fail to allow them time to give a complete answer. A pause in any conversation is filled with a certain level of tension. It's awkward. There is a tendency to want to rush in and fill it. Professional interviewers know and use this tension effectively. The psychologist, counselor, detective and good reporter know to let this tension work on the person being interviewed. Professionals will use the pause to their advantage. The source will often become nervous and elaborate on an incomplete answer without further questioning. Sometimes the interviewer can indicate the answer is not complete by a short query—"Yes?" "And then . . . .?" "He did?" etc.

Change the subject to ease tension. If the tension of a source seems to be inhibiting answers, the interviewer can back off and change the subject for a time. He or she might engage in idle conversation for a time, tell a joke, or move to a less controversial area temporarily.

Reschedule the interview. If the circumstances of the interview or the state of mind of the source make it impossible to conduct a productive interview, reschedule the interview if publication or broadcast deadlines make postponement possible. If the problem has been constant interruptions by office workers or phone calls in the source's office, he or she will probably agree to holding the interview at some other site, where the source won't be disturbed.

Taking Effective Notes

Most beginning interviewers probably take more notes than they need. An interviewer may not have as good a memory as Truman Capote who said he trained himself to remember every word in an hour long interview when he was researching material for his journalistic novel, *In Cold Blood.* But a writer's memory is better than he or she might think. If, as Capote did, he or she puts the memory of an interview to paper immediately after it ends, the writer will have most of the essentials. That does not mean the interviewer should not take notes, but he or she does not have to take down every word. The writer should get the essentials on paper—names, dates, places, figures, good direct quotes, general and specific points made, strong opinions.

Notes are an individual thing. Each interviewer takes notes for a specific purpose. The interviewer can use any technique that fulfills that purpose. The notes can be in fluid shorthand; they can be in an individual shorthand understandable only to the interviewer; they can be extensive or brief. They must serve only the interviewer. They only need to be accurate and comprehensive enough to cover the story.

Using a Tape Recorder Effectively and Ethically

Modern tape recorders are so efficient and so unobtrusive they are a real boon to anyone who has to conduct interviews. They should be used with these restrictions:

They should always be used openly. Anyone making a tape of any conversation is ethically compelled to inform anyone taking part in that taping that a record is being made of the conversation. If a source declines to be taped, that is his or her right.

They should be used unobtrusively. Tape recorders can inhibit sources if they are too apparent. With earlier models, interviewers could not avoid making the source constantly aware of the recorder. The mike had to be held close to the source's mouth. The recorder often was noisy. The recorder was quite large and hard not to see constantly. Those deficits no longer apply. Mikes are sensitive enough to pick up answers from several feet away. Tape recorders are small, quiet and long running. After the first few minutes, sources will probably forget about the recorder and lose any inhibitions aroused initially.

Augment tape with written notes. Like anything mechanical, tape recorders can fail. The interviewer does not want to be left at the end of an interview with only a blank tape. He or she should still take written notes. If the tape fails, the interviewer, like the astronaut, has a backup system. Both notes and a tape will come in handy when the writing starts. Nothing can beat a combination of a good memory, good notes, and a verbatim tape. The general story can be written from memory with reference to notes. The notes will also serve as an index to the tape, which can provide exact details.

THE PROFILE INTERVIEW

All of the procedures recommended for the information interview would also apply to the profile interview, with some differences. Those things that would apply to the profile interview in addition to the informational interview would include:

—*Placing emphasis on the person being interviewed.*
—*Asking different kinds of questions.*
—*Observing the actions and mannerisms of the interviewee.*
—*Trying to establish a theme in questioning the interviewee.*
—*Interviewing others about the subject to be profiled.*

Emphasizing the Person Being Interviewed

In preparing to interview someone for purposes of writing a profile about that person, writers gather not only basic biographical information about the interviewee, but personal information. They want information about the person's hobbies, idiosyncrasies, character, personality, and other experiences, both professional and personal, aspirations, victories or defeats. They seek specific personal anecdotes, examples, incidents of humor, tragedy, pathos, happiness, sadness, honor and embarrassment. They seek not only the positive, but a bit of the negative. The writers of a profile want to delineate a person, not a saint; a specific human, not a stereotype; a rounded personality, not a cardboard character.

Asking Different Questions

The kinds of questions asked of a person profiled should develop the personal material mentioned above. The interviewer should ask the profile interviewee such questions as:

—What was your most inspirational experience?
—What was your most discouraging experience?
—What was your most humorous experience?
—What was your most embarrassing experience?
—What was your most rewarding experience?
—What was your most frightening experience?
—What is your pet peeve?
—Why did you participate in that demonstration against ERA? Nuclear Energy? the Palestinians? Israel? Marijuana? Censorship? Ronald Reagan?
—Why did you participate in that demonstration for (all of the above)?
—Were you ever arrested?
—Why were you arrested in June of 1980?
—Would you do the same thing again if it meant arrest again?
—Etc., in the same vein.

It is important in interviewing a person for a profile to get good anecdote material and good opinion quotes. You have to be persistent to get the anecdotes with some interviewees. The questioner might have to bait the interviewee on occasion to draw out strong feelings. This is a tricky business, but done near the end of an interview it can often produce good quotable material. Mike Wallace once baited Burt Lancaster about his "bad temper." Lancaster tried to keep his cool and switch the conversation, but he finally blew up and stomped off the screen. That was before Wallace's 60 Minute stardom, and one suspects there was more showmanship involved than journalism on that occasion. Wallace did, however, prove his point quite graphically. In doing profiles, it is not unusual for either print or broadcast interviewers to probe for personality or character traits.

Observing Actions of the Subject

Because interviewers are interested in creating a picture in the mind of the reader of the person being profiled, they will make note of the subject's mannerisms and actions. Including descriptions of actions and mannerisms in the profile gives the reader/listener/viewer a better mental picture of the person being profiled. The writer might make such observations as:

—He paced nervously back and forth as he talked.

—She smoked constantly, lighting one cigarette from the still glowing end of the other.

—She tossed her head back and laughed.

—He slumped lazily in his chair, his feet perched on the polished walnut desk.

—There was a long pause as he seemed to be formulating his response carefully.

—Her answers to the questions were quick, short and to the point.

—Etc.

Establishing A Theme

In profiles, the writer must establish a theme. Such a theme may become apparent in the pre-interview research, or it may arise during the interview. As soon as the potential theme does become apparent, the writer should tailor questions to develop that theme. Again the writer must be flexible. If he or she has selected a theme from pre-interview research and a more interesting one develops during the questioning, he or she must be ready to switch directions. The theme of the profile will usually concern the subject's:

—*Range or type of experience.*

—*Personality or character trait.*

—*Aspirations in life.*

—*Personal achievements.*

—*Philosophy of life.*

There are other possibilities, of course. Writing is a creative activity, and there is always a new way to be found to do something. As with all things in this book, these are just guidelines to help the beginner. With experience, writers will go their own creative way.

Interviewing Others About the Profile Subject

Profiles should not be based only on interviews with the person being profiled. Writers should also interview a variety of other sources to get a balanced picture. They should question associates, employers, employees, relatives, friends, possible enemies. Sometimes profiles are done on persons who decline to be interviewed or can't be interviewed. In the case of people who have died, the profile would necessarily be based on interviews with others. As with any story a writer is working, the more sources he or she has for a profile the better.

USE SECONDARY SOURCES

While much of the information gathered by print and broadcast reporters, advertising writers, and information representatives comes directly from human sources, a sizable amount of information comes from printed sources. Such sources range as broadly as the scope of the printing industry itself and beyond. They include everything from books to typed letters and even cards sent to news outlets. The sources can be grouped roughly into these categories:

—*Research and information books.*
—*Periodicals such as magazines and annual reports.*
—*Newspapers and wire services.*
—*Guides and indexes to newspapers and periodicals.*
—*Public records.*
—*Marketing and public relations handouts.*

Use Research and Information Books

Informational books range from the obvious—the telephone directory—to the exotic: specialized books on medicine, science, art, philosophy. In a sense all books could be included, with the possible exception of some works of fiction. It is essential that any writer become well acquainted with the resources of a library and learn how to make use of those resources. However, the scope of this book does not include a course in library science. Thus, the discussion here will be limited to those library resources writers of pieces for the mass media will use most often and find most helpful. Those include:

Dictionaries of Various Kinds—There are conventional dictionaries of definitions, spelling, pronunciation and word derivations, but there are also dictionaries of synonyms and antonyms such as *Roget's International Thesaurus;* dictionaries of slang such as Eric Partridge's *A Dictionary of Slang and Unconventional English;* and other specialized dictionaries such as Webster's *Dictionary of Proper Names.*

Encyclopedias—Most news or broadcasting facilities have libraries which include an encyclopedia—such as *Encyclopedia Americana* or *Enciclopedia Brittanica.* And of course these and other general encyclopedias can be found in a full service library. General libraries would also have specialized encyclopedias in literature, biography (various *Who's Who in America* editions), history, political science, social sciences, technology, science, arts, philosophy and religion.

Writing and Reporting Aids—Libraries carry such writing aids as John Bartlett's *Familiar Quotations* which gives quotations from the Bible, Shakespeare, and other prose and poetry passages. All are indexed by subject matter. So the next time an author quotes some famous or obscure writer, the reader/listener/viewer should not waste time admiring the author's knowledge. He or she should just consult *Bartlett's Quotations*. The writer, too, can quote the classics. He or she can also find books that will improve grammar, punctuation and writing style.

Atlases—Geographical data, local and worldwide, are available in various atlases which contain maps; names of countries, cities, rivers, oceans, lakes and mountain ranges; data on population, climate and terrain; and other pertinent information of the regions covered. Examples are the *Encyclopedia Brittanica World Atlas* and *Webster's New Geographical Dictionary*. Similar information for local areas is published by the local chamber of commerce and other private publishers.

Guides and Catalogs to Using the Library—Short of taking a library science and use course or becoming a pest to the library staff, a writer can consult books that will help in using the library more efficiently. A couple of general guides to reference books are: *Guide to Reference Books* by Constance M. Winchell; and *Guide to the Use of Books and Libraries* by Jean Key Gates. The librarian can refer writers to others. Catalogs include: *Cumulative Book Index*, monthly listing of books published in English; and *Monthly Catalog of U.S. Government Publications*.

Periodicals: Magazines and Yearbooks

Magazines, both general and specialized, provide an endless source of articles on all manner of subjects helpful to the writer. Articles done earlier on a subject a writer is dealing with can provide invaluable background. Such information can give historical, geographic, economic, or philosophical depth to the piece at hand. Most general circulation libraries maintain either bound copies or microfilm on a wide range of general circulation or specialty magazines.

Certain annual publications are invaluable to the writer and reporter. Most newsrooms will have a dog-eared copy of a general information yearbook at the city desk to consult not only for story background but to answer questions called into the newsrooms. Probably the best known is the *World Almanac and Book of Facts*. Other well known ones are the *Reader's Digest Almanac and Yearbook* and the *CBS News Almanac*. There are other specialized volumes such as the *Yearbook of World Affairs*, *Negro Almanac*, and *Facts on File*.

News Outlets Can Provide Information And Ideas

An important duty of editors and news directors is to read their own and other newspapers and wire services and listen to other broadcast outlets for information and ideas to be used in a variety of ways. Editors and news directors can:

—*Check out and rewrite stories missed.*

—*Evaluate different angles taken by other editors or news directors and amend existing stories if needed.*

—*Localize wire stories.*

—*Get ideas for stories that can be pursued later.*

Such information or ideas are not limited to news columns and newscasts. Advertisements, especially classified advertisements, can often provide ideas for news stories or features. One such classified ad led to an award winning series of stories that was made into a movie. An editor in Chicago noticed a classified ad in which a woman offered a reward for information that would prove her son, then in prison on a murder conviction, innocent of the crime for which he was serving time. The editor turned the item over to a reporter to investigate. The investigation ultimately led to evidence that the convicted man could not have committed the crime. He was released from prison. The story was dramatized in the movie *Northside 777*, starring James Stewart.

Wire services such as the *Associated Press* and *United Press International*, which provide worldwide news items to member papers and broadcast outlets, also provide specific information for individual stories upon request and for an extra charge. For example, if a local reporter is doing a story on an individual previously in the news in a distant city, he or she can request the wire service to send information from that city. The reporter can also have photographs sent over the telephoto wires of the news service. Advance arrangements have to be made, of course, because such individual assignments have a low priority with wire service editors. The cost would be substantial, but probably no more than a long distance phone call, and a phone call would not obtain the photograph.

Welcome To The Morgue

Newspaper and broadcast stations maintain libraries of their own. These libraries contain reference books and other conventional library items, but they also contain clippings of prior news stories dating back many years. Because old news is said to be dead news, the newsroom libraries are often called *"morgues."* But old news is not dead at all. Like Douglas MacArthur's old soldier, old news has just "faded away." Some of it may never be heard from again, but much "buried" news will be resurrected for use in subsequent stories.

Take the case of a man who is in the news when he wins laurels as an athlete in high school and college, again when he is decorated in a war, and again when he is appointed president of the family widgit factory. Even if he doesn't create any waves in widgitry, at some future time something, good or bad, will bring him back into the news. He may be honored or dishonored, killed or live to 100, but he will be in the news. All that dead news about his earlier life will be revived as background for a new story.

While news organizations maintain their libraries for use by their own staff members, most will allow scholars, free-lance writers, visiting reporters from out of town and certain others to use the facilities. Each organization has its own rules about who can use its library and when. Anyone granted the right to use a library of a news organization should use it with care and respect for the rules established.

DON'T FORGET THE MORGUE AS A VALUABLE SOURCE. Ronald Reagan, the sportscaster, is shown in the 1930's when he worked at WHO in Des Moines, and again during the 1984 campaign when he revisited the radio station. The morgue can prove to be a pleasant surprise for even less important figures and information. (Courtesy Wide World of Photos/AP.)

Depending on the size of the news organization and the sophistication of its library system, clippings may be filed only under one heading or there may be several cross references leading to the same clipping. In a good library, a researcher could find an item by subject matter, by the names of any of the principal persons involved, by the names of institutions involved, and by any other reference that forms a vital part of the item. It is a quick and convenient way to get background on a news event. Quickness and convenience in research are necessary in a news operation.

Indexes Help Locate Periodicals

Finding articles in periodicals, including newspapers, is relatively easy thanks to indexes compiled for use in libraries. The best known and most useful general index is *Reader's Guide to Periodical Literature*. The writer can use the guide to find articles previously published on the subject under research. He or she can then get the bound copies or microfilms of the magazines in which those articles were published. This resource is immensely helpful in obtaining background material. The guide lists articles from news and general circulation magazines and articles from specialty periodicals. It is published twice a month and is also bound quarterly and annually and giving entries under author and title as well as subject matter.

Libraries also have specialized indexes to articles on a wide range of subjects including art, publishing, law, literature, agriculture, science, medicine, and business. Librarians can direct the writer to such specialized indexes.

One of the most widely used indexes, in addition to the *Index to Periodical Literature*, is the *New York Times Index*. The *Times Index* is published semimonthly and accumulated in bound copies annually. It provides the date and page on which a story appeared in the *New York Times*. Most libraries will have the *Times* on microfilm.

Some libraries have the same sort of guide, or at least a cross-referenced card system, to the local newspaper. Thus, if writers cannot use the library at the newspaper, they may find the community library can serve the same purpose. If a community library does not have a guide to the local paper, it will have the paper either in bound volumes or on microfilm. If the approximate date of an article is known, it is no great task to find it even if no guide is available.

If the writers do not know the date of the item they are seeking in the local paper, but knows it was in some way tied to a national event, they can use the *New York Times* to find the exact date. Then, reference to the bound copy or microfilm of the local newspaper for that date can be made and the item found quickly.

Public Records And Government Publications Are Open

Because the law requires or custom dictates, most actions taken by governmental bodies at all levels are a matter of public record. City and county councils or commissions, school boards, state agencies and legislative bodies, national agencies and courts at all levels do business in public, keep open records, and issue information in great quantities. And because the news media serve as the eyes and ears of the public, print and broadcast reporters spend much time dealing in government data. At the local level this involves:

—*Covering meetings.*
—*Checking on administrative actions.*
—*Checking official or unofficial monitoring procedures.*
—*Checking on police records.*
—*Covering court actions and checking court records.*
—*Checking on property deeds, transfer documents, assessments, taxes, voter records.*

Covering Meetings Can Be Useful

Most local governing bodies provide members of the news media, and members of the public who express an interest, *an agenda* of what actions will be taken at an upcoming meeting. The meeting will be *open to the public* in most instances. And *minutes of the meeting* will usually be made available at a clerk or secretary's office.

The openness of meetings varies. In states such as Florida, which has a "government in the sunshine law," almost every meeting of government officials, whether official action is going to be taken or not, must be open to the public. Other states require, at a minimum, that any meeting where decisions are made and actions are taken be public. Some states allow municipal bodies to thrash things out at private "executive" meetings and then meet publicly only to take the required votes.

Newspapers and broadcast journalists instinctively fight all efforts to ban them from meetings where the public business is being conducted. The pressure is always kept on those who try to keep public information of any kind from the public.

In a given jurisdiction, the same rules that apply to general meetings will apply to subcommittee meetings, and meetings of advisory boards appointed by elected councils, commissioners or boards.

Administrative Activities Are Tougher

Administrative actions of local elected or employed officials are more difficult to cover than legislative actions of councils, commissions and boards. But the law provides ways reporters can keep tabs on such actions. For example, the *budget* of a public body is a matter of *public record*. The reporter can keep tabs on income and outgo. He or she can find out what money is coming in from tax sources, grants or transfers from other levels of government, public user fees, bank interest, and other sources of income. He or she can also find out what money goes for salaries, building costs, maintenance costs, interest on loans, operating costs, purchases, and expense accounts of employees and officials.

Reporting skills become important in covering administrators. When information is not on the record, the reporters must get it through other sources—human sources. They spend much time cultivating such sources by getting to know them, winning their confidence; learning to recognize and use their ambitions and/or frustrations about their jobs, colleagues, and employers or employees; getting them to tell what they know to be right or wrong about the operation of the public's business.

Monitoring Procedures Are Available

Most local government operations must undergo periodic auditing, usually by independent auditors, or auditors from another level of government such as the state. Reports of these audits are usually available to the public and its representatives. Citizens' groups such as the *League of Women Voters* and taxpayer associations also monitor government actions. Such groups often make in-depth studies of problem areas and can be expert sources of information on governmental operation. In extreme cases, *grand juries* will conduct investigations of various segments of local government operations. While the proceedings of grand juries are always secret, grand juries may issue reports critical of some phase of governmental operations. These reports, which often cover areas a reporter has not investigated, can be valuable sources of information.

Police Records Can Be Obtained

The police reporter, usually either overglamorized or libeled in movie and television dramas, spends a lot of time pouring over police records. Much time is also spent trying to get details that are not automatically available.

Readily available at police stations and sheriff's department offices are *logs* of all calls handled by the communications divisions. Also available are all *arrest records*. The information on logs of calls coming into the department and arrest records is minimal. Usually it is limited to names, ages, addresses, times, and locations. Information on the circumstances of arrests and the status of investigations into complaints or crimes is a bit harder to come by.

The reporter's skill at getting cooperation from sources again comes into play. Willingness of police officers to discuss investigations varies from organization to organization. Some law enforcement officials give their underlings wide leeway in talking to reporters. Others hold a tight rein on information. The reporter has to adapt to the system. Sometimes information can be obtained from sources outside the police department. For various reasons of their own, attorneys, either prosecutors or defenders, may be willing to talk about aspects of a case that police would not discuss. Other sources of information in a given situation are the arrested party, his relatives, witnesses to the arrest, and police department hangers-on such as bail bondsmen. Of course, the quality of information from such sources may be suspect.

Don't Forget Court Actions And Records

Most procedures—hearings, arraignments, trials, appeals—are open to the public in courts at all levels, local, state and national. At the lowest level, *municipal or county courts*, traffic cases, violations of county and city ordinances, misdemeanors (minor infractions of the law) and civil cases of limited amounts are open to the public.

At the next level—*courts of general jurisdiction*—felonies (serious crimes usually involving violation of state laws), probate matters, civil cases involving major amounts, and appeals from municipal or county courts are open to the public. However, some *domestic relations* cases, principally guardianship of children or juvenile offenders, are closed to the public. In some jurisdictions divorce cases may also be closed.

Jury deliberations are always closed, whether they are grand jury deliberations or petit or trial jury deliberations. Conferences among the judge and the prosecuting and defense attorneys are closed to reporters. These conferences might be held quietly at the bench or in the judge's chambers. Sometimes results of these conferences are announced in open court—a recess in the trial, dropping of one or more of multiple charges, or even a changed plea. There have also been occasions when judges have gagged reporters, ordering them not to report something that took place in the court. But usually reporters can print without interference whatever takes place in open court. Pretrial and post-trial information is usually available.

Court calendars of cases are open to reporters. Prosecuting attorneys usually keep reporters informed about upcoming prosecutions, postponements in planned trials, changes in charges, dropping of charges, etc. They obviously do not tell reporters anything about trial strategy unless they are trying to use the press to confuse the defense. The same actions and motives would withhold or bring information from the defense attorney.

After a trial is over, *the complete case,* from arrest in a *criminal trial* to acquittal or conviction and sentencing, is placed on file in the office of the clerk of court. There it can be read by anyone who wants or has a reason to read it. *The same is true of civil trials.* The complete case from the filing of the suit by the plaintiff to a jury verdict in favor of the plaintiff or the defendant will be on file and available.

The Property Deeds, Assessments And Taxes

Complete records on ownership of property in a county are kept in the county courthouse. Depending on the state, property records may be maintained in the clerk of court's office, the office of the recorder of deeds, or an official with some other title in charge of such records. In searching real estate records, the reporter can find out who owns land now, who owned it earlier, when ownership changed, and perhaps how much was paid for the land. If the state taxes the transfer of deeds, and the state usually does, transfer stamps may be attached to the deed. By noting the amount of money represented by the stamps and knowing the tax rate, simple arithmetic will divulge the sales price.

Why would the reporter want to know the ownership of a piece of land? For any number of reasons. It might prove interesting if land the city was planning to purchase as a park site just happened to be owned by the daughter of the mayor. It would also be interesting if the slum rental housing for which poor people were being overcharged was owned by an elder or deacon in the *First Righteous Church*.

Other courthouse records which the reporter might want to inspect include:

—*Assessments*—A study of these could tell if there are any inequalities in the assessment of property throughout the county. And, of course, it could yield assessment information on an individual piece of property.

—*Tax Rolls*—Information from these could tell a reporter if taxes in the county are higher or lower than taxes elsewhere.

—*Voter Registration*—A study of voter rolls would tell whether they are up to date. Most states require cancellation of the registration of voters who have not voted in recent elections.

Check State Records

Availability of state records *does not differ* appreciably from the availability of municipal records. *Agenda, meetings,* and *published records of legislative bodies* are open to the public, as meetings and records of most regulatory agencies.

Administrative activities in some states are not quite so open, but again budgets, income and expenditures are open to public scrutiny. The biggest problem reporters on the state level have is the enormous amount of paper work available. Checking everything becomes a monumental job. A two-month session of a state legislature can produce volumes of reports on committee and subcommittee actions, debates, bills passed, bills defeated, bills tabled.

There is an enormous number of state publications, ranging from driving manuals to personnel information for state employees; from brochures promoting tourism or some other industry to agricultural department handbooks on taking care of your lawns. One of the most useful publications coming from state government is its annual *statistical abstract.* This volume, which every newsroom should have on hand, provides a treasure of information that can be used in a variety of ways.

An example of such a volume is the *Florida Statistical Abstract,* published by the Bureau of Economic and Business Research, College of Business Administration, University of Florida. In a 693 page volume, the writer can find up-to-date figures on:

—*Human resources,* such as population; housing; vital statistics and health; education; income and wealth; labor force, employment and earnings; social insurance and welfare.

—*Physical resources and industries,* such as geography and climate; agriculture; forestry; fisheries and minerals; construction; manufacturing; transportation; communications; power and energy.

—*Services,* such as wholesale and retail trade; finance, insurance and real estate; personal and business services; tourism and recreation; health, education and cultural services.

—*Public services and administration,* such as government and elections; courts and law enforcement; government finance and employment.

—*Economic and social trends,* such as economic indicators and prices; quality of life.

Such readily available data are invaluable to *reporters* in giving perspective to stories they may be working on involving any of these fields.

The data are also invaluable to advertisers in planning marketing campaigns and appeals, and to *public relations professionals* in a variety of writing chores.

Use Federal Records

As a book for beginning writers, this volume is not intended as a training guide for federal government reporters, but there are a few volumes published by the federal government that can be helpful to beginners.

As is true at the state level, the U.S. Congress publishes complete reports on its legislative activities. *The Congressional Record* is issued daily while Congress is in session, which in recent years has been almost all year. Revised versions, issued in bound form after each yearly session, can be found in most libraries.

For nationwide information on the same subjects listed for the *Florida Statistical Abstract,* the writer can consult the *Statistical Abstract of the United States,* issued annually.

A guide to innumerable other publications issued by the federal government is the *Monthly Catalog of U.S. Government Publications,* to be found in the library.

Many publications of the federal government are free, and others can be purchased at small cost. Not all are stocked by libraries, since some are of limited interest and use.

Information Handouts And Marketing Data

Newspaper and broadcasting newsrooms are inundated with information handouts from many private and public sources. A lot of these handouts are promotional or propaganda pieces and not of much use to newsrooms. But much of such incoming mail provides information which can be utilized by the news staffs. One of the functions of editors and news directors is culling useful information from any puffery that may be included. Such routine information as biographical data about government, business, professional, sports and entertainment figures is widely used, as is routine information from annual reports, brochures, company publications, and informational handouts. Competent reporters will double check such information before using it just as they check information from any source. Big newspapers and broadcast outlets will probably rewrite the information to fit their own purposes. Small news outlets will be more likely to run well written pieces as is.

Sources of printed data for writers of advertisements are rather narrowly limited in the sense that the data apply to a particular product or merchandiser. Information about either the product or the institution must come from the manufacturer, wholesaler or retailer.

While most of the information for an advertisement comes from the merchandiser, the writer might want to know a bit about the potential consumer and where the consumer is likely to get his information. This book cannot get into the whole field of marketing, but the *bible* used by writers of advertising to learn about consumers and ad outlets is *Standard Rate and Data Services*. *Standard Rate and Data Services* publishes weekly or monthly editions giving *rates, technical data* and *audience data* in seven areas: newspapers, consumer magazines, business magazines, farm publications, spot radio outlets, spot television outlets and *outdoor advertising*.

SUGGESTED EXERCISES

1. If you were doing stories on the following subjects, which people in your community would you go interview for expert information?

   a. Rights of a woman in inheriting the estate of her husband if he dies without leaving a will.

   b. Which properties in your city are considered historical landmarks and why.

   c. There has been much talk about people being able to shop, pay bills, make appointments, and conduct other business from their homes by using computers. When will that be likely to occur?

d. Your state is losing or gaining congressmen because of reapportionment following the census. How will it affect the state politically?

e. How will the same situation as posed in question 4 affect the state economically?

f. There have been a rash of hotel fires around the country. You want to find out if the local hotels pose any fire risk, and just how severe a risk.

g. The Congress has proposed reducing Social Security benefits for those over 65. What is the local opinion of such a move?

h. Several large oak trees in the city's parks have developed a strange disease and seem to be dying. Why?

i. Test scores of students from your community taking the college entrance exams have dropped from previous years. Why?

j. The FBI crime rate report has indicated that crime in your community has risen by 20 percent. Why?

2. Check the television guide for your area and find out who is scheduled to appear on one of the Sunday interview shows—Meet the Press, Face the Nation, etc. Then make up a list of questions you would be prepared to ask that guest. Listen to the show and see how your questions compared to the questions asked.

3. Plan a profile of an interesting person in your community. Make sure he will talk to you. Find out all you can about the person to be profiled from all sources you can think of. Prepare a list of questions you should ask. Conduct the interview and write it. Try to get it published in your local newspaper if you feel it is of high enough quality.

4. Go to the library and look up the following items of information:

a. How many foreign cars were imported into the United States in 1983?

b. Who won the Pulitzer Prize for editorial writing in 1976?

c. What U.S. Government publications on education were issued in February of 1984, if any?

d. Did your home congressman speak on the floor of Congress during the past month? How many times and on what subjects?

e. What are the 10 largest cities in the world and their populations?

f. Who is your community's most famous person? What does *Who's Who in America* say about that person?

g. What was Peter Jennings' hometown and where did he attend college?

h. What plays have been written by the British author Graham Greene?

i. You want to find a literary quotation on laziness to use in a piece you are writing. Find at least five such possible quotations.

Chapter XI

DISCIPLINE AND PROFESSIONALISM: A MUST

Professionals, whether they are physicians, lawyers, clergymen, teachers, or writers for the mass media, must constantly strive for excellence in the practice of their professions. If they do not have the discipline and dedication to seek excellence, they have no right to call themselves professionals. This discipline and dedication must have led them to:
—A thorough knowledge of their profession.
—A competency in the practice of that profession.
—Unquestioned integrity.
—Understanding and acceptance of the responsibilities of their profession.
—A determination to strive for excellence.
Professional standards and codes (See Appendix B) give the advertiser, journalist and public relations professional guidance in seeking professionalism, but the chief enforcer is the individual. In some professions, such as medicine, law, teaching and religion, professional organizations and societies and even government, enforce standards. That is not true of advertisers, journalists and public relations personnel, except in a narrow sense.

The writer must not only learn what codes and standards should guide him, but he should also learn how to implement the standards he or she has adopted. Living up to the standards for the profession means that the writer must observe certain basic practices. The writer should always strive to be:
—*Accurate.*
—*Objective.*
—*Lawful.*
—*Thorough.*
—*Responsible.*
—*Fair and sensitive.*

Accuracy
Accuracy is the quality most desired by the public in information presented by writers of the mass media. The reader/listener/viewer wants factual stories and advertisements which satisfy the desire of the consumer for the truth. While, as Oscar Wilde said in *The Importance of Being Earnest*, "Truth is rarely pure, and never simple," essential to truth is accuracy.

Part of the discipline the writer must accept is a constant dedication and diligence in getting the facts correct. Accuracy requires checking and double checking everything that will go into a story or ad. It means the writer will:

—Check things *he hears* by looking them up when possible.

—Check things *he reads* by asking the subject if the facts are straight.

—Develop a system to avoid errors while gathering facts, while writing, after writing, and again before printing.

—Use diligently such sources as telephone directories, city directories, dictionaries, atlases, encyclopedias, morgue clippings, his notes, tapes, memoranda, handouts.

—Check all figures, statistics, percentages.

—Check not only *unusual* names, places, ages but all *common* names, places, ages.

—Call the source back. The source won't mind; he or she too wants accuracy.

It also means the writer will *assume nothing.* There is a sign on a post in the newsroom of the Orlando (Florida) Sentinel Star which reads, "Assumption is the mother of all screwups." Always assume that your facts are wrong. Always assume that if anything can go wrong, it probably will. It is better to *double check* facts 99 times only to find you are correct each time than *fail to check* and be wrong on the 100th time. Most journalism teachers will (or at least should) give a paper containing a fact error a failing grade. When teachers do that, they are not being holier-than-thou. They recognize that a failing grade is a mild penalty if it makes the writer more diligent about eliminating errors. An error in fact can:

—Destroy the writer's credibility.

—Destroy the credibility of a newspaper, magazine or broadcast outlet.

—Trigger a libel suit against the writer or an employer.

—Lose an advertising account.

—Destroy or damage a public relations client's business, reputation, campaign.

—Cause the reader/listener/viewer great inconvenience.

—Cost the writer a job.

To illustrate the effect even a minor error can have, assume the writer is doing a story on an upcoming panel discussion a particular reader/listener/viewer wants to attend. Suppose the writer says the event will be held in a downtown meeting hall on Monday night, July 14, at 8 o'clock, when in fact the event is scheduled for Monday night, *July 21,* at 8 o'clock. The person who reads or hears the information broadcast might:

—Have his or her spouse come into town for dinner prior to going to the panel discussion.

—Hire a babysitter at $3 an hour.

—Get clothing cleaned for the event or buy a new outfit.

—Arrive at the site and find a darkened hall and no panel discussion.

"ASSUMPTION IS THE MOTHER OF ALL SCREWUPS," reads a sign in the news-room of the Orlando Sentinel Star. Facts must be checked and rechecked for accuracy. Not only do factual errors destroy the writer's credibility, but they can be the basis for libel actions. (Courtesy Wide World of Photos)

Such a person might write a testy letter to the editor. Having received such a letter, a testy editor certainly would have a discussion with a belatedly concerned and uncomfortable writer.

So the word is *accuracy, accuracy, accuracy.* The writer should get it *all,* but get it *correct;* get it *quickly,* but get it *correct;* write it *brightly,* but get it *correct.* Get it *correct, correct, correct.*

When, for whatever reason, the writer gets it wrong, the writer should correct the error with speed, good humor and grace.

Objectivity

The news writer owes his reader/listener/viewer objectivity. The writer's opinion is just not important. The only opinion the reader/listener/viewer cares about is his own and that of subjects of the story. He wants the unvarnished facts. He will interpret them himself. Objectivity is not all that hard to achieve. The writer merely has to:

—*Write only the facts.* The writer should make certain a story is made up only of facts from reputable sources, facts known to be true from the writer's own background knowledge, and facts he or she has observed. Rumor, unconfirmed reports, and speculations should always be avoided.

—*Write all appropriate facts.* The writer should include all the facts necessary to the reader/listener/viewer's understanding of the story.

—*Keep out of the story.* The writer should write in the second or third person. The only time the first person should be used is if the writer is doing a story on a momentous personal experience.

—*Qualify facts and opinions of others.* The writer should always tell where information came from. The reader has a right to know the source of the information. Any opinions included should always be attributed to the person expressing the opinions.

—*Treat all sides of a controversial story fairly.* In writing about a controversial subject, the writer should present the viewpoints of all responsible parties. If one faction in a disputed story declines to talk or cannot be reached, the writer should so inform the reader/listener/viewer.

—*Make certain the facts in the story relate clearly to one another.* The writer should organize his story logically and with good transition so the facts are clearly related and can be seen by the reader/listener/viewer in proper perspective.

—*Present the facts responsibly and not sensationally.* The writer can maintain objectivity by presenting facts in a responsible way and not in a way that will mislead the reader by distortion or sensationalism. A writer should try to make a story interesting, of course, but a story can be interesting without being misleading.

Some people will argue that objectivity is not possible. They will say that all writers and editors bring their own prejudices to their work. There may be some truth in that position. Everyone agrees that the reporter can *attempt* to be objective. He can *try to overcome* his prejudices and preconceived notions. He *must try.*

A reporter must realize that if he or she succeeds in being objective in a controversial story, only those readers who have no strong opinion on the question at hand will see that objectivity. Those with strong opinions on the subject will see a truly objective story as biased because it does not wholly agree with their viewpoint. Being objective in some instances means being alone. Good reporting and writing will earn the writer the respect of the uninvolved reader and other professionals.

Of course, objectivity does not apply for writers of advertisements, promotion material, editorials, speeches, or any advocacy pieces. Such writing is argumentative, and no attempt is made to present a balanced view. The writer is trying to persuade the reader/listener/viewer to purchase a product, use a service, vote for a candidate, adopt a point of view, etc. But the reader/listener/viewer undersands the role of a clearly marked advertisement and/or editorial. Neither an advertisement nor an editorial should ever be disguised as something else. Reputable publishers and broadcasters always separate news from both advertisements and editorials so clearly that the reader/listener/viewer cannot mistake one for the other.

Qualification

The reader/listener/viewer has a right to know not only what the facts are but where they come from. A reporter should almost always qualify information by giving its source. By citing the source of information the writer gives the reader/listener/viewer an added dimension to use in determining acceptance of the information. If a writer predicts there will be a recession in the months ahead, it makes a lot of difference to the reader/listener/viewer to know that information came from a qualified economist.

Attribution to sources is not as important in giving noncontroversial or nontechnical information. The writer can say that the economist cited is a graduate of the Harvard School of Business Administration without quoting him, but should attach the name of the source to any economic pronouncements made or opinions expressed. Anything not attributed to another source will be attributed by the reader/listener/viewer to the writer.

The writer should not fear giving too much attribution. Even when quoting the same source for several paragraphs, don't hesitate to repeat the attribution several times. Of course, attribution should always be made clearly when a new source is quoted. With the new source make the attribution either directly by starting the quote with . . . John Jones, partner of Evans, said . . . . etc., or indirectly by some transitional phrase such as . . . Evan's partner, John Jones, agrees with that assessment. He said . . . Etc. Do *NOT* change sources by starting with the quote and citing the new source at the end. This confuses the reader, who will think Source A is still talking and will not find out it is Source B till the end.

In quoting a source, the writer can use exact words if it is felt those words are most effective. Or he can paraphrase what the source said if that is most effective. A paraphrase should never distort what the source said. Although the words may be changed, the meaning must not be changed. To indicate he is quoting the exact word of the source, the writer will begin and end with quotation marks ("). If the writer paraphrases the source, he will omit the quotation marks, but still attribute the information to the source. An exact quotation would look like this:

Mayor Dwyer said, "The city budget will be held down to our income this year. There will be no increase in taxes."

An indirect quotation, or paraphrase, would look like this:

The decision to hold the line on taxes this year will not mean a reduction in city services, the mayor said.

Sometimes the writer will combine an indirect quote with a direct quote of just a small part of the statement. This is done to emphasize a few strong words, as follows:

There will be no new city taxes proposed in the budget for next year, Mayor Dwyer said today. The city's taxpayers are already "carrying too heavy a financial burden."

In the three illustrations above, the attribution was handled in three different ways. In the first statement, the attribution came at the beginning; in the second statement, the attribution came at the end; and in the third example, it was in the middle. This illustrates the writer can vary the placement of the attribution to make the piece read more smoothly and avoid monotony of style.

Finally, the writer should never be afraid of the word *"said."* Beginning writers often feel they should not repeat words, and seek synonyms for the word "said." Such writers have sources *stating, declaring, averring, avowing, alleging, adding, continuing, going on to say,* etc. The word *"adding"* may be all right if what the writer is adding is what the source said immediately following what had been previously quoted. But often that is not the case. The same applies for *"continuing."* That word implies an unbroken order. Most of the other words should probably never be used. Most sources *"say"* things, and that is what the writer should indicate. The writer can use *"said"* ten times on a page if that is the correct word. The novelist has no hesitancy in using the word *"said."*

There may be rare occasions when the source says something in a colorful way. If the words really apply, the writer can say the source *"whispered," "thundered," "snorted," "pleaded," "threatened," "joked."* But for the sake of accuracy, the writer should use such words *only* if they truly represent what happened and are not prejudicial. Such *"opinion"* words should be used with great care.

LEGAL CONSIDERATIONS

Two things fill my mind with ever-increasing wonder and awe, the more often and the more intensely the reflection dwells on them: the starry heavens above me, and *the moral law within me.*
—Immanuel Kant, *Critique of Pure Reason*

The writer for the mass media should be guided by the *"moral law"* within him or her in all professional efforts, but must also be aware of the law outside of self. That too must be observed.

In addition to obeying all civil and criminal laws that apply to everyone, writers for newspapers, magazines, and other printed materials and broadcast outlets must be concerned with laws involving:

—*Libel.*
—*The right of privacy.*
—*Obscenity.*

Writers for broadcasting also must be concerned with the added provisions of their Federal Communications Commission licenses that call for:
for:

—*Equal time for political candidates.*
—*Fairness in presenting controversial subjects.*
—*Serving the public.*

Libel

One of the most precious possessions a person has is his or her reputation. As Shakespeare said in Othello:

> . . .Who steals my purse, steals trash . . . . But he that filches
> from me my good name robs me of that which not enriches him,
> and makes me poor indeed.

English common law, from which American law is largely descended, has long held that it is an offense against a person to rob him of his name or reputation by publishing false and damaging information about him. That person who has been libeled can bring a civil suit for damages against the publication or broadcast facility that disseminates such false information. The extent of monetary damages juries have returned can be monumental. Juries have returned high awards in libel suits. A libel suit can be an expensive journalism lesson indeed. Even if the jury finds no damages have been inflicted, the trial costs can be considerable.

What constitutes libel? The basic elements a plaintiff has to establish in suing for libel are:

—*The information was false.*
—*The information was communicated to others.* (In the case of news that means it was published or broadcast.)
—*The person claiming to have been libeled was identified.* (Not necessarily by name, but so that the public would understand to whom the story referred.)

231

—The information caused damage. (Either financial loss, damage to the plaintiff's reputation, or humiliation and/or mental anguish.)

—The publisher of the information was at fault. (Either through negligence if the plaintiff is a private individual; or having known the information was false or having had serious doubts as to its truthfulness in the case of a public figure).

These definitions are somewhat vague and shift from court decision to court decision. Therefore, writers and editors always have to be on the alert to avoid accidentally libeling someone. The easiest way to avoid libel, of course, would be never to print anything controversial or of borderline legality. To keep from being impotent, however, newspapers, magazines and broadcast outlets must at times print material on that borderline. Those decisions are made by senior editors, and writers usually do not get involved in such obviously borderline cases. However, writers should know how to avoid libel.

Writers need to have some idea of the difference between public and private individuals. Broadly, public individuals are those *"public officials"* (not all public employees) who are basically responsible for the conduct of governmental affairs; and those *"public figures"* who are celebrities and have substantial power and influence or private individuals temporarily involved in a public issue. Elected officials, police officers, and administrators such as city managers would qualify as "public officials." *Dan Rather* and *Jerry Falwell* would probably qualify as *"public figures."* A *private individual* who has voluntarily thrust himself into a controversy over nuclear energy and is acting as a spokesman for a protesting group would be a *temporary "public figure."* It is important the writer knows who public individuals are because he will be writing about them more often and is more likely to get into the area of possible libel. It is comforting to know that public individuals have a much more difficult time winning libel suits than do private individuals.

The whole area of libel is so laced with booby traps the writer needs a mine detector to avoid the traps. Some common types of libel are *false statements* which:

—Cast doubt on a person's honesty or competence in his profession or business.

—Falsely accuse a person of belonging to a generally disreputable organization such as the communist party.

—Accuse a person falsely of being involved in a crime.

The Right of Privacy

The right of privacy laws are closely related to the libel laws. They are involved with a person's right to be let alone. Violations involve matters that are not in any way public. For example, if a person sunbathes in the nude in his fenced-in backyard, a photographer would be invading the sunbather's privacy if he stood on a chair to get a picture of that person and his paper published it. On the other hand, if that person undresses and takes a shower in the fountain in front of city hall at noon, it would be no invasion of privacy to photograph him and publish the picture.

This may be an oversimplification, but violations of the right of privacy usually involve an *intrusion* on a person's privacy even if there is no publication; publication *of private matters* of health, sex activity, deportment, economic affairs, etc. and/or *using a person's name or picture in a commercial way* (as in an ad) without permission.

Bruce W. Sanford, author of *Synopsis of the Law of Libel* and the *Right of Privacy* suggests that writers can avoid libel and invasion of privacy suits by:

—Avoiding slipshod and careless reporting.

—Being not only truthful but determining if they can prove what is written is truthful.

—Basing any comment or criticism on facts which are fully stated and true.

—Being careful of the "routine story," which may slide past the editor more easily. (Sanford points out that routine stories "account for more libel cases than all of the investigative reporting and human interest stories combined.")

—Trying to get the "other side of the story."

—Taking particular care with quotations.

—Being precise and specific in stories.

—Being sensitive to the private and non-newsworthy parts of a person's life.

—Avoiding unauthorized use of names and pictures for advertising and commercial purposes, and gaining consent for use of all pictures not clearly part of a public news event.

—Consulting an attorney in preparing a retraction so as to avoid compounding the libel or invasion of privacy.

There are five basic defenses against libel which may lessen the risk: *truth; privilege* (a statement that would be libelous except that the public interest in the event reported—a trial, for example—outweighs the interests of the individual); *opinion or fair comment* (as in a critique of the performance of a public official); *consent* of the plaintiff to the publication or broadcast of the material; and *right of reply* (publication of the defense of a person against the attack of another person).

There can be other mitigating circumstances that can reduce the dangers of conviction. But that is the area basically for lawyers. The best defense is no offense. If the libel or invasion of privacy is not committed by the writer and passed by the editor, there will be no case to defend.

Obscenity

Under U.S. Supreme Court rulings, each community sets its own standards on what constitutes obscenity. If a local jury finds material obscene, that in effect establishes the community standard. But, of course, another jury in the same town can make a more liberal interpretation on similar materials.

Actually, there is small chance that any community publication or broadcast outlet will have a problem with obscenity. Most community publications or broadcasters will so police themselves that obscenity is not likely to occur short of an accidental or unusual set or circumstances.

If the writer uses minimum care and good taste, he will steer clear of using anything remotely resembling graphic pornography. Undergound publications can expect strong local reaction to openly published and distributed pornography. But almost any serious treatment of sex, bodily functions, or any other subject of a sensitive nature is acceptable today.

Broadcast Regulations

In addition to the laws that govern all publications and dissemination of materials, broadcasters must observe regulations enforced by the Federal Communications Commission, such as:

—*Giving equal time for political candidates.* Exclusive of news stories, broadcasters cannot hold debates, panel discussions or other appearances by one or more candidates for a given office without giving equal time to all candidates, serious or frivolous. This ruling has not proved a problem in smaller community elections with a limited number of candidates. It has, however, virtually prohibited such appearances on the national level, where there are a great number of minor party candidates with no serious chance to gain office. Exceptions have been passed by Congress for such presidential debates as those held by John F. Kennedy and Richard Nixon in 1960 and those held by Jimmy Carter and Ronald Reagan in 1980 and those permitted in the 1984 Democratic primaries.

—*The Fairness Doctrine.* Under regulations of the Fairness Doctrine of the FCC, broadcasters are urged to editorialize, but must give air time to responsible groups or spokesmen of differing or opposing viewpoints. At the time of this writing the FCC was seriously discussing the possible elimination of or changes in this regulation.

—*Public Service Role of Broadcasters.* When a broadcaster's license comes up for renewal every three years, among the things the licensee must do to gain renewal is prove the licensee has served the community well in operating a radio or television station. Part of this proof traditionally has been to show the station has used a portion of its air time to promote local public service organizations. Thus news departments of broadcasting facilities are encouraged to air news items, announcements and free promotions for such community endeavors.

Completeness

The writer of a story or advertisement for print or broadcast owes the reader a story that is complete for its purposes. Of course, all pieces have a limited function. Obviously the writer is not going to write everything known about a subject. But he or she should leave no questions raised in the story or ad unanswered. Length of the piece is immaterial. A piece can be three paragraphs and complete or it can be 20 pages and incomplete. Some examples:

—If an advertisement suggests the reader/listener/viewer write in for a coupon book, it better also tell where to send the letter.

—If a story tells the reader/listener/viewer that a city commissioner collapsed at city hall, it better say what caused the collapse and whether or not the commissioner recovered, entered the hospital, or died.

—If an obituary reports that services will be held Wednesday at 2 p.m., it better say whether they will be at a funeral home or church, and which funeral home or church.

Occasionally the reporter cannot get the information needed to make a story complete by deadline. If so, he or she should tell the reader so. That at least answers the question as to why the information is missing.

It is just good professionalism to think about any questions the reader may have, and to answer those questions.

Responsibility

A writer's *first responsibility is to him or her self. The writer should never forget that.* He or she will encounter many pressures from the public, from sources, from clients and from employers. *If the writer does not have a strong personal code of ethics and values, those pressures may be difficult to resist.* Even ambition can assail that personal code, but most of those who would tempt a writer to compromise will respect the writer who resists such temptation.

In addition to his or her responsibility to himself or herself, the writer is also responsible to:

—*The reader/listener/viewer.*
—*The publication, broadcast outlet or client.*
—*Sources.*

The range and extent of responsibilities varies with the type of assignment. *News and feature writers* for print or broadcast organizations are responsible *first to their readers/listeners/viewers; second to their employers;* and *last,* to their sources. *Advertising* and *public relations* writers are also *primarily responsible* to their *readers/listeners/viewers* although that responsibility is not as deep as is that of newsmen. Advertising and public relations writers are also *much more* responsible to their *clients* and employers than newswriters, and *more* responsible to the *sources,* who are often also their clients.

THE REPORTER'S RESPONSIBILITIES

The *scope* of the responsibilities newswriters have to their readers/listeners/viewers is broad indeed. It includes serving as:

—*Purveyor of essential information.*
—*Watchdog over government activities.*

—*Consumer advocate.*
—*Educator.*
—*Guardian of civil rights including the public's right-to-know.*

The chief responsibility of newswriters to readers/listeners/viewers is to bring them the essential information they need to function and want to enhance enjoyment of life. The needs and wants are spelled out in the front page index to the paper or a listing of the items of news and public affairs in a day's operation of a broadcasting outlet. The newswriter's role is to *plow* through the flood of information available each day, *analyze* it thoroughly, *arrange* it, *condense* it, and *present* it in an accurate and efficient form for relatively easy consumption by the readers/listeners/viewers. In the comic strip, Frank and Earnest were amazed that there is always just enough news each day to fill up the newspaper. Editors dream that it could be that easy.

In the role as *watchdog for the public* over governmental operations, newswriters also perform an important service to society. The watchdog role creates an adversary relationship with government officials, but both groups have learned to live with that often tense arrangement with surface equanimity.

The press comes under sometimes intense economic pressures to soft pedal consumer information detrimental to business interests, but good newspapers and broadcast outlets not only ignore that pressure but aggressively act as the *consumer's advocate*. It is not unusual for newspapers and broadcast outlets to air criticism of products advertised in their publications or on their air time. Newswriter's loyalty to the consumer outweighs loyalty to the advertiser.

The *education aspect* of a newswriter's responsibility to the *readers/listeners/viewers* is both *incidental* and *direct*. *Incidental* of course is the vast variety of information a person learns just from reading a newspaper or listening to or watching broadcast news and public affairs shows. The *direct education* involves all of the how-to-do-it features printed or aired on everything from cooking recipes and household hints to playing bridge or making out income tax returns.

Guarding the public's right-to-know is a responsibility in which the newswriters are in the front line. They are constantly fighting to keep open the lines of information and activity to the public. To give some dimension to that battle, consider the activity taking place within a one month period in just one state. In Florida in one month there were court suits or other organized challenges to alleged violations of Florida's "Government in the Sunshine" law in ten different cities in the state. Politicians find it much more comfortable to conduct public business in private. That is understandable. But it is not desirable. Shortcuts in procedures, conflicts of interest, favoritism, inefficiencies, and the occasional frauds wither when exposed to the light. Defending the public's right-to-know (it's not a reporter's right exclusively) is a never-ending struggle most accept with their press cards.

Responsibility to their employer differs only slightly from the responsibility all employees have to their employers. They owe employers their *best efforts* and *faithful service*. In addition, as professionals they are *on duty at all times*. They do not punch time clocks although their hours are usually regular. But when a story develops, all worthy of the name are immediately on duty. Newswriters *should never get involved* in any writing or reporting activity that in any way *conflicts with their duties to their primary employer*. However, most reporters write for publications other than their employer's where no conflict exists. Reporters in small towns are often "stringers" (correspondents) for news organizations in larger towns. Others write for magazines, syndicates, or book publishers where no conflict results.

Finally, newswriters owe a responsibility to their *sources* including reporting that is accurate and without misrepresentation and protection of confidentiality. Modern reporters will, and have, served time in jail rather than reveal the name of a confidential source. However such a responsibility only applies if the source tells the reporter beforehand that the information he is about to give is confidential. The reporter need not keep in confidence information given without that understanding. A source will often try to go "off the record" after he has given sensitive data. The reporter need not accept such an after-the-fact request unless he feels it is in his best interest to avoid antagonizing his source.

THE ADVERTISING AND/OR PUBLIC RELATIONS WRITER'S RESPONSIBILITIES

Writers of *advertisements* and *public relations releases, promotions* or *other materials* have a strong, perhaps primary, responsibility to the *readers/listeners/viewers* of their efforts. They have essentially the same responsibility as do reporters for *accuracy, completeness*, and fairness of the *information* they provide.

Advertising writers provide a major portion of the marketing information that citizens depend on to guide them in the purchase of products they need and want. The homemaker could hardly function without the information advertisers disseminate on old and new products available, variety of choices, prices for comparison shopping, and catalogs and direct mail for at-home shopping. Advertising journalism is as old as news journalism. Early newspapers were often made possible only through the income from advertising. Advertising is such a key part of the American journalism and the American economic system, it is difficult to imagine what either would be like without advertising. Professional advertising writers can never forget their job is to communicate with the readers/listeners/viewers on behalf of their clients.

Public relations writers in the responsible discharge of their function must also keep tuned to the wave length of readers/listeners/viewers. The public relations writers are the communicators whose function is to deliver a message from an untrained or even inarticulate client in a form acceptable to readers/listeners/viewers. They do so in a direct manner through promotion letters, brochures, annual reports, even advertisements; and indirectly by news releases to newspapers and broadcast outlets.

Responsibilities of the *advertising* and *public relations writers* to their *clients and employers* are *much stronger* than are responsibilities of newswriters to their employers. Most work done by advertising and public relations writers does more than bring information to the public. It either promotes sales, introduces products, creates or polishes images, or influences opinions or actions. In filling such néeds, advertising and public relations writers are often a part of a sales or promotion campaign staff and other members of the campaign staff have much to say about what and how advertising and public relations writers will write and what they will not write. Of course, editors to a degree have that same role with reporters' copy, but both are journalists. In the case of the advertising and public relations pieces, the copy changes are often made by persons who are not advertising or public relations writers.

The responsibilities owed to *their sources* by writers of advertisements or public relations pieces are in a sense much stronger than the responsibilities owed their sources by newswriters. Often the sources for writers of advertisements or public relations pieces are also their clients or employers. Even when the sources are not clients or employers, some sort of close relationship does exist that makes writers of advertisements or public relations pieces more sensitive to the approval of the sources than newswriters would normally be.

FAIRNESS AND SENSITIVITY

In being accurate, objective, thorough and responsible, most writers in most situations will also automatically be fair. But writers should be constantly alert to lapses which may inadvertently be unfair to a source by quoting someone incompletely or out of context. In writing and rewriting, writers should keep fairness in mind.

Newspapers and broadcast outlets usually make every effort to permit people who think they have been treated unfairly in a story or editorial to respond through letters to the editor columns or air time.

Many of the best news organizations now employ ombudsmen, whose function is to listen to aggrieved persons and set things right. Far-sighted editors give ombudsmen considerable leeway in criticizing staff members if that seems in order.

By the same token, most advertisers and marketing organizations have consumer relations departments to deal with complaints customers might have. If such departments do not exist, good advertising and public relations personnel will quickly advise businessmen that establishing such a service is a good investment.

In attempting to be fair to readers/listeners/viewers, most news outlets today are more willing to *make appropriate corrections* and display them better than was the case in the past. It is only fair. Big news organizations have a tremendous amount of power. Generosity of spirit by the powerful should come easily and promptly.

Journalism and marketing are tough businesses, but there can still be room for *sensitivity* and even *kindness*. Without withholding essential news from the public, writers and editors can, on occasion, *decline to publish* sensitive details of some stories. For example, even when a coroner issues a ruling of suicide, some responsible papers will omit such details from an obituary if the suicide was not performed in a public or spectacular way. The public has a *right to know*, in most cases, but does not always have a *need to know* something of vicarious interest only that will cause anguish to others.

APPENDIX A

A summary of the Associated Press and United Press International Stylebook featuring the most commonly used style elements.

NUMERALS

1. In general, spell below 10; use numerals for 10 and above.
2. Numerals used exclusively for dimensions, speeds, sums of money, election returns, times, highways, ages, proportions, dates.
   Use for address numbers, but spell out First through Ninth as street names; use figures with two letters for 10th and above: 20 Sixth Ave., 140 15th St.
3. Fractions: decimals preferred except with stocks, recipes. Spell fractions less than one: one-third. For mixed numbers use 1 1/2, 2 5/8, etc., with a space between whole number and fraction.
4. Distances: numerals for 10 and above. Spell out one through nine: five miles, 14 miles.
5. Sums of money: 70 cents, $1, $1.25, $2,350, $675,000, $1 million.
6. Percentages: 70 percent, 5 percent.
7. Temperatures: 95 degrees, 3 degrees.

CAPITALIZE

1. Common nouns as part of proper name: Democratic Party, Elm Street, J. Wayne Reitz Union; lowercase common nouns in plural uses: Main and Elm streets.
2. Principal words in names of books, movies, historic periods, plays, holidays.
3. Only formal titles used before a name. Lowercase titles following a name. Lowercase false titles (job descriptions): attorney John Smithers.
4. Lowercase academic departments: department of journalism.
5. Specific regions: the Midwest. Generally lowercase sections of state or city: northern Ohio. Lowercase direction: They drove west.
6. Nationalities, peoples, races: Cherokee, Chinese, Negro, but lowercase descriptive words: black, white, yellow.
7. Lowercase parts of proper nouns when they stand alone: union, university, council.

ABBREVIATE

1. States with six or more letters that follow cities; spell out Alaska, Hawaii, and all with five or fewer letters. Spell out all states standing alone.
2. Months with more than five letters with a specific date: Aug. 20, June 6. Spell out when standing alone.
3. Jr., Sr., after a person's name. Co., Corp., Inc., Ltd. in company names.

4. Some organizations are widely recognized by initials: CIA, YMCA, etc. Use full name if needed for clarity.
5. Dr., Gov., Lt. Gov., Mr., Mrs., Rep., the Rev., Sen. and certain military titles before a name. Spell out titles not used with a name, following a name, and set off from the name by commas.
6. Spell out and capitalize formal academic titles, such as president, professor, before a name. Lowercase such modifiers as history Professor Bob Handline, or department in department Chairman Bill Risen.
7. Spell out academic degrees: a bachelor's degree, a master's.
8. Use Ave., Blvd., and St. in numbered addresses: 1600 Elm Ave. Spell out without a number: Elm Avenue.
9. Abbreviate compass points and use periods with addresses: 220 E. 42nd St., 600 Oak St. N.W. Do not abbreviate if number is omitted: East 42nd Street.

DO NOT ABBREVIATE
1. Names: as Robt., Chas., unless person does so.
2. United States when it stands alone.
3. Names of days of the week, unless in tabulated material.
4. Percent as %.
5. Cents as ¢.
6. And as &.
7. Christmas as Xmas.

COMMAS
1. Omit before "and" in a series: red, white and blue.
2. Omit between name and Jr. or Sr.
3. Commas and periods are placed inside quotation marks.
4. Use to separate a city from a state or nation: Her journey will take her from Dublin, Ireland, to Fargo, N.D., and back.
5. Use to set off complete, one-sentence direct quotation, but not partial quote: Wallace said, "She came back speaking Spanish."
6. Use to separate person's hometown from name: Joe Smith, Miami, and Jill Jones, Ocala, were there. Use of "of" without a comma is preferable: Joe Smith of Miami and Jill Jones of Ocala.
   Use "of" with name, age, hometown to eliminate comma after hometown: Joe Smith, 44, of Miami and Jill Jones, 31, of Ocala, were there.

MISCELLANEOUS
1. Semicolons are gramatically proper to separate main clauses (sentences). However, it is preferred to use a period and begin a new sentence, or use a comma and conjunction to join the clauses.
2. The semicolon separates phrases containing commas to avoid confusion: The party consisted of J.L. Jones; Mrs. Ed Kelly, his secretary; Mrs.

Jones; Mrs. Edna Brown, her nurse; and three servants.

Or for more than one element in a series: Sarah Riley, Gainesville, president; Jan Morgan, Lake City, vice-president; . . .

3. Time of day or amounts of money don't take extra zeros: 6 p.m. not 6:00 p.m.; $40 not $40.00.

4. Days of the month take only the numeral, not *nd, rd, th*: Aug. 2 not Aug. 2nd; Sept. 3 not Sept. 3rd; Oct. 4 not Oct. 4th.

5. Mr. commonly used only with Mr. and Mrs. combinations.

6. Time: Today, tonight is proper. Use day of the week rather than yesterday, tomorrow.

7. Hyphenate compound adjectives: four-year study, 12-member council, 19-year-old man.

8. Collective nouns take singular verbs and pronouns: group was (not were); council scheduled its (not their) meeting.

Appendix B

PROFESSIONAL STANDARDS AND CODES

Professionals in the mass media adhere to codes of standards and professionalism that assure the public that minimum standards of responsibility and professionalism will be maintained. The standards for broadcast and print journalists, advertisers and public relations professionals are set by organizations and professionals in the various fields. Specific standards and codes follow.

STANDARDS FOR REPORTERS AND EDITORS

Giving guidance to reporters and editors of newspapers, broadcast outlets, magazines, and wire services, and to free-lance writers is the *Code of Ethics* of the *Society of Professional Journalists, Sigma Delta Chi,* adopted by the national convention on November 16, 1973:

The Society of Professional Journalists, Sigma Delta Chi, believes the duty of journalists is to serve the truth.

We believe the agencies of mass communication are carriers of public discussion and information, acting on their Constitutional mandate and freedom to learn and report the facts.

We believe in public enlightenment as the forerunner of justice, and in our Constitutional role to seek the truth as part of the public's right to know the truth.

We believe those responsibilities carry obligations that require journalists to perform with intelligence, objectivity, accuracy, and fairness. To these ends, we declare acceptance of the standards of practice here set forth:

Responsibility. The public's right to know of events of public importance and interest is the overriding mission of the mass media. The purpose of distributing news and enlightened opinion is to serve the general welfare. Journalists who use their status as representatives of the public for selfish or other unworthy motives violate a high trust.

Freedom of the Press. Freedom of the press is to be guarded as an inalienable right of people in a free society. It carries with it the freedom and the responsibility to discuss, question, and challenge actions and utterances of our government and of our public and private institutions. Journalists uphold the right to speak unpopular opinions and the privilege to agree with the majority.

Ethics. Journalists must be free of obligation to any interest other than the public's right to know the truth.

1. Gifts, favors, free travel, special treatment or privileges can compromise the integrity of journalists and their employers. Nothing of value should be accepted.

2. Secondary employment, political involvement, holding public office, and service in community organizations should be avoided if it compromises the integrity of journalists and their employers. Journalists and their employers should conduct their personal lives in a manner which protects them from conflict of interest, real or apparent. Their responsibilities to the public are paramount. That is the nature of their profession.

3. So-called news communications from private sources should not be published or broadcast without substantiation of their claims to news value.

4. Journalists will seek news that serves the public interest, despite the obstacles. They will make constant efforts to assure that the public's business is conducted in public and that public records are open to public inspection.

5. Journalists acknowledge the newsmen's ethic of protecting confidential sources of information.

Accuracy and Objectivity. Good faith with the public is the foundation of all worthy journalism.

1. Truth is our ultimate goal.

2. Objectivity in reporting the news is another goal, which serves as the mark of an experienced professional. It is the standard of performance toward which we strive. We honor those who achieve it.

3. There is no excuse for inaccuracies or lack of thoroughness.

4. Newspaper headlines should be fully warranted by the contents of the articles they accompany. Photographs and telecasts should give an accurate picture of an event and not highlight a minor incident out of context.

5. Sound practice makes clear distinction between news reports and expressions of opinion. News reports should be free of opinion or bias and represent all sides of an issue.

6. Partisanship in editorial comment which knowingly departs from the truth violates the spirit of American journalism.

7. Journalists recognize their responsibility for offering informed analysis, comment, and editorial opinion on public events and issues. They accept the obligation to present such material by individuals whose competence, experience, and judgment qualify them for it.

8. Special articles or presentations devoted to advocacy or the writer's own conclusions and interpretations should be labeled as such.

Fair Play. Journalists at all times will show respect for the dignity, privacy, rights, and well-being of people encountered in the course of gathering and presenting the news.

1. The news media should not communicate unofficial charges affecting the reputation or moral character without giving the accused a chance to reply.

2. The news media must guard against invading a person's right to privacy.

3. The media should not pander to morbid curiosity about details of vice and crime.

4. It is the duty of news media to make prompt and complete correction of their errors.

5. Journalists should be accountable to the public for their reports and the public should be encouraged to voice its grievances against the media. Open dialogue with our readers, viewers, and listeners should be fostered.

Pledge. Journalists should actively censure and try to prevent violations of these standards, and they should encourage their observance by all newspeople. Adherence to this code of ethics is intended to preserve the bond of mutual trust between American journalists and the American people.

STANDARDS FOR WRITERS OF ADVERTISEMENTS

Writers of advertisements for either print media or broadcast media can be guided by these sections of the *Standards of Practice, American Association of Advertising Agencies,* adopted in October, 1924, and revised on April 28, 1962:

WE HOLD THAT a responsibility of advertising agencies is to be a constructive force in business.

WE FURTHER HOLD THAT, to discharge this responsibility, advertising agencies must recognize an obligation, not only to their clients, but to the public, the media they employ and to each other.

WE FINALLY HOLD THAT the responsibility will best be discharged if all agencies observe a common set of standards of practice.

To this end, the American Association of Advertising Agencies has adopted the following Standards of Practice as being in the best interests of the public, the advertisers, the media owners and the agencies themselves.

These standards are voluntary. They are intended to serve as a guide to the kind of agency conduct which experience has shown to be wise, foresighted and constructive.

It is recognized that advertising is a business and as such must operate within the framework of competition. It is further recognized that keen and vigorous competition, honestly conducted, is necessary to the growth and health of American business generally, of which advertising is a part.

However, unfair competitive practices in the advertising agency business lead to financial waste, dilution of service, diversion of manpower and loss of prestige. Unfair practices tend to weaken public confidence both in advertisements and in the institution of advertising.

1. Creative Code

We the members of the American Association of Advertising Agencies, in addition to supporting and obeying the laws and legal regulations pertaining to advertising, undertake to extend and broaden the application of high ethical standards. Specifically, we will not knowingly produce advertising which contains:

    a. False or misleading statements or exaggerations, visual or verbal.

    b. Testimonials which do not reflect the real choice of a competent witness.

    c. Price claims which are misleading.

    d. Comparisons which unfairly disparage a competitive product or service.

    e. Claims insufficiently supported, or which distort the true meaning of practicable application of statements made by professional or scientific authority.

    f. Statements, suggestions or pictures offensive to public decency.

Other sections of the advertising code refer to non-writing aspects of advertising agency operations such as contracts, client relationships, credit, and other business standards.

STANDARDS FOR PUBLIC RELATIONS PROFESSIONALS

The public relations worker can find guidance in the *Declarations of Principles: Code of Professional Standards for the Practice of Public Relations with Interpretations,* Public Relations Society of America:

Members of the Public Relations Society of America acknowledge and publicly declare that the public relations profession in serving the legitimate interests of clients or employers is dedicated fundamentally to the goals of better mutual understanding and cooperation among the diverse individuals, groups, institutions, and elements of our modern society.

248

In the performance of this mission, we pledge ourselves:

1. To conduct ourselves both privately and professionally in accord with the public welfare.

2. To be guided in all our activities by the generally accepted standards of truth, accuracy, fair dealing and good taste.

3. To support efforts designed to increase the proficiency of the profession by encouraging the continuous development of sound training and resourceful education in the practice of public relations.

4. To adhere faithfully to provisions of the duly adopted Code of Professional Standards for the Practice of Public Relations, a copy of which is in the possession of every member.

CODE OF PROFESSIONAL STANDARDS FOR THE PRACTICE OF PUBLIC RELATIONS

This Code of Professional Standards for the Practice of Public Relations is adopted by the Public Relations Society of America to promote and maintain high standards of public service and conduct among its members in order that membership in the Society may be deemed a badge of ethical conduct; that Public Relations justly may be regarded as a profession; that the public may have increasing confidence in its integrity; and that the practice of Public Relations may best serve the public interest.

1. A member has a general duty of fair dealing toward his clients or employers, past and present, his fellow members and the general public.

2. A member shall conduct his professional life in accord with the public welfare.

3. A member has the affirmative duty of adhering to general accepted standards of accuracy, truth, and good taste.

4. A member shall not represent conflicting or competing interests without the express consent of those concerned, given after a full disclosure of the facts; nor shall he place himself in a position where his interest is or may be in conflict with his duty to his client, employer, another member or the public, without a full disclosure of such interests to all concerned.

5. A member shall safeguard the confidences of both present and former clients or employers and shall not accept retainers or employment which may involve the disclosure or use of these confidences to the disadvantage or prejudice of such clients or employers.

6. A member shall not engage in any practice which tends to corrupt the integrity of channels of public communication.

7. A member shall not intentionally disseminate false or misleading information and is obligated to use ordinary care to avoid dissemination of false or misleading information.

8. A member shall be prepared to identify to the public the source of any communication for which he is responsible, including the name of the client or employer on whose behalf the communication is made.

9. A member shall not make use of any individual or organization purporting to serve or represent some announced cause, or purporting to be independent or unbiased, but actually serving an undisclosed special or private interest of a member of his client or his employer.

10. A member shall not intentionally injure the professional reputation or practice of another member. However, if a member has evidence that another member has been guilty of unethical, illegal or unfair practices, including practices in violation of this Code, he should present the information to the proper authorities of the Society for action in accordance with the procedure set forth in Article XIII of the Bylaws.

11. A member shall not employ methods tending to be derogatory of another member's client or employer or of the products, business or services of such client or employer.

12. In performing services for a client or employer, a member shall not accept fees, commissions, or any other valuable consideration in connection with those services from anyone other than his client or employer without the express consent of his client or employer, given after a full disclosure of the facts.

13. A member shall not propose to a prospective client or employer that the amount of his fee or other compensation be contingent on or measured by the achievement of specified results; nor shall he enter into any fee agreement to the same effect.

14. A member shall not encroach upon the professional employment of another member. Where there are two engagements, both must be assured that there is no conflict between them.

15. A member shall, as soon as possible, sever his relations with any organization when he knows or should know that his continued employment would require him to conduct himself contrary to the principles of this Code.

16. A member called as a witness in a proceeding for the enforcement of this Code shall be bound to appear unless, for sufficient reason, he shall be excused by the panel hearing the same.

17. A member shall co-operate with fellow members in upholding and enforcing this Code.

In addition there are interpretations for the parts of the code relating to certain specific situations. The public relations practitioner should obtain a complete copy of the code and interpretations. He gets a copy automatically upon joining the *Public Relations Society of America* or the *Public Relations Student Society of America.*

INSTITUTIONAL CODES

In addition, there are codes and standards adopted by various associations of editors, publishers, radio broadcasters and television broadcasters. For the most part they cover the same grounds on writing practices covered in the codes printed here. In addition they cover aspects that have to do with managerial responsibility and which will be adequately covered by other sources which professionals will encounter. Suffice it to summarize a few briefly:

—The *American Advertising Federation* and the *Association of Better Business Bureaus International* have a code of practices encouraging truth in advertising, responsibility, taste and decency, and explicit guarantees, and condemning attacks on competitors, bait advertising, false price claims and false testimonials.

—The *National Association of Broadcasters* has radio and television codes prescribing integrity and responsibility in the treatment of controversial public issues, community responsibilities, political broadcasts, advancement of education and culture, religion and religious broadcasts, dramatic programs, and programming for children.

A SELECTED AND ANNOTATED BIBLIOGRAPHY

The Associated Press Style Book, Rev. Ed. The Associated Press, New York, 1984.

Berner, R. Thomas, *Language Skills for Journalists*, 2nd Ed. Houghton Mifflin Company, Boston, 1984 (Excellent guide to word usage, spelling, grammar and punctuation for writers of material for the mass media.)

Bernstein, Theodore M., *The Careful Writer.* MacMillan Publishing Company, New York, 1973. (A book on proper word usage and style by a former New York Times editor.)

Bremner, John B., *Words on Words, A Dictionary for Writers and Others Who Care About Words.* Columbia University Press, New York, 1980. (A witty and specialized dictionary written by a man who loves words and the language for writers and readers who also love words and language.)

Cappon, Rene J., *The Word, an Associated Press Guide to Good Writing.* Associated Press, New York, 1982. (Good sections on writing feature stories and on using colorful words.)

Cohen, J.M. & M.J., *The Penguin Dictionary of Quotations*. Penguin Books, New York, 1960. (A reasonably priced collection of quotations from the classics.)

Cohen, J.M. & M.J., *The Penguin Dictionary of Modern Quotations*. Penguin Books, New York. (Quotations from authors after 1900.)

Flesch, Rudolf, *The Art of Readable Writing*. Collier Books, New York, 1962. (A classic study of the anatomy of writing. Provides excellent measurements to determine the readability of a piece of writing.)

Griffith, John L. and Weston, Edward G., *Programmed Newswriting*. Prentice-Hall, Englewood Cliffs, N.J., 1978. (A programmed text on the basics of writing news, one the student can use outside of a classroom.)

Gunning, Robert, *The Technique of Clear Writing*. McGraw-Hill Book Company, Inc., New York, 1952. (Book by a readability counselor detailing ways to measure the quality of writing.)

Hayakawa, S.I., *Language in Thought and Action*. 3rd ed. Harcourt Brace Jovanovich, New York, 1972. (A book on the English language by a noted semanticist.)

Hohenberg, John, *The Professional Journalist, Guide to the Practices and Principles of the News Media*. 4th Ed. Holt, Rinehart and Winston, New York, 1978. (Excellent comprehensive reporting text covering both print and broadcast general reporting, public affairs reporting and specialized reporting.)

Leggett, Glenn, Mead, C. David, Charvat, William. *Prentice-Hall Handbook for Writers*, 8th Ed. Prentice-Hall, Inc., Englewood Cliffs, N.J., 1982. (Excellent comprehensive handbook for writers of English. Good examples and good exercises.)

Malickson, David L., Nason, John W., *Advertising: How to Write the Kind that Works. Basic Guide to Creating for Print, Direct Mail, Radio and T.V.* 2nd Ed. Charles Scribner's Sons, New York, 1982. (Excellent text on writing advertisements for all media.)

Maloney, Martin, Rubenstein, Paul Max, *Writing for the Media*. Prentice-Hall, Inc., Englewood Cliffs, N.J., 1980. (Good book on writing scripts for television shows, documentaries, screen plays, T.V. ads.)

Mencher, Melvin, *News Reporting and Writing*, 3rd Ed. Wm. C. Nrown, Dubuque, Iowa, 1984. (This basic reporting and news writing text is excellent. It is used throughout the country in news writing courses.)

Metzler, Ken, *Creative Interviewing*. Prentice-Hall, Inc., Englewood Cliffs, N.J., 1977. (Highly specialized and in-depth book on interviewing.)

Newman, Edwin, *A Civil Tongue*. The Bobbs-Merrill Company, Indianapolis/New York, 1976. (A witty attack on unclear and imprecise language by a noted television newsman.)

Newman, Edwin, *Strictly Speaking: Will America Be the Death of English?* The Bobbs-Merrill Company, Inc., Indianapolis/New York, 1974. (An attack by a noted television newsman on the threat to the English language from American gobbledegook.)

Newson, Doug, and Siegfried, Tom, *Writing in Public Relations Practice: Form and Style.* Wadsworth Publishing Company, Belmont, CA, 1981. (Writing text for the public relations writer with good chapters on persuasion, research, speeches, newsletters and brochures, memos and letters.)

Sanford, Bruce W., *Synopsis of the Law of Libel and the Right to Privacy.* Rev. Ed. World Almanac Publications, New York, 1981. (Excellent condensed explanation of laws of libel and privacy. List of dangerous words for writer to avoid.)

Strunk, William Jr., White, E.B., *The Elements of Style.* 3rd Ed. MacMillan Publishing Co., Inc., New York, 1979. (Short, 85 page classic book on writing English. Tightly written and highly praised little volume of the basics.)

Watkins, Floyd C., Dillingham, William B., Martin, Edwin T., *Practical English Handbook.* 5th Ed. Houghton Mifflin Company, Boston, 1978. (Comprehensive English writing instruction book. Good examples.)

Watkins, Floyd C., Dillingham, William B., Hiers, John T., *Practical English Work Book.* Houghton Mifflin Company, Boston, 1978. (A workbook with exercises on basic grammar, punctuation and word usage to go with handbook by same authors.)

Webster's New World Dictionary of the American Language, 2nd College Edition. Simon & Schuster, New York, 1982. (The dictionary used by the Associated Press for the first preference for spelling, style, usage and foreign geographic names to augment the Associated Press Style Book.)

Westley, Bruce W., *News Editing.* Houghton Mifflin Company, Boston, 1980. (Excellent book on print editing. Standard college classic.)

index

A

Accuracy; 225; by checking facts, 226; checking all names, 226; checking figures, statistics, 226; consequences of errors, 226; developing a system, 226; never assume, 174; rechecking, 226; using sources, 226

Advance story, use of unique angle, 100

Advertising, *American Association of Advertising Agencies*, 170

Advertising, appealing to needs and motivations, 37

Advertising, subliminal motivation, 75

Advertising Creative Code, 170

Advertising layout, role of whitespace, 73

Advertising writing: AIDA formula, 71; arousing interest, 73; attracting attention, 72; benefits defined, 71; creating desire, 71; creative motivation, 71; direct mail appeals, 117; double duty of headline illustration, 74; hard sell, 114; headline function defined, 74; institution ad, 116; moving to action, 75; product ad, 114; selling a service, 116; soft sell, 116; theme, 71

Arousing interest: exploiting fear, 34; exploiting human nature, 31; future, 33; human nature, 31; people in action, 31; people's experiences, 31; progress, 32; quoting people, 30; relating to people, 30

Associated Press, 125, 213

Associated Press Managing Editor Association, 175

ATEX computerized typesetting system, 58

Attribution: dangers of opinion words, 231; frequency, 229; placement, 230; use of word, "said", 230

Audience: common denominator, 65; magazine audience, 65; magazine audience diversified, 69; mass audience, 65; newspaper audience defined, 67; radio audience defined, 67; specialized audience, 65; specialized audience and variety, 67; television audience defined, 67; universally interesting data, 65; writing for different audiences, 1

Audience Interests: basic interests, 29; conflicts and competition, 31; conflict, many forms, 31; fear, 34; human interest, 30; living is conflict, 32; measuring intensity, 37; oddity, 35; progress, 32, self, 29; sex, 34; suspense and drama, 33; sympathy, 35

B

Basic skills, iv

Beginnings: advertising headlines, 11; analogy lead defined, 19; anecdote leads, 20; contrast lead defined, 20; cumulative lead defined, 19; dialogue lead defined, 20; direct address lead in advertisements, 20; direct address lead defined, 20; exageration in leads, 18; find unique angle, 6; five W's, 13; flashback lead defined, 19; freak lead defined, 22; functions of, 5; gaining attention, 5; headline is not lead, 12; hypothetical leads, 23; identification in leads, 14; make them active, 6; modified summary lead defined, 17; narrative lead defined, 18; P.R. leads, 22; pointless anecdotes, 23; punch or jolt lead defined, 18; quotation lead, use sparingly, 17; say nothing leads, 22; should induce further reading, 8; should set angle, 10; should set tone; 9; summary lead, 13; summary lead length, 14; suspended interest lead defined, 19; things to avoid, 22; too many details, 23; vary the length, 11

Brisbane, Arthur, 173

Broadcast commercial: form, 76; sound effects, 76

Broadcast regulations: equal time for political candidates, 234; Fairness Doctrine, 234; public service rules, 234

Broadcast writing: characteristics, 109; editing of tapes, 111; public service announcements, 110; use of taped segments, 111

Broadcasting, advertising on television, 68

Burke, Edmund, 61

Byline, 4

C

CBS News Almanac, 212

Capote, Truman: 1, 207; *In Cold Blood*, 207

Carter, Jimmy, 234

A Civil Tongue, 126

Chicago (Ill.) Sun Times, 58

Churchill, Winston, 2

Completeness, explaining, 70

Confidential source, 237

Congressional Record, 220

Copy preparation: 43; for broadcast stories, 47; for optical character scanner, 56; print advertisements, 48; print stories, 43; public relations releases, 47; radio commercial, 49

Copyediting marks: for advertising, 55; for broadcasting, 55; for public relations handouts, 47; use by reporter, 53

Correction of errors, 53

Cosell, Howard, 78, 224

Courts: calendars open to press, 218; domestic cases, 218; judges can gag reporters, 218; jury deliberations always closed, 218; open to public, 218; property ownership is public information, 219

Craft; an energy of its own, 1; framework for art, 1

Craftsmanship; acquired asset, 1

Critique of Pure Reason, 231

Cumulative Book Index, 212

D

Dreiser, Theodore, 2

E

Encyclopedia Americana, 211

Encyclopedia Brittanica, 211

Encyclopedia Brittanica World Atlas, 212

England, Arthur, 125

Ethics, reporter, 245

Exorcist, The, 186